Visitations

I read *Visitations: Conversations with the Ghost of the Chairman* with great ambivalence. On the one hand I turned each page with eager anticipation of what these two great souls, one dead and one alive, would reveal next about one of the great revolutionary struggles of our time. And yet, on the other hand, I knew that this heroic struggle waged, in their own way, by the scholar diplomat, Francis Mading Deng and the liberation leader, John Garang de Mabior has ended tragically with more ghosts of a once hopeful people. This book is essential reading for anyone interested in knowing how the hopes of one generation can so tragically and so quickly turn to the hopelessness of another generation!

—*Vasu Gounden, Executive Director,*
African Centre for the Constructive Resolution of Disputes (ACCORD)

Writing literary form gets to be whatever you want it to be. I appreciate that you told the story in this way as I think it is more interesting than reading a straight memoir on the topic. Also, I very much like the Chairman. He is direct and matter-of-fact, and incredibly wise. There are definitely two voices here and both are interesting and contribute much to the story. I find this fiction/nonfiction blend a clever approach to writing a memoir.

—*Michelle Poff, PhD, Communication Scientist, Accomplish, LLC*

Artful, delightful, and fascinating storytelling with the seriousness of lifelong purpose, Dr Francis Deng has written an arresting account of South Sudan's struggle for independence. This book turns a global diplomat into a passionate master narrator of complex history, broad concepts, long term vision, and per-sonal experience. Deng, a former Under-Secretary General and Special Adviser to the United Nations Secretary-General on the Prevention of Genocide and now a peacemaker, has effectively employed the art of storytelling to convey messages of nation building and peace-making to his people and beyond. I have read countless narratives but this stands out as the easiest for many Afri-cans to relate to.

—*Dr Mehari Taddele Maru, Professor of Law, Addis Ababa University*

South Sudan's most prominent intellectual Francis Deng has written a rich, in-novative, and fascinating meditation on his new country's continuing challenges based on a highly original form of dialogue he has with the ghost of South Sudan's martyred 'Founding Father' John Garang in this fascinating novel of ideas.

—*Professor Adekeye Adebajo, Director,*
Institute for Pan-African Thought and Conversation, University of Johannesburg

This is an exceptionally well crafted sophisticated autobiography, which, in style and conceptionalisation, is out of this world. Dr. Deng will amaze his readers with the medium in which he opted to present his life long experience through the late Chairman's visitations from the other side. He brilliantly did that without having to say things which would make the reader uncomfortable, being aware that the conversations are indeed between the ghost of a dead dear friend and a living intellectual giant who wanted to honor his late intellectual comrade in thought by implicitly dedicating his autobiography to him. I am thrilled and proud. A master read.

—*Dr. John Gai Yoh, Formerly Ambassador and Minister of Education*

The publisher wishes to acknowledge and thank Dr. Douglas H. Johnson for his invaluable help and support for Africa World Books and its mission of preserving and promoting African cultural and literary traditions and history. Dr. Johnson and fellow historians have been instrumental in ensuring that African people remain connected to their past and their identity. Africa World Books is proud to carry on this mission.

ISBN (Paperback): 9780645110906
ISBN (Hardcover): 9780645612745

Cover design, typesetting and layout: Africa World Books
Unit 3, 57 Frobisher St, Osborne Park, WA 6017
P.O. Box 1106 Osbourne Park, WA 6916

Visitations

CONVERSATIONS WITH THE GHOST OF THE CHAIRMAN

FRANCIS MADING DENG

Dedication

To Mama Rebecca Nyandeeng de Mabior, widow of Dr. John Garang de Mabior, the Legendary Founding Leader of the Sudan People's Liberation Movement and Army, SPLM/A, the loving mother of their six children, and Mother of the Independent Nation of South Sudan.

As her husband's trusted commrade-in-arms and devoted partner, Nyandeeng's dedication to his Vision and Mission for the Nation has been reinvigorated by his martyrdom and the myriad challenges facing South Sudan, the country for which he made the ultimate sacrifice.

May this book be a modest reaffirmation of my friendship and solidarity with them in pursuit of the cause of justice and human dignity for our people.

Table of Contents

Preface

This story is a medley of myth and reality in which the ghost of the late Chairman of the Sudan People's Liberation Movement/Army (or SPLM/A), and I, designated by him as his Messenger, relive our experiences in this world through a series of visitations and conversations. The Chairman, of course, for dramatic purposes, exists as an intangible spirit, but he comes to me as a ghost through some form of physical image.

The story involves many people with whom we shared common experiences. Some of them, like the Chairman, have passed on. Others are still with us. To protect both the living and the dead, the names of the people with whom we interacted in real life have been omitted or recast to conceal their identities. But their relationship to the story retains significance. What is described here is a fictionalization of what actually happened—a blend of myth, 'faction', and reconstruction.

Much is said through this format that would not normally be said, even though it needs to be said. This format, therefore, offers an opportunity to do what needs to be done but is not otherwise easily doable. And that was indeed the Chairman's motivation in initiating his program of visits and conversations with me.

For most of our adult life, the Chairman and I engaged in a stimulating exchange of ideas about the challenges facing our country and the vision of a New Sudan, which the liberation movement he led postulated for our country. To be sure, we approached this vision from our different vantage points, he as the Chairman and Commander-in-Chief of the liberation movement and its military wing, and I as a research scholar, diplomat, and international civil servant. Nonetheless, we collaborated closely, both explicitly and implicitly, on how best to pursue a vision we both agreed was a noble one and worth our devoted commitment and sacrifice.

The themes and issues that surfaced in our conversations reflect history, contemporary experience, and dreams for a better future for our people and our country. They developed over the course of several decades through our sustained dialogue and cooperation in our practical endeavors until his tragic and untimely death. Memories of those exchanges have inspired this book, which is mostly fact, with just a thin veneer of creative fiction.

I hope this format will both entertain and inform or enlighten the reader about what we tried to do together and individually for our country.

Prologue

One night, in my room, I heard a voice that I surprisingly recognized. I was startled—in fact, shocked and bewildered. The Chairman suddenly appeared in front of me, exclaiming: "*Raandit*" (Big Man, a Dinka term of respect for age).

"*Benydit* (Big Chief), where are you coming from?" I responded. "I thought you were long dead!?" I was genuinely perplexed. The Chairman appeared as alive as I remembered him.

"This is the biggest myth you will ever experience," he said, rather teasingly. "It's a complicated story, but, as you can see, I am alive."

Confused as I was, I felt truly delighted that the Chairman was after all alive and that the story of his death must have been some monumental misunderstanding—the biggest myth I would ever experience, as he put it. I felt a huge sigh of relief that the leader in whom our people had placed so much faith was still alive to fulfill his vision for the nation. Perhaps the story of his having died had only been a nightmare from which, thank God, I was waking up.

Suddenly, I drifted into consciousness, and into the disappointment that it was his being still alive that had all been just a dream. The Chairman disappeared as suddenly as he had appeared. We did not even have enough time to reflect on what was going on and far less to discuss what had become of our people since his death and whether he had any advice on how to confront the many crises and challenges facing the new nation he had liberated.

I sincerely wished and hoped that the Chairman would appear again and have enough time for us to dig deeper into the major challenges of development and nation-building confronting our country and to which he is supposed to have given much thought, and even designed plans. Developments that I did not foresee at the time would create a process that would help bridge the Chairman's new world of the dead and my world of the living.

Session One: Setting

It all began with an accident. I was attending a two-day meeting on African conflicts. I had established and was directing an African Studies Program at a leading think tank in Washington, D.C. The meeting was organized by another institute that focused on peace research for which I was a member of the board. It was held in an idyllic conference center outside Washington, in fact in Virginia. It was in a rolling well-groomed scenic landscape of green grass, hedges, and trees spread over a vast stretch of land next to a golf course. With the conference building at the center, participants were accommodated in cottages spread over the spacious grounds. We checked into our rooms before attending the opening session at dinner in the conference center building.

Walking back to my accommodation, the grounds were dimly lit, adding to the romantic ambience. I exited the dining area and strolled through the beautiful garden of flowers and hedges leading to the lane that would take me to my quarters. Suddenly, I found myself flat on the pavement, having fallen down, out of the garden that was, in the dark, invisibly elevated about four feet from the adjacent lane, with no barriers.

I must have instinctively extended my right arm out to shield my head and the rest of my body. Someone saw me and rushed to me to make sure that I was alright. I said I was fine. But I was not. They called the ambulance and I was taken to a nearby hospital. Fortunately, no bone was broken, but an MRI test would need to be taken anyway, to look for what else might have gone wrong. I attended the meeting the next morning but, although I had been given painkillers, I was still in a fair amount of pain.

Back in Washington, I had an MRI test and found the real damage. My rotator cuff was badly torn; the arm on which I had landed had shot through my shoulder, possibly saving my life by keeping my head from cracking on the pavement, but shattering the muscles and the rotator cuff. It could of course have been much more tragic, for had I landed on my head, there would have been a very different story told—*about* me, and not *by* me.

I needed to be operated on, urgently. The operation was carried out by a very well reputed surgeon who spoke with an Eastern European accent. The post-operation pain was excruciating, even though I was heavily medicated. The medication itself had seriously disorientating consequences. But I was glad to be allowed to go home.

We had a lovely house at Takoma Park at the borderline between Washington, D.C. and Maryland. It was an old Victorian, with the dome on the third floor shooting prominently into the sky. It was the biggest house in the neighborhood. The first floor of the house was well designed with a good-sized entry hallway, a spacious living room to the left, and an equally spacious dining room to the right, next to (again) a spacious kitchen. There was a screened-in deck facing a large garden in the back lined by trees and hedges that shielded us from the neighboring houses. The house also had a large open front deck, which we hardly ever used because it was too close to the street, across which was the Takoma Elementary School.

I was being nursed by my wife in our master bedroom on the second floor, where there were three additional bedrooms, one of which I was using as my study. A shared bathroom was at the center-back of the floor. On the third floor, there were additional rooms and the attic from which the dome shot up.

The story in this book really began the night of my return from the hospital. It had been a very tormenting night for me. I had just had that major operation for the badly torn rotator cuff that the surgeon said was the worst he had ever seen. I believe that was probably why he gave me what I was told was the strongest painkiller available, which he said he rarely prescribed. Although I had been released from the hospital and was back at home, I was in severe pain and taking that exceptionally strong painkiller, which helped at least a little.

As in the hospital, the medication made me feel awkward—hallucinating, seeing human figures without clear shapes. I was talking to someone or myself and moving about in ways I thought embarrassing for others to see. So I locked my door. My wife was worried about my condition and my locking myself up alone. But I was adamant, and she conceded.

To give me space and respect my privacy, my wife moved to another room, but kept her door wide open in case my situation needed her attention.

Not long after my door was closed, someone tapped me gently on the shoulder, precisely on my incision. It hurt sharply. I almost screamed, but I feared that I would prove my wife right in her opposition to locking the door. This was utterly bewildering. The door was closed, indeed locked, and there was no other way anyone could have entered the room. But I was, of course, not thinking clearly. I was in a tormented void. A voice accompanied the tap on the shoulder, saying, "Do not be afraid. I am not going to hurt you." The voice sounded familiar, but only very vaguely.

It was dark. A lamp on the table at the corner of the room shed dim light that made the man talking only faintly visible in some mysterious shape. "Who are you? And how did you get into my locked room?" I asked, visibly shaken, but vaguely curious.

"I am someone you used to know very well, but now do not know at all," the voice answered. "And I got in through a mysterious way you will not understand."

"I certainly do not understand anything about you; if I once knew you very well, how can I now not know you at all?"

"What I mean is that while you once knew me very well where I was then, where I am now, you cannot know me at all."

"Where were you then? And where are you now? And really, who are you? I still want to know how you came in here! And why?" A stream of questions flowed from me, one after the other.

"You ask too many questions without waiting for answers," the voice responded. "I was once with you. Now I am somewhere amorphous that you cannot see or understand. How I got into your locked room is part of the mysteries of who I am now in an amorphous world. And I came to you because I want you to be my Messenger to your world."

"Your Messenger? My world?! And what is your world?"

"Yours is the world of the living. Mine is the world of the dead."

"You are dead? And how can you be talking to me? Who really are you? And why are you choosing me to be your Messenger?"

"I used to be known as the Chairman."

"You *used to* be known? Whose Chairman were you? And what are you *now* known as?" More questions flowed.

"I say 'was' because I am no longer. I was the Chairman of our liberation movement. You can say that I am now his ghost. Or, if you prefer, consider me his spirit."

I could not believe my ears. Our beloved Chairman himself? Back in this world alive and talking to me? I wanted to scream with a mix of joy and fright. But I could not. I could not really comprehend what was happening. And I was very frightened that something ominous was happening to me. Was I going insane? "Please tell me why you chose me," I said, still not comprehending what was going on.

"I chose you to transmit my message because you were both a friend and an elder. That is why I always called you *Raandit*. I also chose you because I always thought that we shared the same ideas. Or should I say ideals? And we held similar views on issues."

As the Chairman continued to speak, I began to calm down and absorb what he was saying. I could not really see him, but I could recall the image of the man I knew. He was not tall by our people's standards, but he was not short either. He was somewhat stocky, but not fat. His bald head was compensated by thick hair around the bald spot and a bushy beard that was graying. His eyes, small relative to his head, penetrated sharply, radiating his intelligence. Occasionally fierce looking, he always softened his stern appearance with his wit, humor, and a winning smile. The picture came vividly to my mind as I interacted with a figure I could not really see.

His distinctive voice came back: "But that is not the whole story. My real reason for wanting to talk to you is not so much to carry my message, but actually to talk about you."

I was even more baffled. To talk about me? Why? What about me would The Great Chairman want to talk about?

"You did so much for our country that only a few people know. So, I want our conversation to be a record of both what you and I did together and what you yourself did for our movement and for our country. That's why I want you to record our conversations and eventually make them available to a wider audience."

I was so shocked and bewildered that I almost forgot the agony of my pain. I was truly beyond myself, not even aware enough to cry out loud. Our legendary Chairman himself, long dead, now coming to pass a message on through me?! And not only about himself, but about me as an old friend, and what I had done for the movement and the country?!

Of course, I always knew that I was close to the Chairman and that we shared many ideas about our country. But why would he now care so much about having my service to the country recognized? Did he really need me as his Messenger out of the multitudes that still revered him? Was all this real or an illusion? Was I myself still alive or had I died in my agony from the operation? Had the strange medicine that was supposed to kill my pain killed me instead? Had I perhaps joined the Chairman in the world of the dead, which was why we were able to communicate?!

I tried to recollect how the Chairman and I had the same ideas and shared the same views on critical issues. Because I was considerably older, the Chairman used to address me deferentially as *Raandit,* Old Man or Big Man, both terms of respect for an Elder.

I eventually gathered myself enough to respond to the Chairman. "I think I know what you mean," I said. "I am deeply touched that you remember how much we had in common." Until now, I was talking with no clear idea about the form of the person I was talking to, whether he was standing or sitting. I decided to be polite anyway, in case it was relevant to the situation. "Won't you sit down?! There is a chair here. I can't even see you well."

The Chairman's reaction confirmed the mystery of his presence. "The dead do not have a physical form to sit down. They cannot and should not be seen by the living. Don't you remember the stories about ghosts as frightening creatures of the night? Those who claim to have seen ghosts are themselves at the borderline of life. If you can see me well, you will have risked becoming one of us."

I laughed, although I knew that what he had just said was no laughing matter.

His remark added to my concern about my own situation between death and life. Since I sort of felt his presence, was I perhaps already one of them? Afraid of the answer, I instinctively redirected my focus. "So, what then is your message?"

The Chairman again displayed his skill in controlling dialogic situations. "My message is long and, as I said, it is really a joint message, and may mostly be about you. I don't think there is enough time tonight for the whole message. Let's arrange for me to visit you again tomorrow evening at about the same time."

"That sounds good," I said, with some sense of relief, trying to understand what had occurred and be better prepared for the next round. I was exhausted and quite confused.

"But please do not tell anyone that I visited you. For one thing, you will not be believed. They will probably think that you are going out of your mind. For another thing, they will just think it was a dream and dismiss it lightly. All this, including the message we are discussing, is strictly between you and me. When you are ready to share it, you can do so without revealing how it was collected and packaged. But at that point, you can do pretty much what you want to do. You will be your own judge."

"I see what you mean," I said, wondering whether I really saw what he meant and whether I was not indeed going mad or dreaming. I wanted to fall asleep and go back to the dream world where that encounter appropriately belonged.

Session Two: Background

The next morning, I felt better but was still in pain. I remained bewildered about what had happened the night before. As the Chairman said, talking about it would have been dismissed as a dream, which he knew it was not, or worse, be taken as a sign of madness. There was also the possibility that people might see that as self-promotion, claiming to be the chosen reincarnation of the Chairman, a remote but conceivable distortion. I chose silence.

My interaction with the Chairman began to trigger memories of my relations with him: the time we first met in the United States of America; his return to the Sudan and defection into the first South Sudanese liberation movement; his absorption into the Sudanese army; his postgraduate studies back in the United States; his re-defection to form the latest liberation movement; his life as the leader of the movement; his tragic death in a helicopter crash just three weeks after assuming the first vice-presidency of the newly reformed government of the Sudan and the presidency of the newly liberated Southern Sudan; and my immediately flying back to the country to accompany the body until the burial.

As I reflected on the world without the Chairman, the loss suddenly weighed very heavily on me, aggravating the pain I continued to feel.

In the evening, I called for my wife to give me my pain medicine. I also asked for my door to be locked. I was still mindful of how the medicine made me behave. I did not want to be seen or to draw attention. My wife had thoroughly prepared our four sons for this unusual situation in which the family had found itself. She disciplined them to respect my privacy and to consider my room out of bounds. The boys were of course deeply affected by the developments, but they obeyed the rules and kept the company of their friends outside the house or brought them home for the lavish meals their mother always prepared for any unexpected numbers. But they kept relatively quiet and serene, away from my room.

It was not long before the Chairman reappeared around the agreed-upon timing. "*Raandit,* do you remember me, or should I again introduce myself?" he asked me jokingly.

I laughed before responding: "How could I have forgotten you? You have not left my mind since I last saw you. I still don't understand why you chose me out of the multitudes of the people you related to in this world and who still remember you with great fondness and are still devoted to your memory." I then shared with the Chairman the concern that had crossed my mind. "I am also concerned that people may think that I am trying to promote myself as your successor—if not politically, then intellectually. This is of course absurd, since I was never a member of your movement and do not have the military and political combination of your leadership. But you never know the things people can concoct."

The Chairman reacted with characteristic wit. "I wouldn't worry about that. After all, what do I have for you to succeed me? Whatever I had has already passed on. It is no longer mine."

The Chairman was clearly being humorous and we both laughed. He continued.

"Actually, I also need to clarify that. Please do not think that you are the only one I am contacting. And remember that, instead of asking you to carry my message, I want us to remember together and especially about what you yourself did in your own right. It will then be for you to take what you make of it as a message. To be frank, I do the same with many others in different ways and I leave it to each one of them to carry whatever they get out of it."

I was of course very much moved by what he said. I had never doubted our friendship, but I had never realized fully what it meant to the Chairman. I also had a concern which I chose to share with him. "*Benydit*, I am of course deeply honored and flattered by what you are proposing. But I am still concerned that if people see it as me promoting myself, that might indeed defeat the very purpose you have in mind. I am worried about the implications."

"Look my friend, of course you are right that there will be people who will take it negatively that way. There are also people, perhaps the majority, who will take it positively. Do you think I could have done what I did if I worried about what people would say?"

He was of course quite correct. After all, he not only had many enemies, there were challenges to his leadership from within the movement that led to some violent confrontations and to the death of many people.

"Let us not be concerned about your competitive, perhaps envious, contemporaries and record our experiences for well-meaning people and for posterity."

Whether I was predisposed to agree with him or not, I thought the Chairman made a convincing case. I accepted his generous offer. "I appreciate what you are saying. So, let's go ahead. Where do we begin'?

"Wherever you wish," he responded in the same generous spirit.

"That's a blank check," I said.

"It is, but in an account probably with insufficient funds.," he said. We both laughed.

"Let me take the risk," I said and went back to the beginning of our relationship. I had already been reflecting on the history of our friendship since our last meeting. I began with the occasion when we first met. "It was in Philadelphia in the United States in the mid-1960s. Since you want this to be also a message to others, I will try to give details which you probably remember. It was the first gathering in which we formed a South Sudanese Students' Association in America. I was then finishing my doctoral studies in Law at Yale University and most of you students from South Sudan had just enrolled in American colleges. As I recall, after graduating from high school in Tanzania, you were accepted at Grinnell College, Iowa."

Details of our first encounter began to unfold as I continued. "As you will recall, I was elected President of the Association. The oldest among you refused to serve on our committee. I thought that he was protesting my election. Having come from the field as a member of the liberation movement, I suspected that he felt he should have been the one elected President. So, I offered to decline the presidency, but all of you insisted that I should abide by the will of the group as determined by the election."

Although I did not really want to bring tribal politics into my recollection, I thought I should say more on that issue. "Some people thought that their colleague was protesting the fact that I was elected because most of you were Dinka and he was a Nuer. I did not think so myself. I believed he just thought he was better qualified on political grounds. Since I was not a member of the movement, I thought he had a point. That was why I offered to step down. Actually, he and I later became good friends and colleagues in the government—he in the regional government and I at the center."

The Chairman seemed uncertain about his recollection of events. "All this is somewhat fuzzy in my memory," he admitted. To my surprise, he drew attention to himself: "Tell me more from the meeting in Philadelphia?"

I felt confident enough about our friendship to be candid with him. "To be frank, my memory of you was that you were exceptionally quiet. You hardly spoke. But I am not flattering you when I say that whenever you spoke, you impressed me with the depth of your thoughts. However, again to be frank, I never thought you would become the leader you became."

We laughed. Indeed, the Chairman seemed amused by what I said. Certainly, he did not appear offended by it. After all, his leadership had become widely acknowledged, which should make modesty a virtue.

"It's always good to be underestimated, and to surprise people in a positive way." He was magnanimous and kind in his recollection about me. "With you, I saw in you someone whose ideas I admired and hoped to learn from and befriend, as indeed I did."

Again, I felt touched, especially as I realized that he was sincere. "Well," I replied, "you certainly acted upon that when you and your Iowa friend visited me in New York. I had joined the United Nations Secretariat after obtaining my doctorate at Yale."

The Chairman had evoked my recollection of a particularly significant event. "Shortly after that pleasant time in New York, as I recall, you graduated with a Bachelor's degree in 1969, and although you received a scholarship to pursue graduate studies at the University of California, Berkeley, you chose to go back to study agricultural economics at the University of Dar es Salam in Tanzania. I am not sure why, but my vague recollection was that you were expected to return to Iowa. What I vividly recall is that your Iowa colleagues lost contact with you and I began to receive frantic calls from them wondering where you were. We all worried that something terrible might have happened to you. It was only after exhaustive enquiries that we learned that you had joined the Liberation movement. The rest, of course, as they say, is history."

Then, as though those recollections caused him some discomfort, the Chairman ended the session rather abruptly. "I think we have had enough for today. I will see you again tomorrow. But let me say again, please keep all this to yourself. I don't want people to think that I claim to be another Jesus rising from the dead. I am no longer of your world. I am dead and I have not arisen; and I have certainly not ascended to Heaven. I can only live in the memory of those who care about what I did or tried to do in real life. That is the immortality our African people believe in. And, of course, I am counting you among those who will remember me … and perhaps document the story of my life—along with yours, of course."

"I am sure many will. No one who knew you can forget you. And it would be an honor and a source of pride to document the story of your unforgettable life and your great achievements."

"On that reassuring note, let's continue tomorrow," the Chairman concluded and suddenly disappeared.

I lay on my back and reflected on all that had happened, wondering whether it was real. The Chairman coming back "alive" and choosing to reconnect with me to share our experiences and in particular to promote recording my contribution to our people and our country! It was all too good, or too strange, to be true. I took my medicine and gradually faded into sleep.

Session Three: Dynamics

My wife continued to be concerned about my state of mind. She realized that the pain had lessened, but I still needed the painkiller. I remained in our bedroom on the second floor. She served my meals in the room. And although the door was locked and no one could enter, she could still hear me talking, at times laughing. I can only imagine her growing concern, since this was not at all my behavior through the entirety of the time she had known me and lived with me.

Our four sons were, of course, well aware of what was happening. But their mother was very stern about their keeping a distance. I once heard our youngest son ask his mother why I was talking in the room alone. He was hushed into silence. I suspected that they thought their father was mad and that their mother was covering up. And they respectfully complied with her motherly wisdom.

I looked fine during the day and my wife apparently did not want to raise issues that might offend my sense of vanity, which she knew well. And of course, she did not want the rumors to spread around about my condition. So she nursed her concerns in silence.

Everyone in the family had now come to expect me to follow the routine of going to bed and taking my medicine. I also made sure that my door was locked. She had stopped listening to the sounds from my room, obviously choosing to let the sleeping dog lie. And the boys also kept their distance.

My mind was shifting to the encounters with the Chairman when the sounds of movement and some shadowy image told me that he had arrived. I was not sure when to expect him, since we had not fixed a time. But I thought it would be about the time he had first appeared: mid evening.

"*Raandit*, I assume you have been expecting me and gathering your thoughts on what we should talk about today," the Chairman opened the conversation. "In our last session, you said I had caused you and my American friends great anguish over my disappearance, only to resurface in the bush in South Sudan. I was a student turned rebel. But it was not long before the war came to an unexpected end through the Addis Ababa Agreement of 1972. I understood that you played a role in the process that led to peace. What did you do?"

"That's quite a flattering beginning. Good evening! Well so many prominent names were involved in bringing peace to the country. My role was minor in comparison," I said with a genuine sense of humility.

"Perhaps, but it is your role specifically I am interested in now."

I thanked the Chairman and gave him a brief account of what I knew about the developments leading to the Addis Ababa Talks and my role in the preparations. "Of course, virtually every Southerner had in one way or another suffered the anguish of the war and engaged in the search for peace in a variety of ways. I do not recall any occasion when South Sudanese sat together and talked about anything that did not in one way or another involve what was then labelled the Problem of South Sudan before you made it the problem of the whole Sudan. But the precise process that led to peace began with the military takeover of power by a leftist group of officers in October 1969 under the leadership of Colonel Jaafar Nimeiri. They were quite young, most of them below the rank of colonel. The portfolio on the South was given to a well-known and respected South Sudanese lawyer. He was one of the prominent communist leaders."

"Being respected did not mean being politically popular, since communism was quite unpopular in the Sudan."

"That's right, although most Northerners did not associate Southerners with communism, he was clearly an exception. The junta made a Declaration that promised peace based on autonomy for the South, which was in line with the long-standing position of the communist party in the Sudan. The Southern communist leader was known to have been the brains behind that Declaration. The government also announced amnesty for the rebels who put down their arms. That was when the government first offered me the position of minister plenipotentiary and deputy head of mission in our London Embassy. In his letter to me, the communist Minister of Southern Affairs emphasized the need for qualified South Sudanese to join the Foreign Service, which did not include any Southerners. As the war was still going on, I politely turned down the offer, offering as an excuse the post-doctoral fellowship I had just received from Yale Law

School to conduct research on the crisis of national identity in the Sudan."

It suddenly dawned on me that I was giving a historical account that the Chairman must know very well. "Why am I saying all this to you, when you know it all?" I said to him, after a brief pause.

"Remember, you are not just talking to me or informing me; we are making a record of your achievement or at least experience for others to know. So, please continue."

"Thank you. But please forgive me for recounting details that might be common knowledge to the unknown audience we are addressing." I sensed a gesture of agreement.

"Two years later, the communist wing of the leftist regime tried to stage an internal coup. I was then in Khartoum on my way to a UN conference in Gabon. I had just had a very lively discussion with the Minister of Southern Affairs. I had known him from the time he was in what was then Rumbek Senior Secondary School and I in Rumbek Junior Secondary. He and I later developed a warm personal relationship.

"I was trying to mediate a better understanding and cooperation between him and his Southern colleague in the government, another respected lawyer whom I had also known from our days at Rumbek. We later became colleagues in the faculty of law at the University of Khartoum, although he was senior to me. After graduating, he had served as a judge before joining politics to focus on the cause of the South. The two ministers were widely known to be competing to influence the government's Southern policy."

"Another instance of the North always trying to divide the South," the Chairman interjected.

"Well, in this case, I think it was a combination of the divisive politics of the North and the ideological differences between the two Southern leaders. The communist minister appreciated my initiative to reconcile them, but complained that there were no mediators among the Southerners in Khartoum, all of whom had taken sides. He said that the standoff between them had reached a point of no return. As a result, nothing was being done for the South. The impasse had to be resolved to determine who really was in charge of the Southern policy. He was clearly confident and jubilant, verging on euphoric. I had no idea why he seemed certain that he would soon win the contest he was describing."

"I think he was right in saying that Southerners tend to take extreme positions on Southerners in politics," the Chairman again interjected. "You are either with them or you are against them. I also agree with him that you were somewhat exceptional in that respect, largely because you were nonpartisan when it came to the internal politics of the South."

I agreed. "I soon learned why he had been so confident sounding," I resumed. "That late afternoon, the coup plotters struck. Roads were blocked in many spots in the city. Streets were flooded with soldiers. I was driving with a friend and my elementary school headmaster when we were stopped at a checkpoint. A soldier peeped into the car pointing his gun at us. When he let us go, the headmaster turned to us and wondered aloud, 'Was that gun loaded?' I was later intercepted just outside the house of a friend with whom I was staying by a soldier who demanded a document of identification. I wondered whether he expected all Sudanese to carry identity documents or saw me as different. In any case, I showed him my UN card from New York. I am sure he did not know what it was. After gazing at the document for some time, pretending to read it, he handed it back to me and reluctantly let me go."

"He obviously could do nothing else," said the Chairman.

"He would have been completely crazy to shoot or even arrest me, the unarmed, obviously benign civilian that I was. The announcement of the takeover, followed by martial music, kept being repeated on the radio. Power was in the process of changing hands. But intense fighting was still going on. Civilians were confined to their homes. The airport was closed. I could not fly out to my conference for several days."

"It has always puzzled me that the communists could be so reckless, knowing the culture of hostility against them in the Sudan. And their leaders were also very bright individuals," the Chairman observed.

"They were probably carried away by the surprise that the army was prepared to do for them what they could never achieve politically. It is ironic that the Muslim Brotherhood would do the same twenty years later in the so-called Revolution for National Salvation. The Islamists were probably more successful because they learned from their kindred opposites, the communists."

"I think I know what you mean by kindred opposites. But please, continue with the story."

"When I say that the Muslim Brothers and the communists are kindred opposites, I believe they are not as ideologically committed and divided as they appear. What I think unites them is their shared rebellion against the conservatism of their society. But since there is no ideological base for this rebellion, they had to look for something. In the process, they saw Communism and the Muslim Brotherhood as the effective bases. This is where they tactfully or operationally differ. Even then, their differences do not endure. Most communists turn conservative with time and age and most Muslim Brothers also shed their Islamic robes in due course. I have known quite a number of them personally and I cannot believe the transformation they undergo."

"That's fascinating. It's certainly more than I knew. Let's go back to the story of the regime and the communists."

"In Gabon," I continued, "I heard the news of the developments at home on the BBC. After three days during which the President was virtually gone, the coup attempt failed, and the President reemerged triumphant. The communist leaders responsible had been tried and executed. They included my friend, the Southern Minister, and the party's Secretary General, who was a household name in the Sudan. I was deeply saddened, not only because I had lost a friend who was a prominent Southerner, but also because of what must have been a sham trial, a slaughterhouse of injustice."

Again, I paused, feeling self-conscious about speaking too long on issues that might be either too well-known, or of no particular interest to the Chairman. "Are you still with me?" I asked, implicitly wondering whether he was interested. "I am concerned that our project is becoming one of me telling my own story, rather than you transmitting your message through me."

"Of course I am with you. It's all very interesting. And remember, my objective was more to give you the opportunity to share your own experiences and reflections. I know what I did and I believe most of our people are aware of what I did as a public figure. But even I, who knew you relatively well, do not know well what you did, especially before we got much closer in the latter part of your life. So, please tell us your part of the story and we will pick up mine at the appropriate stage of our conversations. Continue."

"Thank you. I appreciate that.

"I returned to Khartoum on my way back to the United States. The composition of the government had changed. The other Southern member of the Cabinet had been given the responsibility for the Southern policy. Although he differed ideologically from his communist colleague, he was truly a decent man and a strong believer in the rule of law. He could not possibly have been comfortable with the response of the government to the coup attempt. But he obviously owed it to the South to take their cause in a more representative direction.

"Foreign Affairs had gone to a man who was also vehemently anti-communist and who had been the permanent representative of the Sudan to the United Nations. He was a very liberal-minded intellectual. I had come to know him well and had developed a warm personal and professional relationship with him."

"He was indeed a very progressive scholar," interjected the Chairman. "He was vehemently supportive of the cause of the South, and indeed of the marginalized groups in the country, which is why he became one of the eminent Northerners to join our movement. But I am going too far ahead of your own story. Please continue."

"That's very pertinent, even to the developments I am recounting. While still in Khartoum, I was one day suddenly informed by the Ministry of Foreign Affairs that the President wanted to see me. I wondered why, but I was sure that it had been at the initiative of the Minister. I went. With the President was his new Minister of Southern Affairs. The President sat at his desk while the Minister and I sat in front of him on opposite ends of the desk. It was a simple modest setting, different from the grandiose office aura the President would eventually grow into.

"The President was in his military outfit, looking as though ready for battle. He was one of those Sudanese who was very Northern, but not typical in his physical looks. Contrary to the Black color reflected in the very Arabic name of the country, Sudan, he was light brown, more Egyptian looking than a regular Sudanese. He was stern looking, with snuff bulging under his lower lip. But he was otherwise cordial and friendly in demeanor. The Minister was a contrastingly slender and gentle person. He was quiet, soft spoken, and unpretentious, but very dignified, a characteristic for which he was well known."

"He was one of those few leaders whom power never corrupted," the Chairman interjected.

"Absolutely. As I sat with those two national leaders, I had very mixed feelings. On the one hand, I felt very uneasy about being with the President, a man who had the blood of prominent citizens, including my friend, the Southern Minister, on his hands. Many years later, the President would say to me, 'Ever since I slaughtered Farouk Hamdalla (a close colleague and friend of Nimeiri and one of the military officers who staged the abortive coup against him and was tried and executed), I no longer fear any decision'. I was shocked by his use of the brutal word 'slaughtered'. But that was indeed what he had done, and what I detested. On the other hand, although I felt uneasy about meeting a man I considered a murderer, I sympathized with him because those people wanted to depose and perhaps kill him. I also appreciated the fact that he was with the Minister, a man for whom I had high regard. There must be something good in him, I thought, to gain the confidence of that decent man."

"I think the Minister saw him as a necessary tool for pursuing a noble cause," the Chairman commented. "It must have been a case of the end justifying the means."

"I guess so. Feeling somewhat uncomfortable and with no agenda for discussion, I eased my discomfort by taking the initiative to discuss the situation in our sensitive border area of Abyei, where the horrors of the war still prevailed. Only months after the military seizure of power, our father got terminally ill and died in Cairo, where my brother, a medical doctor, and I had taken him, hoping for a miraculous treatment.

"We checked into a hotel, but an old friend, a journalist politician from a neighboring Dinka tribe in the South, who had been a member of the National Assembly that Nimeiri's Revolution had dissolved, came and insisted that we stay with him in his house. His Dinka tribe had such a close affinity with our tribe that we both were considered virtually one tribe. His father and our father were age mates, initiated into adulthood together, and were close friends. He himself was also personally close to our father."

"I know that you yourself became very close friends and colleagues with him and that you collaborated on many issues over the years, including with us."

"Correct. Although we do not always agree and in fact often disagree on issues, we have remained good friends and collaborators on both personal and public issues. Before leaving for Cairo, I made a hint to Father to designate a successor to himself as Paramount Chief. I told him that since we did not know how long he would be away, should he not name someone to act for him in his absence? Father seemed to understand the hint. After all, he was a brilliant man. He looked at me with suspicious eyes and said, 'When I left, did I not leave someone in charge, or is there something else you want to tell me?' I could not say anything further, except to gesture without words, 'I understand'.

"Two things happened while my father was in the hospital that would feature significantly in my work for the country. One occurred while my journalist politician friend and I were visiting Father. As we were leaving the hospital, my friend exited first, leaving me alone with Father for a few minutes. Father said to me, 'That friend of yours is a man. Work closely with him.' And indeed, as I have said and as will be evident in our conversations, he and I have worked very closely ever since.

"Another incident involved another friend, a law school classmate at the University of Khartoum, who, after obtaining a Master's degree in Law at Howard University in Washington, D.C., had briefly joined the United Nations and then returned to the country on the occasion of his father's illness and eventual death. Father invoked the case of my classmate by raising the rhetorical questions: 'Was your friend not with you in America and has he not returned to his country? Which one is your country? Should I survive this illness, I want to have a serious talk with you.'

"That was quite a series of challenging questions."

"They sure were. I explained to my father the political circumstances that had led to my going to the United States to pursue my post-graduate studies. The understanding was that I would return after obtaining my doctorate to resume my position as lecturer in law to which I was appointed after graduation. My appointment had been interrupted by political differences, which had been resolved by the time I went to the States. When I tried to return to the University in accordance with the initial understanding, the response I received made me feel as though I were a foreigner applying for a job. So, I joined the United Nations instead of returning home.

"My father nicely surprised me with his understanding. He said, 'In the ways of our Dinka people, when a man leaves his tribe in protest to an offensive way he is treated by his tribe, it is incumbent upon his people to fetch him and persuade him to return with honor and dignity. Wait, they will fetch you'. I was deeply moved. And my father's prophecy would be fulfilled only a year later. And I returned to national service less than two years after, with the honor father stipulated, as Ambassador with an important posting abroad, and at the young age of thirty-four."

"That is the spiritual power of an elder and divine leader."

"I can only agree. But I have strayed from our main theme. Let me go back to my father's illness, eventual death, and the challenge of taking his body home. It was a rainy season and travel by road or air was undependable.

Traveling by land, if at all possible, was only by military trucks, and that would take days. Because of the rains, landing strips were not functioning and flights were ruled out. Then, miraculously, we were told that it had not rained in Abyei for some time and that, with some leveling of the ground, a plane could land. With the help of the government, we flew the body home to find a war situation in which the commanding officer was terrorizing the population with arrests, torture, and killings."

"It means that the latest developments toward peace that were underway in Khartoum had no effect in the periphery. That is evidence of the marginalization of the rural areas that we in the movement were addressing."

"I have always understood and supported that. The day my brother and I arrived with the body of our father, we learned that a close uncle had been killed the previous day by the security forces. Our father's sister, a very close aunt, had been tortured and her hands bound and nearly crippled. Since our family quarters were crowded with mourners, we were initially to stay in a dilapidated rest house to be guarded by tribal warriors who carried only spears. So, when the commanding officer invited us to stay with him in his house, we immediately accepted.

"That night, we heard a lot of commotion. In the morning, when the officer joined us for tea, we questioned him about the security situation. In his account, he admitted that he had surrounded our home with soldiers at night because they learned that the rebel leaders might come to pay their last respects to their deceased uncle.

"After fully assessing the situation, we contacted our cousins nearby to either join us in managing the security challenges or removing themselves from the area. The officer initially resisted any

21

contacts with the rebels, but we eventually persuaded him, as an effort to ease the security situation. Besides, we reminded him that the government had offered amnesty to the rebels. We also tried to ensure the cooperation of traditional leaders, especially our younger brother who had just been installed as successor to our father as Paramount Chief, with the security forces in the area.

"After a month of nearly impossible attempts to try to restore peace and security, we left a precarious situation that was still experiencing a reign of terror. Worse, our young brother, who had succeeded our father as Paramount Chief, was assassinated by security elements who had not been held accountable."

"I can see why you wanted to seize the opportunity to discuss with the President the critical situation in Abyei. But in the national crisis situation he was managing, I doubt if Abyei could feature significantly in his priorities."

"I was essentially appealing to the President to take appropriate measures that would build on the strategic historic role of Abyei as a peaceful and harmonious bridge between the North and the South. I thought that would give them a national vested interest in what might otherwise be a remote situation, as you correctly point out. The President and the Minister seemed attentive to what I said. The President might have been perhaps only courteous, but he responded very positively to my request."

"That was a smart way of turning a crisis situation into an opportunity. And a very appropriate and effective one."

"It's interesting you say that, because strategic optimism and looking for opportunities in crises are among my guiding principles in life."

"I was discreetly stating what I knew about you, which you have just confirmed."

"I suspected that you probably knew me that well. Anyway, going back to the story of my encounter with the President, I then took the initiative to end the meeting by saying, 'Having made my case on my small area of Abyei, let me now leave you to deal with the big issues of the country.' Although I did not know it at the time, it would become obvious later that the meeting was in fact intended as an interview for a position in the government. And that was, of course, the work of the foreign minister, who was so discreet that he never hinted to me what he was doing."

"Obviously, though, of course not surprisingly, you passed the test without bending to the calculations of the president for wanting to see you. Perhaps this is the place to explain how Abyei happened to be administered in the North. But I suggest we leave it for our next session."

"Thank you. I expect it to be a long account. So, I agree."

We ended the conversation rather abruptly, which made me wonder whether the Chairman had really been interested in what I had said. The situation was in every way rather awkward and ambiguous. Since the Chairman ended by saying that we should discuss the history of Abyei between the North and the South, he could not have been disinterested in what I had said. I gave him the benefit of the doubt and retired for the night.

Session Four: Abyei

I was really enjoying my conversations with the Chairman and looked forward with great anticipation to his visitations, which of course were not visits in the normal sense. In fact, they were mysterious and rather mythical, but they were to me an almost tangible reality.

I was particularly interested in the topic of our next session, since it involved my home area, which had been of great interest and concern to me since childhood. I also realized that it had been an issue of considerable interest to the Chairman. After all, fighters from Abyei were among his closest comrades and the most committed supporters of his leadership.

When the Chairman next appeared, he opened our session by noting that Abyei had been a matter of particular concern to him. He launched right into the topic, as if it had been on his mind. He said he thought the issue of Abyei had been resolved by the Comprehensive Peace Agreement and the special Protocol on Abyei. He recalled that on his visit to Abyei after the conclusion of the peace agreement, he declared his intention to make Abyei a model for peace and development cooperation between North and South Sudan. Now, he could see that the issue of the political status of the area between Sudan and South Sudan remained unresolved. He said that the cause of Abyei was one of the issues he most regretted not resolving before his demise.

He then reminded me to tell the story of how Abyei ended up being administered in the North in the first place. He said that while Southerners overwhelmingly support the cause of the Ngok Dinka, only a relative few know the circumstances that took Abyei to the administration of the North.

I tried to be brief but comprehensive at the same time. "This is a story that has often been told, but it does not seem to register with our people in the South. The story goes back to the time of my great grandfather, Arob Biong. It was during the Mahdiya. Our people were still being hunted by the Arab slave traders, using mostly our neighboring Missiriya Arabs. But our people fought back heroically and at times overwhelmed the Arabs. Mind you, the weapons of war in those days were spears on both sides. The Arabs had large spears called *rek* that were used for face-to-face combat, with the Arabs on horses. Our people had slim-shafted spears called *tong* that could be darted at an enemy from a distance."

"That's why the word for war or fight among the Dinka is *tong*," observed the Chairman. "I suppose they must have changed, now that wars and even local fights involve guns, no longer spears. Our people have also moved from spears to guns, which is now causing havoc in tribal wars that used to be fought with the much less destructive power of spears."

"Really tragic! It is quite extraordinary that, as children and even as young men, we witnessed tribal wars being fought with spears and shields, and now I have them displayed on the wall of our house in America as historical trophies. That's the speed of change in our contemporary world. When scores of people were killed in tribal wars with spears, that was considered a tragedy remembered in history. Now tribal conflicts, even between clans, result in the deaths of hundreds. It's really a tragic development.

"Going back to the history of Abyei, defeated in battle and with large numbers of their herds captured when they entered Ngok territory for their seasonal search for water and grazing, the Arab Chief, Azoza, approached my great grandfather, Arob Biong, and sued for peace. He is said to have told my great grandfather that he was no longer seeking the return of their captured cattle. All he wanted was peace and brotherhood so that their people could live together as relatives.

"It is said that my great grandfather and his Arab counterpart entered into a pact of brotherhood. They symbolically bled themselves and mixed their blood to become brothers. That pact has been kept with that Arab clan to this day, although now strained to the breaking point by the more recent history of hostilities. There were times when these Arab 'relatives' contributed to the payment of bride wealth of our marriages and shared in the distribution of bride wealth coming into our family. The Arabs offered the Dinka gifts of horses and received gifts of cattle from their adopted Dinka 'kindred'.

"Those leaders were far more tolerant and accommodating than the leaders of today. The fact that differences of race, religion, and language did not inhibit their developing close ties is remarkable."

"Absolutely. Then the Mahdiya replaced that friendly Chief with one of their own men who was one of the most aggressive slave hunters. My great grandfather then offered the former Arab leader, with his faction of the tribe, refuge and protection in the Ngok Dinka area known as Baar Aliil. This is documented by English historians, among whom was the administrator and scholar, K.D.D. Henderson."

"That's important, because, with the shift from oral to written history, what our people now believe is what is written. Unfortunately, it is leading to what you might call a cultural intellectual inferiority complex—a very difficult condition to treat," asserted the Chairman.

We laughed at the intellectual-medical linkage. "That's true. But worse, even what is written must be Western to be respectable and credible. It is not only history, but even the documentation of our culture is only acknowledged if done by foreign writers. I must confess that this is a condition from which I myself suffered at one point in my life. It took me quite a while to recognize and appreciate Jommo Kenyatta's book about his people, the Kikuyu, *Facing Mount Kenya*. I am glad I liberated myself in time to write about our own culture."

"Which at least some of us—and, I believe, increasingly, most of our people who read—much appreciate."

"Thank you. Anyway, to go back to the story of the Ngok Dinka, my great grandfather is said to have gone to the Mahdi with his Deputy, Allor Ajing, from another spiritually powerful clan, to complain against his Arab neighbors. Some Arab elders, whom I interviewed about relations, claim that he was indeed taken to the Mahdi by his Arab friends or relatives. It should be noted that, generally, the Dinka initially welcomed the Mahdi as sent by God to redeem the people of the Sudan from foreign domination. They even composed hymns in his praise, calling him the Son of Deng, the powerful Dinka spirit next to God in mythology. That hymn, as I recall, has verses that include the words:

It is Mahdi, the Son of Deng Acuuk
To whom we ants on Earth pray.
Our people have suffered for eight years.
It is Mahdi to whom we pray."

27

"They probably didn't think of him as an Arab, only a man of God."

"That's correct. Even the fact that he was a Muslim leader was probably less significant to them than the fact that he was a messenger of God. In fact, when, later on, the Mahdist revolution proved to be a power of the slave traders, the Dinka opposed it and even sang the hymns in praise of the Mahdi as a redeemer against the Mahdi as an Arab slaver.

"When my great grandfather, Arob Biong, visited the Mahdi, he was still seen as a redeemer. It is reported by the Arabs that my great grandfather converted to Islam and adopted the name Abdel Rouf. Although the version of the Ngok Dinka does not refer to this alleged conversion, it acknowledges that my great grandfather and the other Ngok leader, Allor Ajing, who accompanied him, prayed with the Mahdi.

"The story among the Ngok has it that after the prayers, my great grandfather's companion, Allor Ajing, asked him whether he saw God when they were praying. My great grandfather's response was, 'Allor, I did not see God, but let us leave matters as they are.' It is said by the Ngok Dinka that the Mahdi recognized my great grandfather as the leader of 'All the Black People'.

"That probably meant the Dinka, which would not be surprising since our people, with their limited view of the wider world, used to consider themselves the only people God created Black."

"That's right. It should also be noted that the Ngok Dinka were then administered in the Southern Province of Bahr el Ghazal, together with their neighboring Twic, while the Ruweng Dinka were administered in Upper Nile Province, but were closely associated with the leadership of my grandfather. This would also be why my great grandfather considered himself the leader of the Black people, since those Southern neighbors were the only other Blacks they knew. I was later told by a leading Rek Dinka Chief of an important Dinka tribe that they did not know the Arabs, and that the Ngok Dinka leaders were their intermediaries with the Arabs. He said that prominent Chiefs from all Dinka tribes would make contributions to the authorities in the North, to be channeled through Ngok Dinka leadership. Major Dinka Chiefs would all gather periodically and meet with my grandfather to deliberate on the affairs of the country. It was a form of Dinka Tribal Confederation. He went as far as saying that the fact that our Dinka people survived the upheavals of that period was largely due to my forefathers. It was a very moving and humbling testimony. Of course, the Mahdi's knowledge of the Black peoples was also very limited, which is probably why they readily accepted my grandfather's claim to be the leader of all Black people."

The Chairman added, "For the Mahdi, probably, those who were not Arabs were all Black. I find all this very informative. I am sure most of our people have no idea about these historical details. Continue with your fascinating account."

"When my great grandfather and his companion, Allor Ajing, left," I continued, "the Mahdi ordained that my great grandfather would beget a son to be named 'Mahdi' and Allor would beget a son to be named 'Sabah.' He also freed the Dinka slaves and handed them to my great grandfather to take back with him. In the periphery of Abyei village, there is an area called '*Mit-rok*', 'Pulling the Fence', where my great grandfather had an enclosure made in which he accommodated these freed slaves and called their Dinka chiefs from the South to come and identify their people to take back with them. The Mahdi gave my great grandfather a sword as a sacred symbol of his authority and assured him that his people would no longer be raided for slaves. The two leaders had sons who were named Mahdi and Sabah as the Mahdi had ordained."

"Our people would probably interpret these historical facts as evidence that you had been turned into Arabs and Muslims, which would of course be a misreading of the way people perceived these things in their historical context. There was really no racial notion of an Arab or having a religion in their scheme of things. There was probably a tribal name and a perception of God and the spiritual world that was a cultural way of life and not a formal institution called religion. The Mahdi for them represented this spiritual world view, though with culturally different practices, such as manner of praying. And of course, your great grandfather was being pragmatic in adjusting to the ways of those who were stronger than them and wielded power over them."

"That's the baggage we carry for compromising to redeem our people from evil, which people now second-guess and become wiser in hindsight. Later on, when the British and the Egyptians defeated the Mahdiya under the Khalifa, the Mahdi's successor, and established the Anglo-Egyptian Condominium rule, the Missiriya, under the veteran Mahdist, were still raiding the Ngok Dinka and the neighboring Twich and Ruweng Dinka tribes for slaves. That's when both my great grandfather and the leaders of the neighboring Dinka tribes complained to the new government. The government then decided, in 1905, to transfer the Ngok Dinka, the Twich of Bahr el Ghazal, and the Ruweng Dinka of Upper Nile to Kordofan in the North, both for administrative convenience and to provide them with better protection against Arab slave traders. Later, in the 1940s, the Ruweng and the Twich were returned to their previous provinces in the South, while Ngok Dinka remained administratively in the North."

"It is interesting," interjected the Chairman, "that Southerners believe that only the Ngok Dinka were administratively connected to the North. If they knew that other Southern groups were also affiliated administratively with the North, they would not see the Ngok Dinka as an anomaly between the North and the South. They would see them as Southerners the way they see the other groups that had historically also been administered in the North."

I resumed: "The Ngok Dinka under the leadership of my grandfather Kwol Arob chose to remain under Kordofan as gatekeepers to protect the land of the Dinka from Arab incursions. When the British tried to persuade my grandfather to return to the South and even sent Dinka leaders from the South to go to persuade him, my grandfather explained to them that he was there to protect the land of the Dinka. If he were to join his people in the South, those Arabs that appreciated being granted seasonal access to water and grazing land would claim that the land was theirs and would try to take it by force. He asked his fellow Southern leaders to wait patiently for an appropriate time to join them."

"Your grandfather was prophetic; what he foresaw is what has now happened. He was obviously following the wisdom of the classic saying, 'If you can't beat them, join them'. People sometimes refuse to see the obvious, at the risk of being suicidal."

"That's unfortunately the case. And our people, not fully appreciating the circumstances under which that decision was made, criticize it on the basis of the situation today. My father followed in his father's footsteps for more or less the same reasons. Before the British left, they gave our father the same option and even invited him to visit Bahr el Ghazal before making his final decision. In 1951, he visited several towns in Bahr el Ghazal, including Aweil, Wau, and Tonj. One of my brothers and I accompanied him. We were newly admitted to

Rumbek Junior Secondary School. Father was headed for Rumbek when he decided that he had been too long away from his sensitive border area and turned around for his journey back home, having apparently made up his mind. Although the issue was very controversial among the Ngok, Father eventually decided to remain in the North for various reasons. He certainly was not impressed by the overall situation he found in the South, particularly the status accorded the chiefs, compared to their Northern counterparts. But a major consideration in his decision had to do with the 'bridging' role his area had played between the North and the South. Father was particularly known for describing himself as the needle and thread that stitched the North and South together."

"This was evidently a complex strategic decision which cannot be easily understood by our people today, but I do understand it fully," the Chairman noted. "The challenge is how to make our people understand."

"I think our Dinka elders from the South also understand. As I have already said, in my interviews with Dinka Chiefs after the Addis Ababa Agreement, the protective role of the Ngok Dinka on the borders was widely acknowledged. The critical question was whether the time had come for the Ngok Dinka to join their kith and kin in the South. The Ngok Dinka and the South Sudanese generally felt that the justification for joining the South had already been demonstrated by the suffering of the Ngok Dinka in the North and their participation in the South Sudan liberation struggle.

"It is certainly a complex situation. On the one hand, identifying with the North and demanding equality within unity can be an effective form of struggle. On the other hand, when that strategy ceases to work, other forms of struggle, including separation, become imperative. That's what the Ngok Dinka did then and are doing now. It is not that different from what the South did earlier and has now done. But if that too proves difficult, as seems to be the case over Abyei, people must be creative in seeking alternatives.

"That's what I keep telling our people: that even water, that does not think, when its flow is blocked keeps meandering around until it reaches its destination in the sea or the ocean."

"Keep saying it," the Chairman encouraged me, "and more importantly, keep doing it yourself."

The Chairman then suggested that we end the session and resume our discussion of the steps leading to the 1972 Addis Ababa agreement in our next session.

As I reflected on our session, as had become my practice, I really appreciated the Chairman's generosity of spirit. The whole session had been devoted to my area of Abyei, which most Southerners regarded as marginal to the main concerns of the South. And yet, here was the Chairman, whose agenda was the whole Sudan, focusing on Abyei, appreciating the historical context in which the crisis situation had evolved, the decisions taken by the leaders in that context, and the challenges now facing contemporary leaders of the country to find appropriate remedies to the historical wrongs that shaped the destiny of the people. I felt much closer to the Chairman. And if I had told my wife about my discussion with the Chairman, I was sure she too would have shared my sentiments. But that was a secret I felt I must keep to myself, even from my wife. As was the pattern, I called out to her, took my medicine and transitioned myself into sleep as I reflected over my conversation with the Chairman.

Session Five: Recruitment

Although my right arm was still in a sling, I was now able to move around the house and often changed the scene by sitting on the deck to marvel at the quietness of the garden that screened us off from the hassles of the city. Anticipating the sessions with the Chairman had become a program that required some preparation by thinking about the topic we would discuss. The more I thought, the more specific events came to mind. The problem then became one of selecting those that were of direct significance to our agenda. And increasingly, our discussions seemed to focus on my experiences, largely due to the Chairman's generous encouragement. After all, we both knew that his record of achievement was well known. He wanted mine to be better known, partly because he thought it was only fair, and partly because he knew that we had much in common in our ideas.

As our usual time for the sessions was approaching, I was getting restless in my anticipation. And as always, the Chairman suddenly appeared the moment I stopped anticipating his appearance. "Good evening, *Raandit*. I hope this is roughly the time you are expecting me." I heard the voice and tried to look around for the Chairman's figure. The Chairman was generally quite punctual in his visits. And I had become well-tuned to his timing. Not that we had any set time; only a vague mid-evening time between 8 and 9.

"Good evening, *Benydit*," I responded. "Yes, you are always punctual because we have no precise time in mind," I added as a purely factual and jocular statement, to which we both laughed.

"Are you diplomatically telling me that I have no sense of time? If you are, you would not be wrong, for in our world of the dead, our sense of time is different from yours."

"That was not the way I was thinking about it. But since you have raised the issue, what is your sense of time?" I asked, again being purely curious.

"In our world, the issue does not really arise, and for that reason, it would be difficult to answer your question or for you to understand what I would say. I suggest we go to the topic of our session."

"Very well," I said and went straight to the peace process following the aborted leftist coup attempt and the appointment of a new minister for Southern Affairs. "In our last session, my account of the process leading to the 1972 Addis Agreement was side-tracked by the case of Abyei, which became the topic of my meeting with the President and the new minister of southern affairs. The new minister immediately embarked on preparations for negotiations with the rebels. His predecessor had wanted appropriate institutions for socialism to be first grounded in the South before autonomy could be implemented or negotiation with the rebels undertaken. Southerners, who were vehemently anti-communist, were strongly opposed to his socialist agenda and policy position on the South. The new minister was also known to be against that policy. He now had the trust of the President to proceed with his own alternative policy, which favored entering into negotiations with the rebels."

"I doubt that the President was taking sides on the substantive positions involved. It was sheer political opportunism. He had backed someone who turned against him. So, he turned to the opponent of his enemy who would actually just serve his interest by negotiating an agreement that was favorable to his regime. It is that simple."

"I entirely agree with your analysis. At the start of the preparations with the rebels, I happened to be in Khartoum again on my way to a UN meeting, this time in Zambia. I was invited by a Khartoum University colleague to attend a meeting of South Sudanese intellectuals and politicians discussing issues to be negotiated with the rebels. The room was filled with the Southern political elites of Khartoum. The precise issue under discussion was the definition of South Sudan.

"The meeting seemed to agree that South Sudan comprised the three provinces of Bahr el Ghazal, Equatoria, and Upper Nile, as defined by the 1956 colonial borders. Of all those gathered, no one thought of the people of Abyei, who were fighting and dying in the struggle alongside their Southern kith and kin. Although I was a guest, I raised my hand and asked whether they were not leaving out some areas of South Sudan. All laughed and recognized immediately that I was alluding to Abyei. The definition of the South was then changed to include areas that were culturally part of the South, meaning Abyei.

I feared that specifying Abyei might have generated controversy. In retrospect, I was probably wrong."

"Did you really think that they had deliberately overlooked Abyei? Or were they aware of the political sensitivities which they were trying to avoid by being shrewdly evasive?" remarked the Chairman.

"This is a very good question, for which I have no answer, but the spontaneous way they reacted to my reminder made me believe that they were at least subliminally aware of the issue but had inadvertently overlooked it. But how all of them could have been oblivious to that omission is difficult to fathom. You must have been following this process in the jungles of the South?"

"Not at all. We vaguely heard that something might be brewing, but we did not take it seriously. We were so far apart with the North that no possible agreement was conceivable."

I then resumed my account. "Later, when the preparations for the talks intensified, at the initiative of an old friend, one of the prominent personalities in Southern politics, the new minister of southern affairs asked me to join him to go to London from the US to meet with members of the liberation movement to prepare for the talks. My brother, who was practicing medicine in England, joined us in the talks. We spent days in intensive discussions that began early in the day and continued into the early hours of the next morning."

"You were endeavoring to end the war we were fighting when we, the fighters, were in the dark. People knew what they were fighting for. Would the peace you were negotiating address their concerns? As you probably know, I myself was suspicious and eventually opposed to the talks as a risky, unacceptable compromise. Even then, I had in mind the Vision of a New United but totally transformed Sudan. I certainly did not want our army to be absorbed with the Sudan Army. I wrote my concerns in a letter to our Commander-in-Chief on January 24, 1972, asking, 'How would the Agreement address our concerns?' Let us leave that for later discussions. Continue your story."

"It's interesting you raise that question," I responded. "I remember at one point in our discussions, late into the night, when some people were dozing off, I said I had a small point to make. I then argued that, for the war to end, and for peace to be achieved and sustained, the men who had been fighting—some for a long time—must find value in it for them. What would a peace agreement offer them that would make it worth their while to stop fighting? Although it seemed like an

35

obvious point, it was met with a surprising response. There was dead silence for a while, which indicated that my remark was either a total surprise or was explosively sensitive."

"It's quite possible that they were aware of the issue but considered it too sensitive to raise. It's an example of what you say in your famous article, that what is not said is what divides."

"Probably. Then a senior member of the rebel movement, who had been lying down, seemingly sleeping, sat up and said, 'That's it! That's the crux of the matter. I have nothing else to say.' He said that and fell back to sleep. Again, dead silence followed. Then one of the leading members of the delegation to the talks spoke, 'Like our Brother, who began by saying that he had a small point to make, then dropped a bomb, I too have a small point to make.' I don't remember what his small point that was a potential bomb was, but my remark led to our proposing that the fighting men in the rebel movement be absorbed into the Sudanese Security Forces. Now, in hindsight, with their absorption taken for granted, my initial proposal may sound trite. But, at the time, it was an intriguing bombshell. You are probably right, that they knew about it but considered it one of the hidden issues to be raised at the right time.

"That's what I meant when I said that you have much to report. These may seem insignificant now, but when seen in their context might have significantly contributed to reaching the agreement, a compromise that I personally felt uncomfortable with.

"One of the most touching moments for me is when one of the leaders who had represented the Southern movement in Europe for many years, said to me shortly before his death that it was I who made him understand the Northern point of view, which enabled him to look for a common ground. My main argument with Southerners was that we should always be open with Northerners, to explain our point of view and to listen to theirs. I also argued for a compromise that would balance Northern commitment to the unity of the country and Southern demand for self-determination. This could be achieved through autonomy for the South. In any case, our people needed peace to have a reprieve, to strengthen themselves and build their capacity for a future round of the struggle, if need be. My discussions with the representative were ongoing and we met every time I passed through London. Shortly before his untimely death, he said that, in appreciation of the role I played in influencing his position in the quest for peace, he would leave his papers to me in his will. Knowing that the practice of writing wills is still alien to our people, I am not surprised that I never received his papers. But I remain deeply appreciative of what he said to me."

The Chairman noted, "That's another detail that is worth letting our people know. How many of our people do you think would expect a leading spokesman for the South to tell you that you made it possible for him to find a basis for negotiating peace with the North? Please keep talking."

"What is interesting is that the initiative and the process that led to peace was very much engineered and sustained by the African Council of Churches working closely with a regime that, at least initially, was leftist and Arabist. Although they broke with the communists, their color did not change radically, as shown by their creating what they called the Sudan Socialist Union. It, of course, helped that the process involved a minister who did not share that leftist leaning, with Emperor Haile Selassie hosting and guiding the process."

"It was perhaps a marriage of convenience," the Chairman surmised. "Even the Devil could be welcomed as a peacemaker, whatever his interest or hidden agenda."

"The regime, having alienated both the right and the left, clearly needed the middle through peace with the South to consolidate its power base. The results of our discussions were shared with the minister who led the government delegation in the Addis Talks. The Addis Ababa Agreement was concluded in March, 1972. The integration of forces became a central provision in the Agreement. The Agreement also gave the people of Abyei the right to decide by plebiscite whether to remain in the North or join the South."

"That was precisely what I had feared and opposed. I wanted our two armies to co-exist separately for five years and then carry out a merger for another five years during the transformation of the country into a New United Sudan. Anyway, it was after the Agreement that you accepted an appointment in the government?"

"Yes. Shortly after the signing of the Agreement, I received a letter from the Minister of Southern Affairs, emphasizing the importance the government attached to the justice system in the country and, on behalf of the President, offering me the position of a Provincial Judge, Chief Justice of the Province, later State of Kordofan. Despite my high regard for the minister, I did not think that, with my post-graduate specialization and international service, I was suited for a provincial assignment. The mistake I made was that I did not even respond to the letter, for which I later apologized.

"Not long after that offer, I received another letter from the Minister of Foreign Affairs offering me the position of ambassador to the Nordic Countries, with a residence in Sweden. I had just gotten married to an American and immediate relocation abroad had not been in our plan. So I procrastinated, reflecting on how to respond. The minister later told me that when he first discussed the appointment with the President, he was told that they were still waiting for my response to the offer of the provincial judgeship and he explained to the President that he did not think I would accept that offer. He of course knew me well and must have thought, as I did, that becoming a judge was not in line with my academic and professional qualifications.

"Then came another letter, this time from the Deputy Minister of Foreign Affairs, who had also served as Permanent Representative to the United Nations. He and I had in fact become friends. In his letter, he referred to the earlier letter that had offered me the Ambassadorship to Scandinavia and said that if I wanted a more active position, the post of Deputy Minister of Foreign Affairs, his own position, was available for me. I later learned that he was assigned an important ambassadorship to the Organization of African Unity in Addis Ababa.

"That was when I told my wife that I could not turn down four offers and still expect to be ever asked to serve my country in any capacity. She wondered how her family would take our living abroad, which they had not expected. We had just gotten married in what the media projected almost as the wedding of the era of changing race relations. She is an American of German background. She was then doing her doctorate at Columbia University in bilingualism under Margaret Mead, the famous anthropologist. She was also collecting conversation style in world languages for a project with the famous folklorist, Alan Lomax. She was told that I was the only Sudanese who spoke a Sudanese local language besides Arabic. That was how we met.

"The wedding took place in the United Nations Chapel in New York. Our family was represented by my doctor brother and a female cousin. My wife-to-be called the *New York Times* for an announcement, but got connected to the social page, whose editor got interested in the story. They turned what was to be a brief announcement into a relatively long substantive article, with our wedding photograph, giving details of our academic and professional positions, an elaborate description of the dress she wore, traced back to the wife of the Secretary of War under President Woodrow Wilson, her doctoral work under Margaret Mead, and the political and occupational status of our respective parents. I went back to Yale to find the *New York Times* article posted on an office wall of the Faculty of Law. The article was reproduced in the *UN Secretariat News Bulletin,* the *International Herald Tribune* in Europe, the *US Embassy* in Khartoum, and many national newspapers. As I say, it was as though the moment was ripe to display to the world support for mixed marriages. With the way the Western world is behaving these days against foreign infiltration into their countries, this trend appears to be reversing itself."

"This is transient, representing only a phase," the Chairman responded. "They cannot stop the march of history and the globalizing forces of interracial fusion. After all, the powerful scientific and disciplined system of Nazi Germany failed in its racist policies and strategies. Many people around the world feared that the evil apartheid system of South Africa was too powerful to be reformed, even at the dawn of its collapse. So, the racists are facing an inexorable current they cannot block."

"I couldn't agree with you more," I admitted. "Anyway, it was under those circumstances when I had just become affiliated into my new American family that the national job offers came and my wife was concerned about the reaction of her close-knit family. I suggested that we seek her parents' opinion. We did and they advised us to accept the position of Ambassador. I also thought that the position of Ambassador would be a better transition for my wife than plunging into a job inside the Sudan."

"That was very wise. Given the fact that her family expected you to live in the United States, I can fully understand her concern. But her parents also responded very responsibly. It would have made your position very difficult had they not supported you."

"Actually, they were to prove consistently very supportive of our marriage. That issue resolved, I then had to plan to carry out the challenge of my new assignment. I outlined in writing how I proposed to build on the positive achievement of peace as a basis for promoting international partnership for the post-war reconstruction and development of the country. I sought official endorsement of my proposed approach from the Minister and the President and it was granted."

The Chairman then interjected, "Your wife, whom I of course got to know well, adapted very well not only to your serving the country abroad, but also to your later service inside the country."

"Actually, I thought she did better than me in her relations with our very large family. And that was in fact the way I wanted it, because I did not want our people to think that marriage to a foreigner had taken me away from them. In fact, my doctor brother, who attended our wedding in America, said he would pray to our ancestors to bless my marriage and ensure that, if I was lost, I would be lost in the right direction. I think that if I am at all lost, with my wife, I am lost in the right direction."

"I can certainly testify to that. I was always very impressed by how graciously she received people. And from my own observations, there was always enough food in your house for any number of people who turned up. It was also most unusual that a woman who was a scholar and a professional in her own right would be such a good cook, a devoted mother, and a home maker or keeper. And as I always said, you are indeed a very lucky man.

"Perhaps we should stop here," he suggested, "and in our next session talk about your foreign service to the country."

The session ended on these very moving reflections on my wife, about whom there had indeed been unanimous approval when we got married. My wife's father had told us that while they fully supported us, we should remember that mixed marriages were very difficult and that most of them ended in divorce. With time and the blessing of children, they complimented us on the success of our marriage. And most of the credit was of course due to the way this American of German descent adapted to my African context with an unprecedentedly large and close-knit family. Over the years, I would hear the words, 'She is a great lady' said about her by Sudanese, Americans, and others who got to know her. And the Chairman indeed knew her well.

Session Six: Diplomacy

Anticipating our next session, I was feeling increasingly ambivalent about relating my experiences to the Chairman. My shoulder was hurting, and I was torn between awareness of the pain and sorting out my thoughts for the session with the Chairman. *Was all this worth the painful effort?* I wondered. But it also felt good to recall my experiences. Perhaps I had made more of a difference than I thought I had. So I decided to continue.

At that point, I heard sounds that I associated with the Chairman's arrival. "I am here, *Raandit,*" the Chairman announced his presence.

"Welcome, *Benydit,*" I responded, with obvious enthusiasm. And indeed, by that point, after several visits from the Chairman, I began to feel a greater kinship with the man whom I had known fairly well in life, but quite differently from the way I was beginning to see and feel him now. I cherished his individualized attention to me, which was clearly enhanced by the fact that he was now a spirit, sacred. I felt deeply honored that he was listening to my life stories, which indeed I came to see a bit differently as a result of relating to him.

The Chairman opened the session with the reminder, "I am here, *Raandit.* And, as we agreed last time, we are to talk today about your diplomatic career. I am all ears."

That day, I had been to the physiotherapist for one of those grueling exercises and was still in pain. In fact, I had taken the liberty of increasing the dosage of the painkiller. Perhaps for that reason, I was feeling rather groggy. But I did not want to mention any of that to the Chairman.

My diplomatic service under the regime of President Nimeiri—the regime that had ended the devastating war in the South—was, at the time, the highlight of my professional life. It was perhaps my most tangible and important contribution to the country. But I also had a deep-rooted concern about my original home area of Abyei and my people, the Ngok Dinka, for whom I felt both an inherited and acquired responsibility. Before undertaking my diplomatic assignment, immediately after being sworn in, I focused on the situation in Abyei. In my account to the Chairman, I began with recollecting my swearing-in ceremony.

"As you know, I had been offered a diplomatic position in Sweden, which I gratefully accepted. I went to Khartoum with my wife to undertake my new position. At the swearing-in ceremony, the President and group of his ministers and senior aides stood watching, and the Bible and the Koran lay on the table. I was to choose which one of the Holy Books to swear on. I waved my hand over both before resting it on the Bible. All laughed.

"At the time, I probably meant it as a joke. But, as I reflected later, I realized that there was more to my symbolism than a joke. Choosing between the two implied different commitments to different approaches to God. The Truth should be One to the One God. That divided symbolism could mean acceptance of religious diversity or could be an indication of competing religious identities, which could lead to conflict. The Addis Ababa Agreement provided the framework for the first, acceptance of diversity, which was later reversed to the second, competition of religions, and generated conflict. I joined the government at the time when mutual accommodation was the norm."

The Chairman appeared to appreciate the depth of our shared vision for the country. "That should have been recognized as only a stop-gap arrangement that should lay the foundation for a progressive evolution toward a more integrated New Sudan. That was the essence of my letter to our Commander-in-Chief in reaching the talks in Addis Ababa. It would take a while for that idea to be more fully developed. But I am getting too far ahead of your story."

"You are not going too far ahead," I reassured the Chairman, "because, although I did not use the term New Sudan, that was exactly the way I took the long-term significance of the Addis Ababa Agreement. In fact, I documented that in my postdoctoral research project at Yale Law School, which was cut short by my appointment, in the thin book I published under the title, *Dynamics of Identification: A Basis for National Integration in the Sudan*, and another book on the Agreement, *Peace and Unity in the Sudan: An African Achievement*, which the Foreign Minister asked me to prepare for the President to present to the heads of state and government of the Organization of African Unity, to commemorate the first anniversary of the Addis Ababa Agreement."

"Another example of our shared vision for the country."

"Absolutely. After the swearing in, my wife and I went to the South to see the situation first hand. We were very well received by the government. The atmosphere was still euphoric with the achievement of peace. The President of the Regional Government with several of his ministers took us for a ride outside Juba. They explained that before the peace agreement, it would have been impossible to take such a ride. They showed us a farm in which people grew a variety of crops. Peanuts had ripened and one minister pulled out of the ground a clump full of nuts. My wife, who had never seen the nuts in their natural growth, remarked, 'I always thought peanuts grew on trees.' Part of the problem is that Americans call them peanuts, not groundnuts."

"Most people eat things which they do not know how they grow. It's a problem of the city taking over the country."

"Sadly, this is increasingly becoming true of our country, contrary to your call for taking the towns to the people in the countryside. In the South, amidst the euphoria of peace, we found the people of Abyei very distraught that the Agreement had not included them in the South. They had fought and died alongside their fellow Southerners as Southerners. They felt betrayed and very bitter. There was not much I could say to them, except that the Agreement granted them the right to decide to join the South. It was now for them to organize their people to exercise that right.

"In Wau, we found an even more outraged community of the Ngok Dinka, many of whom had fought in the war. It was a very difficult situation to manage and all I could do was to repeat what I had said in Juba.

"Back in Khartoum, my wife fortuitously acquired a painful insight into the Northern prejudice against Southerners. A classmate from the university invited us to a wedding in his family. My wife was taken to the women's area while I stayed with the men. She was introduced as the wife of an ambassador. And she reported on our visit to the South and the warmth and hospitality shown us. The reaction was essentially one of surprise, as Southerners were perceived as a wild primitive lot who could not behave in such a dignified manner. As she was White, it was obvious that they assumed that she was the wife of a foreign ambassador to the Sudan. My classmate's sister apparently alerted them to the facts in Arabic. Embarrassment sank in, but nothing could be done; the bitter truth was out."

"Of course, what was unusual was the circumstance under which she got that insight and not the prejudice itself. But had that situation not offered that insight, you would never have had that insight."

"Yes. It reminded me of a somewhat similar situation that occurred when we were at Khartoum University and which our lecturer and his wife reported to me years later. They had invited us Southern Sudanese students to their house for a meal. Their cook was a Northerner. When he saw us on our arrival, he was reported to have said to his employers, 'You made me do all this work for these slaves?' This was said to me and my host family at Yale. The message was so unbelievable that I felt outraged with the messenger. I could not believe that any Sudanese would say that about university students, even Southerners. It took me time to believe that it must indeed have happened. And in fact, I began to recall many small incidents of a similar nature."

"Once you appreciate the moral weakness we all share in our prejudice toward 'the other', then you feel more sympathy than anger. After all, our people are really just as prejudiced against 'the others'," the Chairman pointed out.

"I totally agree with you. Going back to our visit to the Sudan, both in Khartoum and Juba, I discerned a clear lack of will to implement the provision of the Addis Ababa Agreement on Abyei. Some people even suspected that I had influenced the decision in line with my father's choice to remain in the North. I left feeling a personal sense of responsibility for finding a solution for the crisis in Abyei.

"Back in the United States and before leaving for my post in Scandinavia, I came to a conclusion on what to do about Abyei. I decided to build on the positive historical role Abyei had played as a bridge of peace and cooperation between the North and the South. Instead of being torn apart by the conflict between the North and the South, and now abandoned by both after the peace agreement, it should be supported and empowered to once again play that role as a symbol of peace, reconciliation, and integration. This could be done by granting the area 'mini autonomy', modeled after the autonomy of the South, and providing social services and a robust development program as well as fostering cordial ties with the neighbors to the South and the North, especially the Missiriya Arabs. This would make the people of Abyei see tangible benefits in their border role between the North and the South, belonging to both."

"It sounds like an element in our New Sudan Vision," the Chairman interjected.

"I shared the written proposal with a friend of mine in the government, who was visiting the United States, and he supported it. I then shared it with the Minister of Foreign Affairs, whom I asked to share it with the President, who welcomed it. It was also shared with the Minister for Local Government and the President of the Regional Government, all of whom were supportive. Apparently, the proposal got them off the hook on Abyei.

"I then went with my visiting friend to Harvard University to request the cooperation of the Harvard Institute for International Development in the implementation of the Project. They enthusiastically accepted. We then approached USAID for funding. Although it took time for the project to be fully developed, it was finally approved formally by the government and by USAID.

"As soon as the President approved the proposal, he decided to visit Abyei to formally announce his new policy for the area. I was to accompany him, but, by the time his visit took place, I was being urged to take up my new assignment and was about to leave for Sweden. The President went, accompanied by my friend, whom I requested to brief our people on my proposal to prepare them for the visit. Apparently, that did not happen. The President was very well received, with social and cultural performances, but he was delivered a very hostile message against Abyei being in the North and calling for joining the South."

"That must have been a bitter pill for him to swallow," commented the Chairman.

"It certainly was," I replied. "The President was so offended that he decided to leave without honoring the lavish hospitality that had been prepared for him. It took much effort for my friend to persuade him to stay. But he left without announcing his policy on Abyei and did not hand over the gifts he had taken with him as the foundation of the policy. It would take quite some time before I could put the project back on the government's agenda."

"In cooperation with the Minister for Local Government and the Southern Sudan Regional Government, we had a well-qualified administrator from Abyei seconded to head the administration of the area. And we had Ngok Dinka staff from various ministries in the North and South seconded to the area to work in the areas of their expertise. A ministerial committee comprising the key ministries in the areas of social services and development, particularly in agriculture, was constituted. Although I was an ambassador posted abroad, I was appointed a member of the ministerial committee."

"The irony in all this is that decisions that would have a historic impact on large communities are left to individual whim," the Chairman interjected. "It was of course good that you were able to influence the situation the way you did. But where was the will of the people? And what about the many communities which may have that level of representation in the power structure!?"

"Even with the kind of individual influence I was fortunate to have, there was no public debate on issues so that people would understand why decisions were made and decide whether to support them or not."

As I was beginning to feel drowsy, I posed a question to the Chairman that had occurred to me earlier. "Why do we always have our sessions at night? Why don't you ever come during the day?"

"Remember, you are communicating with me as a ghost. Have you ever heard of a ghost appearing during the day? Besides, which of us goes to the other? Do I come to you or do you come to me?"

I was baffled by the question. I had no doubt that he came to me. But what if all that was my own delusion? What if the ghost were all a fiction of my imagination? I chose not to debate the Chairman. "I guess I know what you mean. I surely do not understand the mysteries of the dead talking to the living."

The Chairman must have noticed that I was getting quite sleepy. He suggested that we end the session and in the next one focus on my diplomatic work.

It was now quite clear that our conversations had become mostly about me. I was somewhat embarrassed by this, but I had come to accept it, with appreciation of the Chairman's generosity of spirit. The question however remained as to what in the vast quantities of life experience was important or relevant enough to cover. The obvious answer was that I should not include all experiences of my diplomatic or political life, but only those that were relevant to the main issues of mutual interest and concern with the Chairman. Even that was not easy. I thought I should raise this issue in our next session.

Session Seven: Identity

It was getting to the time the Chairman usually arrived. I waited in eager anticipation. No sign of the Chairman. It was obvious that I had begun to look forward to his visits more and more with each passing session. In fact, I found myself spending many if not most of my waking daytime hours reliving aspects of our last sessions. I also pondered what I would say to the Chairman at our next session. Having him in my life through those sessions was oddly thrilling!

I wondered whether I should share this strange aspect of my mysterious life with my wife. After all, she had also known the Chairman in life and admired him—the Chairman had been not just my friend, but a friend of the family. But the nature of my new friendship was different. I really did not feel that it was proper to share that with my wife. I knew she would not understand. So I decided to keep the new friendship with the non-physical Chairman private and indeed secret.

I knew that my wife felt that something suspicious was going on in my life. She wondered why I often had a distant look in my eyes as the evening approached and why I was often distracted and seemingly reflective. But I realized that she associated that with my health condition and not a new relationship with someone I was talking to in my room at night. I saw the concern in her face as she looked at me and checked my medication dosage and the number of pills remaining in the bottle.

I was absorbed in these thoughts when I suddenly heard the voice of the Chairman. "I am here, *Raandit*," I felt a sensation of relief that the Chairman was still in my life.

"Welcome! Welcome!" I said with some excitement. "I am so happy to see you!"

"How are you feeling today?" the Chairman asked, obviously remembering how I felt at the end of our last session.

I told the Chairman that I was feeling much better and thanked him for asking. The Chairman reminded me that our session was to be on my diplomatic service. He recalled that my contribution to the country had mostly been in the area of diplomacy, although he realized that there was no separation between foreign service and domestic leadership, as shown by our earlier discussion on Abyei. The first leg of my diplomatic service, of course, began in Scandinavia.

I decided to introduce the subject of selection of issues to focus on. "*Benydit,* I have been thinking about our conversations and the issues we have been talking about. I realize that you have generously focused our discussions on my experiences. But then, with that focus, I would like us to discuss what areas we should cover. Of course, I know what your agenda as a liberation movement was, but what, more precisely, are the areas of interest you want us to focus on?"

The Chairman seemed touched by my question. "I think you have already laid the basis for answering your question. You know that my main goal in the liberation struggle was to create a New Sudan of full equality for all individuals and groups, where there would be no discrimination on any grounds. Is that a precise enough theme for focus?"

"Absolutely. And I am sure this is a topic to which we will come when we discuss the objectives and programs of your movement."

"But before we get to that, let me turn your question around and ask you what you yourself consider to be a theme of focus in our discussions?"

I pondered. "Thanks. I have actually been thinking about that question. It is really interesting that what I would consider to be an important theme of focus fits in very well with your broad theme of New Sudan of full equality and no discrimination on any grounds. If I were to offer one word that provides an umbrella for my ideas as reflected in policy-oriented scholarship and professional experience, I would say 'Identity'.

"I introduced the debate on identity as a factor in conflicts and nation building in the Sudan in a study that was published in one of my shortest books, *Dynamics of Identification: A Basis for National Integration in the Sudan,* which Khartoum University published in 1973. My thesis was that the evolution of the conflicting identities in the Sudan took place in a historical context in which conversion to Islam, speaking Arabic, becoming culturally Arabic, and claiming descent from Arab ancestry elevated one to a level of respect, while being a Black African and a 'heathen' made one a legitimate target for enslavement. Since Islam and

Arabism encouraged such a liberal process of self-promotion, 'passing' became a well-documented trend among the indigenous populations of the North. Southern identity, on the other hand, evolved as one of resistance to Northern slave raids and Arab racial, cultural, and religious hegemony."

The Chairman responded as I had expected. The idea resonated with him very well, as it was an indication of the historical root of the problems that their movement sought to address in the Vision of the New Sudan. "You must have read my mind. Or, to be more exact, you of course know not only my mind, but my policy agenda in ideas and action. I wrote my letter to our Commander-in-Chief in which I first introduced my vision of New Sudan at about the time you were writing your book, and the arguments were the same."

"I see the case of the Sudan as an example of an even wider global relevance, which I am sure also applies to your New Sudan Vision. It demonstrates the fluidity and adaptability of identity and how it can be shaped and reshaped to serve the interests of the self-identifying individual. With increasing recognition of diversity in pluralistic states and the stipulation of the human rights principle of nondiscrimination, it was my belief that the myth of self-perception of Arabism would be adjusted to the reality of Sudanese admixture and its racial, ethnic, cultural, and religious diversity in national unity. My policy argument was, and still is, that it is not the mere fact of identity differences that generates conflicts, but the way diversity is managed, which usually means that some groups enjoy the status of being first-class citizens who enjoy the full rights of citizenship, while other groups are discriminated against, marginalized, excluded, and denied the rights and dignity of citizenship."

"Here you are sounding very much like a member of our movement. In my letter, I identified the problem as the dominance of Arab nationalism over other nationalities. Of course, I am quite familiar with your ideas, but please recount them so you'll be better ready to explain them to those who do not know as much as I do about them. Remember, our objective in these conversations is not for us to rehash for ourselves what we already know, but to articulate your experiences to be better prepared to share them with others who are not equally informed."

"I realize that. I see identity as both subjective, what people perceive themselves to be, and objective, what they really are by tangible criteria. Scholars emphasize subjectivity as what counts. When subjective self-identification negatively impinges on the rights of others, it should be challenged. Identity can also be exclusive in a discriminatory way or inclusive in a way that accommodates diversity equitably.

"The question," I continued, "is whether inclusivity of identity means accommodating identity differences or reconstructing identity to fashion a new and unified identity. Of course, the first is easier to achieve while the second is more difficult. When we advanced the concept of Sudanism, we were essentially doing both—accommodating diversity equitably and conceptualizing a new integrated identity that was based on mutual identification with the Sudan as a national framework. But of course, that is easier said than done, as we eventually learned.

"Because of these difficulties, identity is a difficult concept to manage. Although it is dynamic and flexible, it is also rigid and dogmatically held and protected. Initially, my ideas on identity conflicts were resisted in the Sudan—and even internationally, including among scholars. In the Sudan, Northerners saw the policy implication of my approach as challenging and threatening their 'Arabness', while Southerners preferred to blame the Northerners on the basis of their self-perception as Arabs. Ironically, *Dynamics of Identification* was misconstrued by some as advocating assimilation into the dominant identity of the North and by others as promoting the 'Africanization' of the North.

"Internationally, there was also resistance to discussing identity as a factor in conflicts. I believe this was in part a reaction to the racist policies of Nazi Germany in which non-scientific bases of differentiating races led to persecution of groups, the worst case being the Holocaust. Identity was also considered intangible as a factor and therefore not negotiable or susceptible to resolution. While I saw identity as central to the analysis of African conflicts in my African Studies Program at the Brookings Institution, and later in carrying out my UN mandates on internal displacement and genocide prevention, I initially met with strong resistance from my scholarly colleagues. It took persistent efforts to eventually turn them around.

"Identity politics is now recognized as a significant factor in the contests for state power in Africa and across the world. But as developments around the world today demonstrate, this recognition does not necessarily mean acceptance of diversity in unity and on equitable bases. In the case of the Sudan, I eventually recognized, as I believe you too did, that I had underestimated the depth and strength of Northern Sudanese commitment to Arabism and the related version of Islam. That was when I and my colleagues in the Task Force on US Policy to end the war in the Sudan proposed the formula, 'One Country, Two Systems', as a means for reconciling conflicting visions of the North and the South for the Sudanese nation in a framework of unity in diversity. Even that compromise was not accepted in the end and the country was partitioned into two independent states."

"Just because an innovative idea is difficult for conservative interest groups to accept is no reason to abandon it. On the other hand, resistance that cannot be overcome requires creativity in seeking strategies for overcoming it and finding alternative means to the same end.

"I believe you have helped identify a central concept or theme that should provide a thread to our discussions, but without putting us in a straightjacket. I suggest we stop here and, in our next session, go back to our topic of your diplomatic experiences, beginning with your diplomatic posting if you don't mind."

"That sounds good," I said, and we ended the session.

Session Eight: Scandinavia

"*Raandit,*" the Chairman alerted me to his arrival. "Remember we agreed to talk in this session about your diplomatic experience in Scandinavia."

"Okay," I acknowledged and proceeded with recollections of my service in the Nordic countries of Denmark, Finland, Norway, and Sweden, better known, collectively, as Scandinavia. "Scandinavia proved to be the right beginning to my diplomatic career. As it removed us from both the US and Sudan, it gave my wife and me a neutral ground for beginning our married life and developing a genuine partnership in discharging my challenging diplomatic work. We indeed spent two enjoyable and productive years in Scandinavia. Given the concern these countries had about the war in the Sudan and the plight of the people of the South, we were able to generate their support for the post-war reconstruction and development of the autonomous Southern Region, very much along the lines of the approach I had outlined to the minister and the president.

"I must confess that I was very highly motivated. I was probably the youngest ambassador in Sudan's foreign service then. It was sometimes not easy for people to tell that I was the Ambassador. I recall an incident at a diplomatic function. I was standing with the Archbishop of Stockholm when a young Swedish diplomat approached the Archbishop and started talking to him. The Archbishop, probably wanting to moderate the intrusion, asked the young diplomat whether he had met the Sudanese Ambassador. The diplomat, looking over my head, to the people around, responded, 'No, I have not had the honor.' The Archbishop explained, 'Here he is, standing in front of you.' The young man was very embarrassed and apologetic. From that time on, he showed me great courtesy, probably to compensate for that unintended slight."

"That's not the kind of slight that offends. It is indeed flattering because it means that you have achieved beyond your age," the

Chairman said, putting a positive spin on the experience. And of course, I knew what he was saying and felt a bit flattered.

"Age, combined with inexperience in diplomacy, accounted for another misstep on my part. I was meeting with the Director General (Undersecretary) of the Norwegian Ministry of Foreign Affairs. He asked why I chose to reside in Stockholm. I said my decision was that of my government and added, 'Isn't Sweden the center of Scandinavia?' He was obviously surprised by my ineptitude. 'Mr. Ambassador, you come to my country to tell me that Sweden is the center of Scandinavia?' I said I was of course speaking geographically. He said, 'Even geographically, if you consider Iceland, Sweden is not the center of Scandinavia.'"

"That was indeed an undiplomatic response on your part." The Chairman was less flattering.

"I believe that my youth and inexperience, combined with being a South Sudanese, made me feel the burden of the challenge in front of me. I felt as though everything I said or did would have important consequences for my country. In a courtesy meeting with the Irish Ambassador—an elderly man, presumably close to retirement—in a stimulating conversation in which he must have been struck by my motivation and dedication to my mission, he said to me, 'Mr. Ambassador, it is admirable to see the level of your commitment and dedication to your job, but please remember that your health must come first.' I have always said that only a man of his age and experience would give that advice."

"You are probably right, but health is becoming widely recognized as the number one priority, and even as a necessary condition for good and productive work. On the other hand, even this wisdom might require experience and perhaps the appropriate age of cognition."

"That's true. My presentations of credentials in the four countries were quite memorable. The formalities in Sweden were spectacular. I was taken by a horse-driven chariot to the palace. After going through several rooms lined with the guards, I came to the king. He received me in a warm, contrastingly informal manner, patting the back of my hand in the fashion of a grandfather. Our conversation took much longer than was expected, according to practice. In the meeting was his grandson, the crown prince who later succeeded him. I was told that this was his first time attending the ceremony of credential presentation, presumably in preparation for the role ahead. At one point, the king involved his grandson by asking him whether we might have met at the UN in New York.

"I had been warned that the King always asks the Ambassador one difficult question on those occasions. Since he was interested in archeology, on which he was very knowledgeable, and had apparently read about the excavations in the Nubia region of the Sudan, I was advised to refresh my knowledge on the subject. Since I had no knowledge to refresh, I did not try. As our conversation was going so well and approaching the end, I thought I had avoided the difficult question. Then the king asked me how wide the Nile was in Khartoum. Of course, I did not know, but I tried to be clever by saying that as the two Niles meet at Khartoum, the merged Nile becomes very wide. 'Exactly how wide?' I decided to make a guess, About half a mile.' I was told later that I was about right.

"My wife, who was watching with many spectators, got into a conversation with a couple who were videotaping the ceremony. They told her that their king was very old and that they wanted him to perform that ceremony, as it could be his last. They later invited us to their home where we watched the video."

"I thought the Swedes were famous for their gender equality. Why did they not allow your wife to accompany you during the ceremony?"

"I wondered about that myself. Anyway, their prediction sadly came to pass, as the king died shortly after. His grandson succeeded him. When I met the young king later, he intimated to me that he would have preferred to remain just a citizen instead of assuming the responsibilities of the king.

"The King of Norway was next on my agenda. Again, I was taken to the palace in a chariot driven by horses. Otherwise the ceremony was simpler. The King and I enjoyed our conversation and he frequently laughed out loud. I cannot recall what I could have said that was so funny.

"In Denmark, the ceremony was even less formal. But I had an incident that was quite comic. I had of course gone from Stockholm. As I thought was the practice in Europe, I left my shoes outside my room to be polished. I looked for them the next morning to get ready for the ceremony at 10 am. To my utter surprise, they were gone, apparently taken by the hotel staff as rejects to be thrown away. It was a crisis averted only by the hotel persuading a shoe company to come to the hotel with a variety of shoes and sizes. I got to the ceremony just in the nick of time."

"That was quite a crisis! What would you have done without shoes?"

"I can't even begin to imagine. Fortunately, all ended well. What stands out in my memory about the ceremony was that the beautiful, relatively young queen, warm and smiling, seemed modestly self-conscious, frequently turned to her husband to respond to me, and he was quite effective in complementing her. Nothing went wrong."

"We tend to forget that royals are only human. It's good that they sometimes show their humanity through their vulnerability," the Chairman observed.

"It did indeed cross my mind that our own traditional leadership goes back much farther than these royals. According to our mythology, the spiritual leadership of our clan goes back to the time of Creation, and the sacred spears that symbolize their spiritual authority were given to them by God. The royal houses of Scandinavia were Napoleonic creations. That's why in bowing I had to strike a balance between the courtesy due to royalty and the dignity of my own claims to divine royalty, diminished only by foreign domination.

"Interestingly enough, in Sweden, the Ambassador of Tanzania, with whom I became good friends, was a tribal leader who retained the title of Chief. His official name was Chief Michael Lukumbuzia. In typical chiefly hospitality, the Chief and his family welcomed us into their neighborhood by lavishly provisioning our new house with food and drink. We became close colleagues and friends. On one of my visits back to Khartoum, I told the Undersecretary of the Ministry about the Tanzanian Ambassador's title and jokingly asked whether I could at least use the title of 'Prince'. His response was, 'We cannot afford that.'

"My experience in Finland was much more normal and went smoothly. There was no horse-driven chariot and the President and I had a cordial, relatively informal conversation.

"While still in Helsinki, I was invited to a huge function spectacularly covered by the media, including television cameras. One man, accompanied by a beautiful, glamorous woman, was being closely followed by the cameras. I felt an urge to talk to him and bluntly asked, 'Who are you and why is there so much interest in you?' Obviously surprised and intrigued by this audacious approach, he smiled at me and offered me his card. I gave him mine and we agreed to be in touch. I later learned that he was an internationally famous industrial artist and a leading celebrity in Finland.

"The next time I was in Helsinki, my wife was with me. I got in touch with the man. We were invited to his beautiful house of silo architecture where we had drinks before going to a fashionable restaurant where he was received with great respect. He took some of his products as gifts to the owner. And, naturally, we were waited on with exceptional courtesy.

"Each of the Scandinavian countries had something to offer us in Sudan, whether it was from the timber and paper industry in Finland, agricultural equipment from Denmark and Sweden, or boat construction, integrated rural development, and infrastructure from Norway. Norway, working with the Church, was particularly committed to supporting the South in various ways and that was where I focused my attention."

"We clearly saw evidence of that. Norway in particular contributed significantly to the post-war development efforts in the South. In fact, for years they remained among our best development partners."

"That's right. Actually, I experienced an interesting example of how deeply rooted the suspicions between the North and the South were. This surfaced early, in regards to our request for support from Norway. I was at first instructed by our Ministry of Foreign Affairs to seek support from Norway for constructing a highway linking the South with Kenya, probably initiated by the regional government of South Sudan. I enthusiastically lobbied for the project and obtained initial interest from the Norwegian government. Then, suddenly, I was instructed not to pursue the project with Norway. Later, while back in Khartoum, I asked for an explanation. I was told that priority was to be given to internal infrastructure of roads before linking to the neighboring countries, which indicated lack of trust in Southern commitment to national unity."

The Chairman observed, "I have always said that even when violent confrontation stops, conflicts that have deep roots persist and need to be addressed in terms of their root causes. Norway was an active member of a Troika with the UK and US, whose involvement eventually ended the war in the country. They are now once again engaged in efforts to end our civil war. Some agreement will probably be reached. But will it succeed in addressing the root causes? We in the movement had our own conflicts that were patched over, but they erupted again. We keep going in vicious circles. Anyway, let's go back to your diplomatic assignments."

"Within a few months of taking up my post in Scandinavia, the Minister of Foreign Affairs asked me to write a book on the Addis Ababa Agreement, which the President would present to his OAU fellow heads of state and government on 25 October, 1973—the Organization's anniversary, as well as our revolution's—as a contribution from the Sudan to the Organization. The title of the book was to be, *Peace and Unity in the Sudan: An African Achievement.* I was given two able young diplomats to assist me. And one of my regular staff also joined the team. We worked very hard on the book and completed the manuscript within a remarkably short time. I then worked day and night with the director and staff of Khartoum University Press to get the book out within two weeks—a publication miracle. The book was very well received, not only within the OAU but also in scholarly circles. As I indicated earlier, I believe that some of the chapters were relevant to the New Sudan Vision that you later developed and promulgated.

"In fact, I built on the thesis of *Dynamics of Identification,* which I had written during my post-doctoral research Fellowship at Yale Law School. That Fellowship was interrupted by my appointment as Ambassador to Scandinavia, but I abridged my research and produced the manuscript that became the book, *Dynamics of Identification.* As I said earlier, that book analyzed the historical process by which the Sudanese identification with Islam and Arabism had evolved and eventually overshadowed the African identity over most of the Sudan, even though traditional identity factors remained thinly veiled under the skin. The moral, social, and cultural framework of the process was that, if you became a Muslim, were culturally Arabized, and could claim and justify Arab ancestry, you were elevated to a higher status of relative respectability and dignity. If you were a Black African 'heathen', you were denigrated and placed into the class of slaves—real, potential, or phenomenal. Islamization and its twin process of Arabization were therefore aspects of self-enhancement in a relatively liberal and permissive environment.

"The process was well documented by the studies of British colonial administrators throughout the North, many of these published in *Sudan Notes and Records.* Since independence, and with the South

Sudanese struggle for equality and greater exposure of both the North and the South to the pluralist identities of the country, I thought that there was an increasing openness to the realities of the Sudan and some distancing from the myths of the divisive Arabism and discrimination based on its religious and cultural connotations. I saw the peace process that eventually resulted in the Addis Ababa Agreement as part of that dynamic. And I saw it as opening doors, whereby recognition of diversity would progressively lead to an interaction involving a cultural give-and-take that would eventually lead to an integrated identity that would not be labeled "Arab" or "African," but rather authentically "Sudanese." Does all this not sound familiar to the Father of the New Sudan Vision?"

"If you mean me, it certainly does," remarked the Chairman. "But it was not just me. It was a movement and, as they say, the devil is in the details, especially as you were a proxy author for an agreement I opposed at the time and a regime we would eventually rebel against. But this is not the place nor the time for that discussion. But, of course, I share your vision, which, as I have already said, had much in common with what I presented in my 1972 letter to the Chairman of our liberation movement. What I proposed is, of course, what happened."

"Anyway," I resumed, "that was the thesis I reproduced in the book I wrote for the Ministry of Foreign Affairs. And since the ideas of the Minister and my own were quite similar, I insisted that the manuscript be read by scholars, diplomats, and political leaders to authenticate its validity as a reflection of the government's policy. I was assured of that at the highest levels. It is quite ironic and indeed paradoxical that political developments would prove me wrong and that I had grossly underestimated the depth of commitment to the Arab Islamic identity and political agenda of the dominant elements in the North, which your movement set itself to challenge, with which I also agreed. And indeed, to reiterate what you already know, what this brief background shows is how much my own thinking has in common with your vision of a New Sudan, whatever devil is in the details."

"That's very interesting. It confirms what both of us have always said: that we share the same ideas and vision for the country. Our only difference is that you apparently had more confidence in the Addis Ababa Agreement as a foundation for building the New Sudan. After

Scandinavia, I believe that your next assignment was Ambassador to the United States."

"That's right. I suggest we make that the subject of our next session."

The Chairman agreed.

At the end of the session, and before reconnecting with my wife and going to bed for the night, I reflected on what had just transpired. My early diplomatic experience in Scandinavia came back to me with a different kind of significance. When I had been going through it, there was a mixed feeling of elation, excitement, and anxiety. Now I looked back with a sense of pride in what I had accomplished at that early age. The fact that I was promoted from that post to more challenging assignments was indeed evidence of my success, as Scandinavia now emerged as an important stepping stone.

I called my wife and asked for my pills. "You look relaxed and in a positive spirit!" she commented. "How is the pain?"

"I feel fine," I said, not conscious of the pain, which was still there, but had been overshadowed by the positive recollections of my past. Although I was not about to reveal my secret conversations with the Chairman, I decided to share with my wife a bit of those positive recollections. "For some reason, I was thinking about our time in Scandinavia," I said to her without elaboration.

"Those were fun days," she responded. "But that time now seems like ancient history. So much has happened in between, most of it also quite positive. We have been quite lucky. We cannot complain."

"Except for this awful condition of mine," I said as I began to feel the pain I had almost forgotten.

"Well, you can't have everything. It would not be life otherwise," she said as she gave me the pills. "Good night. I hope your good memories combine with the medicine to subdue the pain," she said as she left the room and closed the door.

Session Nine: United States

Although my recollections of Scandinavia had seemed exceptionally pleasant, my mind began to shift to the challenging and yet most rewarding experience as Ambassador to the United States. Again, as the usual time frame for the Chairman's arrival came, I kept looking at my watch impatiently, even though we had never agreed on any precise time. I must have looked at my watch several times between 8 and 8:30. I began to wonder whether the Chairman might have decided to change plans. But could he do so unilaterally, without warning? No, he would not, I thought. That was unlike him. So, I waited anxiously, but confidently.

As was the pattern in my life, what you anxiously expect happens only when you stop expecting. The Chairman surprised me with the announcement of his arrival. "*Raandit*, I am here. Am I late?"

"Welcome!" I acknowledged his presence. "You can't be late when we did not agree on a precise time," I said, not sure I knew what I was saying, since I had no idea whether the dead kept our time or even had the means to do so. "In fact, I don't think we have ever talked about time. Do the dead have a sense of time as we know it?"

"You are obviously getting to know the world of the dead a bit better. We think more about daytime, when we become invisible, and nighttime, when we become active, with gradations of the two, when we adjust ourselves accordingly. But remember, we are everlasting in your religious lexicon."

"But what does 'everlasting life' *mean* when you are dead? Our people believe that although the dead continue to live in some form, they also continue to live in the memory of the living. But the living also die with their memories."

"But others come and perpetuate life, including the memory of those who have left your world. Consider it a relay then."

"When does the game end?"

"Did they not teach you that the world will come to an end?"

"Including your world of the already dead?"

"Did they not tell you about the Trinity of Three in One that it is difficult to understand, but that we accept it because God told us so? This is all beyond the subject of our worldly conversation. So, let's get to our subject of today, or rather tonight."

I was tempted to explore more about the world of the dead, especially what they did in the gradation phases of day and night that the Chairman alluded to. But I decided to take the Chairman's advice and not depart from the agenda item we had set for the session. "Shall I get to my service in the United States, as we agreed in our last session?"

"Please do. As I recall, the total time you spent in the US was more than the time of your assignment as Ambassador. But we can begin with your representative role. I am sure we will get to your other activities later. As I understood from you, you spent as much time in the US as you had lived in your own country."

"Actually, longer. But let's begin with my diplomatic mission, as you said. My assignment to the United States was perhaps the most challenging and rewarding in my diplomatic career. As I said farewell to my Scandinavian diplomatic colleagues, the UK Ambassador asked me where I was going next. When I said I was going to Washington, he asked, almost too inquisitively for the usually discreet British, 'As Ambassador?!' he posed a question, accentuated with a tone of doubt or surprise. 'Yes', I said, quite neutrally. 'But you are so young!' he made his doubt explicit.

"My posting in the United States was remarkably productive, as I witnessed the turning of the tide of acutely strained relations into close ties between our two countries. I had wondered whether my close association with a country in which I had studied and married would be an asset or a liability. It certainly proved an unquestionable asset. In presenting my credentials to the US President, I added these elements of personal connections and made jocular anecdotes about our law school professors in a light-hearted conversation. Some of the old-fashioned diplomats at home would later tell me that they thought that these personal aspects should not have been included in such formal ceremonies as the presentation of credentials, but that just revealed their ignorance about the informalities of the American culture, even in diplomacy. These niceties did not in the short run mitigate the monumental challenges facing my assignment. I have always maintained that diplomacy is not only what one learns in professional schools, but an art and skill of human relations with deep roots in culture and upbringing. And indeed, my situation was a challenge of relations."

"Sadly, people with institutionalized myopic vision think they know it all," the Chairman interjected.

"My nomination as ambassador was made in the aftermath of the assassination of the American Ambassador, together with the Belgian and other diplomats in Khartoum, by the Black September Palestinians. We were celebrating the first anniversary of peace in Juba when it happened. The incident was widely interpreted as Arab opposition to the Addis peace agreement. This had the effect of strengthening the national resolve in support of the agreement. I attended the occasion and, at the request of the Minister of Foreign Affairs, ended up drafting the condolence messages on behalf of the President to the countries of the victims. The messages reflected the national outrage. The President publicly vowed to make every day of Black September 'black'."

"That is of course an unfortunate choice of color for a President who was advancing racial equality in the country. On the other hand, that condescending view of the color black is quite universal, even among the Blacks themselves, who do not seem to associate it with their own skin color," remarked the Chairman.

"You are right. It is a universal bias, sadly, even among our people. Why that is so only God knows. And you are also right that our people, ironically, do not associate the negative view of blackness with their own skin color, which they in fact glorify. Anyway, the assassins were tried and were expected to receive severe sentences. In anticipation of retaliation by the Black September terrorists, we were instructed to ask for added protection from the host government, which we did.

"Surprisingly enough, they received imprisonment and were handed over to Egypt to serve their sentences in Cairo where the PLO had their offices. This was seen by the Americans as tantamount to their release. The US almost severed relations with the Sudan, but settled on freezing diplomatic ties, even though the two embassies remained open. The acceptance of my nomination was delayed to a point that, according to diplomatic practice, would be taken as rejection. We later understood that the acceptance eventually came because of the intervention of influential American individuals who knew me personally."

"Everything in life has a human dimension," the Chairman interjected. "People think States are non-human entities, but they are represented by human beings who think and feel."

"I couldn't agree with you more. As Ambassador, I worked very hard with various centers of power and influence, individuals and organizations, even different departments of the government, to reverse the policy in favor of improved relations.

"On a light note, during one of my visits to Congress to meet with the Chairman of the Senate Foreign Relations Committee, I found a lot of commotion. There were policemen all around. I wondered what was going on and was told that Elizabeth Taylor was visiting. As I approached the office, the commotion intensified. I was sitting in the waiting room when the senator opened his office to invite me in. The lady who was with him got up to greet me. In a remarkably casual manner, the senator introduced her as 'Ms. Elizabeth Taylor; she is an actress who has played in many films.' He also introduced me as the Ambassador of the Sudan. I was of course surprised that the senator seemed to think that I did not know that famous actress. I chose to play the game by simply acknowledging her with a nod of the head as we shook hands."

"That was a smart and dignified move. You could have said, 'of course I know the famous actress'. But what you did was better than reacting with excitement."

"What followed was equally remarkable. The senator told me that Ms. Taylor was raising funds for a hospital in Botswana and that I might have some useful suggestions for her. I said the Scandinavians, especially the Swedes, might be interested in such a project. The senator said that he knew the Swedish Ambassador and could telephone him for her to talk to him. Then came the most amusing part; Ms. Taylor, the world-famous actress, said she was too shy to talk on the phone.

"It would have been interesting to probe into the reasons for her being too shy to talk on the telephone."

"That would have been very interesting, but it is rather well known that people who might be extroverted in public might be shy in private. The reasons are better known to psychiatrists.

"One of my pivotal contacts in Washington was the Director of the Central Intelligence Agency, or CIA, to whom our Foreign Minister introduced me. They had both been Permanent Representatives of their respective countries to the United Nations. He was to prove crucial in supporting my mission in Washington. After my first meeting with him at the agency, he made a very flattering remark that he wished he had recorded our discussion to later replay to the concerned congressmen, as they needed to hear the kind of things I had said. He would rise to become Vice President and the President of the United States. I believe calls were coming to the State Department from all over Washington, 'Sudan! Sudan! Sudan!'"

"That was very courageous of you to meet with the CIA at a time when it was virtually taboo for an African official."

"That's true, but our Foreign Minister used to say, the CIA is an organ of the government that you want to do business with. We even exchanged invitations to our homes. I believe he was very helpful to our cause. We eventually broke through and succeeded not only in normalizing relations, but in fostering close ties. In line with my proposed strategy, we consciously and vigorously built on the interconnected domestic and foreign policy implications of the Addis Ababa Agreement. We stipulated the agreement as a basis for promoting constructive partnerships to consolidate internal peace, security, and development and turn the Sudan into a constructive force for regional peace, security, and stability.

"After a meeting with the powerful Undersecretary, which I believe was arranged by both the Hill and the CIA, he called me several days later, while I was nursing a cold in the home of my in-laws in Pennsylvania to say that, as a result of our meeting, they had decided to reverse their policy and begin normalizing relations by lifting the restrictions on the Exim Bank and the Overseas Private Investment Corporation. He asked me to tell my government that this was a first step toward the gradual normalization of our bilateral relations. He went on to tell me that he wanted to give me time to inform my government before informing their own Embassy in Khartoum, because, as he put it, 'I believe in giving diplomats due credit for their accomplishment.'

"Interestingly enough, when the US Ambassador in Khartoum eventually received the information from the State Department, he conveyed the message to the Ministry and added that it did not mean that they were changing their Sudan policy. This was exactly the opposite of what I had sent the Ministry. Our Undersecretary wrote me a letter pointing out the discrepancy in our respective reports. I responded by explaining that I was working to change the policy, while the US Ambassador in Khartoum was upholding existing policy. They understood and acknowledged the difference, with appreciation for my efforts, whose positive results they said they were beginning to see.

"One of the dramatic meetings I had was with the President of the World Bank, who was known to be more favorably inclined toward the Sudan. In fact, my courtesy call on him was as much to thank him for his support as it was to promote closer cooperation with the bank. After reassuring me of his support for our country and its vast potential, especially in the area of agriculture, he was unsparing in his attack on our flawed financial mismanagement and rampant corruption. He gave as an example a 200-million-dollar loan from an Arab financier that was guaranteed by Saudi Arabia, for which he said there was no sound investment objective. He said he could no longer defend the Sudan with any credibility with the donors unless there were a clear and credible reform agenda. I left the meeting appreciative of his candor and his genuine motive to help us. But I felt that this was a delicate message that was better presented in person rather than in a written dispatch. I asked to be given authorization to go back to Khartoum for consultations. The Ministry asked me to send a summary of the message, on the basis of which they would decide whether I needed to deliver it in person. I did. The gist of their response was a very angry reaction to the criticism. How could a responsible person like the President of the World Bank make such unsubstantiated allegations against a sovereign country? The tone was a thinly disguised shooting of the messenger for delivering such a scathing message. I was sure it was not intended to be conveyed to the Bank's President. It is ironic that the issue ended there. There was no authorization for me to return. Nor was the issue ever raised again."

"It is always a dilemma, whether to be transparent in delivering a painful message or sugarcoat it. Truth can be very bitter."

"That's for sure. Our intellectual and engaging Minister of Foreign Affairs had another initiative, in which he asked me to play a major role: to convene a symposium on "Diplomacy and Development." Prominent international personalities from academic institutions and donor agencies were to be invited. I recommended individuals from both. It was a very successful meeting. The Minister asked me to edit the papers presented in a book of the same title, *Diplomacy and Development*, which was produced by the University of Khartoum Press.

"As a side event to the symposium, the Minister asked me to organize a visit by the representatives of the international donor agencies to visit South Sudan, obviously with the objective of gaining their support for the development efforts in the region. I accompanied the delegation. Soon after our arrival, I went to see the President of the Executive Council, the head of the regional government. I found him out of the office and went looking for him to find him literally digging public latrines with the workers. It was a very impressive sight. He agreed to meet with the delegation the next morning.

"That evening, I met with the Executive Director of the President's office and out of courtesy formally placed a request for a meeting with the delegation. I was infuriated when he said that they would first need to see the resumés of the individuals concerned and then submit the request to the President for his approval. I could not conceal my outrage and told him that, for his information, the President had already agreed to see them. I had no doubt that he felt humiliated and I also felt justified that he deserved it. The meeting with the President went very well. The objective of the mission had been achieved."

"That is a good example of the dilemmas of insecurity resulting from the humiliation of domination. In a misplaced effort to reverse such humiliation, one must assert an importance that is really a manifestation of inferiority complex. One paradoxically humiliates oneself by so doing," asserted the Chairman.

"The irony is that we were winning support for our post-conflict reconstruction and development on the basis of our achievement of peace, while those who stood to benefit from our strategic engagement around the world did not appreciate that what we were doing was using foreign policy as an extension of domestic policy, building on positive domestic achievements. I plotted with contacts in the Office of the National Security Advisor, to whom our Minister had introduced me, to introduce the idea of a visit to the United States by our Sudanese President as a fait accompli. One of those intelligence diplomats had served in the Sudan and had developed a special affinity for the country. He was also a personal friend of our Minister."

"That's too subtle a connection for people to understand. And yet it is critically important."

"A reshuffling took place in which the Minister of Foreign Affairs was appointed Minister of Higher Education. But he continued to be involved in the work of Foreign Affairs. The new Minister of Foreign

Affairs was a career diplomat who was deferential to his former Minister.

"I returned to the Sudan to brief the President on my work and his proposed visit to the United States. The President was obviously pleased with my report. After that very constructive meeting with the President, I proceeded to Juba to assess the situation there before returning to the States, especially given the fact that I was using the Addis Ababa Agreement as the domestic basis of my diplomatic mission. While in Juba and only a few days after the meeting with the President, I received word that he urgently wanted me back in Khartoum. Before I could return to Khartoum, there was a cabinet reshuffle and I was appointed Minister of State for Foreign Affairs. The President, however, asked me to continue with my plans in Washington, which meant wearing the two hats of Ambassador for months."

"That was quite a level of confidence," the Chairman said.

"I returned to the United States to continue my mission of normalizing relations and promote a visit by him.

"My role was now strengthened by my new position as Minister of State. An appointment was made for me to meet the Secretary of State. My meeting with the Secretary of State was the final step in the process of normalization. Even meeting him was the result of pressure from many influential circles which we had won over, including prominent senators and the Director of the Central Intelligence Agency, who, as I said, later rose to be the President of the United States. I began my meeting with the Secretary of State with the usual diplomatic niceties. He responded with a tough message, stating that Americans did not take the assassination of their diplomats and the release of the murderers lightly. They still intended to take tough measures on the matter.

"I reacted with controlled rage. First, I politely corrected the statement that they had been released. I then recounted the stern manner in which the Sudan's government had reacted against the PLO, tougher than any Arab country had ever done; the due process by which the murderers had been tried and sentenced to long prison terms; and their being handed over to serve their sentences in Egypt for national security reasons.

"I then explained how the Addis Agreement not only ended the long war and the related suffering of our people but had also turned the Sudan into a force for moderation and the promotion of regional and global peace and security. I ended with a strong, though politely stated, warning: The Sudanese people were very proud and would not accept humiliation. Even the friends of America were now being questioned as to why they were still running after the United States. While it was of course not for me to say what the US policy should be, still, as a friend of the United States, I had to say quite frankly that continuing with their hostile policy toward the Sudan would be counterproductive and would risk losing a friend who shared the same values and principles on the basis of their own domestic policy that was shaping a positive foreign policy."

"You certainly put a much more positive spin on the Agreement than we ourselves saw in it. That was a very effective way of combining diplomacy with militancy, what you might call diplomatic soldiering. How did the Secretary react?"

"I could not believe what followed. The Secretary of State began by saying that he agreed with me, especially when I said that their policy could become counterproductive. I expected a big BUT, which did not come. Instead, he turned to the Assistant Secretary of State for African Affairs and his staff and said, 'Unless you think otherwise, I suggest we reverse our policy.' Since I had already won them to our side, they readily agreed with the reversal of policy."

"That's extraordinary! How was the policy reversal then effected?"

"The Secretary of State advised that the reversal should be done cautiously to avoid a backlash. He then turned to me and said, 'I understand that your President would like to visit the United States'. I said that the proposed visit was indeed the next point on my list of issues to discuss with him. Although I had been 'plotting' the visit with my contacts at the Office of the National Security Advisor, the result turned out far better than I had expected.

"The Secretary of State said that the President would be welcome, but again advised that the visit be conducted discreetly. Although the President would be given the treatment of an official visit, it should be designated as private.

"I then returned to the Sudan to brief the President and accompany him and his delegation on the visit. In putting together the delegation for the visit, I suggested to the President that we should include some representatives from the Southern regional government. Both the President and the former Minister of Foreign Affairs, now Minister of

Higher Education, but still actively participating in our plans, disagreed. I tried to persuade them that the Addis Ababa Agreement was a major factor in our diplomatic initiatives, especially in the United States, and that we should have it reflected in our talks. The President reacted by saying, 'We will reflect it'. He then went on to say, 'Besides, you are the one organizing the entire visit. Why do we need another Southerner?' I responded with some sense of humor, 'Mr. President, I had forgotten that I am also a Southerner, not just a Sudanese'. They laughed.

"You are lucky no Southerner was there to hear you say that," the Chairman commented. "For them, that would have been a denial of your South Sudanese identity."

"I know. Anyway, the visit went exceedingly well. It lasted for three weeks, during which we went to eight states. My message of building on the Addis Peace Agreement and its implications for our domestic and foreign policy was very well received. The President consistently called on me to present our policy. Sometimes, he would begin and then turn to me to complete his presentation.

"At a Congressional Prayer Breakfast, I was asked to introduce the President. I first expressed reservations about introducing my President, for lack of objectivity. I then said that one thing I could objectively say was that apart from Jesus Christ, he was the only other person I knew who rose from the dead after three days. That broke the ice and the conversation proceeded on all the good work the President did after his victory against the communists, obviously an appealing subject for Washington."

"And the President must have felt elated about being compared to Jesus Christ, especially as the Muslims believe in Christ as a Prophet and that he would eventually be a 'born-again' Muslim."

"He certainly joined the laughter at the comparison. We spent the last day at the Rockefeller Estate in Tarrytown outside New York City, hosted by both Nelson and David Rockefeller. As we swam and otherwise lounged around that vast and beautiful estate, Nelson Rockefeller asked the President how he could be away from the country for that long a time. I injected myself into their conversation and responded, 'Just to prove how stable the country is.'"

"I am sure they knew better," the Chairman interjected.

"And they would soon be proven right. Because of the hostile US policy toward the Sudan, the Sudanese President's visit had been quite controversial. In fact, we had planned it in relative secrecy, primarily involving the Former Minister of Foreign Affairs, now Minister of Higher Education, and myself. Among the Ministers in this high-level delegation, hardly anyone else knew what the visit was all about. Our President instructed me to brief them during the flight. I could see that they received my briefing with skepticism."

"I am sure they did not like being treated that way, taken for granted, as it seemed."

"Probably not. There was in fact considerable concern that the Jewish Lobby might do something violent against our President in retaliation against the assassination of the American Ambassador by the Black September Palestinians, popularly believed to have been released. Since I felt personally responsible for the visit, I was delighted that it had gone well."

"So you thought," commented the Chairman.

"Just wait. The truth is coming.

"The Sudanese President initially wanted me to remain behind in the US to follow up on the visit. I thought it was too soon to follow up and that I should perhaps go back and then return after a couple of months to follow up. Two days before the delegation was to return, he told me that he had decided that I should stay behind to follow up. After seeing the delegation off, I went to bed with a sigh of relief that everything had gone off exceedingly well. The visit had been a stunning success with not a single negative incident whatsoever."

"So far, so good. Where is 'the truth'?"

"Here it is: I woke up the next morning still feeling euphoric about the success of the visit. But then I turned on the television and saw the map of the Sudan, followed by the concluding words of an announcement, 'And the whereabouts of the President are unknown'. I was devastated. I felt the personal responsibility of having planned the visit that led to this catastrophe.

"That was what became known as the Libyan Invasion, the attack of opposition groups supported by Libya, with mercenaries from West African countries," the Chairman added.

"Yes. Many people died, but the invasion was successfully repulsed. And a friend of mine, a South Sudanese, as Minister of Information, effectively used South Sudan's regional information system to generate regional support for the government and played a critical role in saving the regime. When our President left Washington to return home, instead of following up on our President's visit, I was instructed to bring the case against Libya to the UN Security Council. Arab mediation, however, argued against an Arab country raising a case against another Arab country, which was said never to have happened before."

"The leader of the opposition, who was also the head of his religious sect and of the largest political party in the country, was tried in absentia and sentenced to death. But he safely remained in the United Kingdom and the government's request for extradition never received a sympathetic hearing, which enraged our President. 'What do they see in the man?', he once asked me rhetorically. 'Don't they know that I could easily kill him in the streets of London if I chose to?' I was disgusted with the thought, but since the 'slaughtering' of the perpetrators of the failed communist coup attempt, nothing would surprise me."

"He probably thought of you as naïve."

"I am sure he did. The government was to reconcile with the rebel leaders and Libya in less than a year. That reconciliation signified the beginning of the undoing of the Addis Ababa Accord as the sectarian parties and the Muslim Brothers who had opposed the agreement joined the government. My friend was one of the Southern Sudanese who opposed the reconciliation. I tried to see the positive side by approaching it as a broadening of the national consensus and even tried to reconcile him with the incoming partners. But the rift with the South would persist and eventually lead to the undoing of the Addis Ababa Agreement.

"Relations with Libya were restored and improved. I was a member of the delegation led by the First Vice-President that went to Libya in the reconciliation talks. After the initial talks, and as I was drafting a statement with my Libyan counterpart, we were informed that 'Brother Colonel' wanted to meet our delegation. I could not join the delegation but expressed the desire to meet the Leader. So, it was arranged that the whole delegation would meet him the next day on our way to the airport.

"Gadhafi received us in his tent, where we all sat on the traditional stools as we listened to the pontification of the Leader. Both in the earlier discussion and in the meeting with Gadhafi, I could not believe the condescending way the Libyans talked to us. And our delegation responded in what I thought was too meek a manner. The Libyans asserted that the attack was by the Sudanese opposition and that all they did was to assist them. Worse, they said that they thought the revolution of the Sudan was dead, but since responsible Sudanese were telling them that the revolution was still alive, they had decided to believe them. They welcomed the initiative to normalize bilateral relations, which should be the normal state; what had prevailed previously was abnormal.

"That was not my first time visiting Libya. I had attended the meeting of the foreign ministers of the Organization of African Unity, during which Gadhafi displayed a very condescending attitude toward the Africans. He claimed that colonialism had distorted the African identity by importing and imposing Christianity and Western culture, when Islam and the Arab culture had been the dominant elements of African identity. He also insisted that most African states were artificial creations of colonialism. He even mentioned a few countries and ended by saying that there were others whose names he did not even know.

"Most of the ministers were in fact Christians. And all, irrespective of their religion, were insulted by the racist attitude Gadhafi displayed against the Black Africans. Interestingly enough, a number of ministers were invited to meet with Gadhafi individually. Among them was the foreign minister of Nigeria, who was a Colonel. He was a very colorful person, who related his militarism to diplomacy. This was demonstrated to me early in our relationship. We were attending a Council of Ministers meeting in Kinshasa, Zaire. I had made interventions in the discussions. During the recess he approached me very casually and asked where I had studied. I told him Sudan, the United Kingdom, and the United States. He surprised me by saying, 'You are very articulate; too articulate for my taste'. He took me so off guard that I could not think of anything to say. Obviously, I could not thank him for saying that I was too articulate for his taste. And I could not quarrel with him for flattering me as articulate. We actually became friends. He later wrote his memoirs under the title *Diplomatic Soldiering*. When he received Gadhafi's invitation, his response was 'Who told him I want to see him?' and refused to go."

"Good for him and for Africa. That's how a true soldier should react to such an insult," the Chairman interjected.

"I was proud of him," I said and went on to elaborate on my activities in the government. "One of the first things I tried to do as Minister of State for Foreign Affairs was to recruit Southerners into the Ministry. In fact, I visited the South for exactly that purpose. I was confronted with two obstacles. One was a seeming lack of interest in foreign affairs among Southerners. The other was the resistance in Khartoum to any preferential treatment of Southerners in the recruitment of diplomats. At first, the President agreed with my plans. But then, on the advice of others, he told me that Southerners should sit for examination and then be given preference in the selection. The combination of these obstacles discouraged me from pursuing my objective and the matter came to rest."

"All that was probably because South Sudanese did not fully appreciate the linkage between the domestic situation and international relations. What I always found remarkable was the way you continued to combine involvement in domestic affairs with your international engagement. And of course, Abyei continued to be one of the areas of your domestic focus. I suggest we go back to that issue in our next session."

"Fair enough," I responded as we ended the session.

Session Ten: Abyei Revisited

As I waited for the Chairman and reflected on the topic we had set for the session, I reflected on the risks involved in my continuing to engage in tribal affairs while my assignment was in foreign relations. A colleague in the Government had once mentioned that to me as something he admired but which most ministers were quite reluctant to do. I was well aware of the sensitivities involved but decided that it was a risk worth taking.

The Chairman arrived and immediately raised the subject. "So, tell us about your favorite subject. Of course, I mean the situation of the Ngok Dinka of Abyei and their relations with their Missiriya neighbors."

"Thank you. Of course, you know that I am aware of the ambivalences involved in combining tribal relations with foreign affairs. Some of my colleagues even jokingly wondered whether I was Minister of State for Foreign Affairs or for Tribal Affairs."

"I wouldn't worry about that. We do not come from nowhere and as they say, charity begins at home," the Chairman injected.

"One aspect of my involvement in Ngok Dinka–Missiriya Arab affairs occurred in 1977, after a tragic incident in which the Missiriya Arabs intercepted a convoy of lorries carrying Ngok Dinkas returning to their area and killed nearly two hundred people, including a brilliant student who was doing his Ph.D. at London University. Nimeiri was traveling abroad. The First Vice-President was in charge. He convened a meeting of the National Security Committee, which he chaired. As the senior Foreign Minister was away, I attended on his behalf. I took the opportunity to explain the security situation in Abyei as I knew it. The committee decided to send the Governor of the State and the Political Advisor to the area. I advised against the idea on the grounds that they were already implicated, as the Ngok Dinka viewed them as parties in the conflict on the side of the Missiriya. People objected vehemently to my characterizing national leaders as parties in a tribal conflict. I defended my position and told them that they would be burying their heads in the sand if they did not recognize the facts on the ground. The First Vice-President said he would go himself. People objected for security reasons, but he insisted. He asked me to accompany him.

"The helicopter that we flew in did not have a door on the side where the First Vice-President sat. I offered to sit there. The Vice-President reacted with apparent indignation. 'Do you think that after all I have gone through in life, I would be afraid of falling off the helicopter?'"

"Were you suggesting that you were braver than a general?"

"Not at all. I was suggesting that I was more dispensable than the First Vice-President of the Republic.

"Anyway, in the public meeting in Abyei, people spoke very candidly and with unmitigated anger, alleging that the army and indeed the government was fully on the side of the Missiriya. They went as far as telling the First Vice-President to go back and return to the area with his army to confront the Dinka who were prepared to fight and die for their rights. The Vice-President listened with patience and apparent understanding and sympathy. But when he spoke, he unveiled his anger at the way people had spoken. He said it was irresponsible and unacceptable to consider the national army a party in a tribal conflict. He said he had allowed them to speak freely because he recognized their pain and anger, but that they must change their perception of the army. I chose not to speak in Abyei.

"We then stopped in Muglad, where we met with the Arab Chiefs. The Vice-President clearly sympathized with the Ngok Dinka and was quite critical of the Arabs. Although I had not spoken in Abyei, I chose to speak in Muglad, to advocate a return to peaceful and cooperative coexistence that had marked relations between the two communities. I also reiterated my familiar theme that the perception of racial division between them was a myth that did not reflect their realities. I asked the Arab Paramount Chief, Babo Nimir, who had been a close ally and friend of my father, 'Uncle, Nazir, you have been to Arab countries, what do the people there look like?' He said, "By God, they are white-skinned.' I then said to them, 'Look at your skin color, where do you think it comes from? It is from those neighbors you consider racially different from you. You do not realize that you are relatives, divided only by erroneous self-perceptions.' They all laughed with obvious understanding of and empathy for my argument."

"That is the myth of self-perception the New Sudan was aiming to explode."

"Not long afterwards, the First Vice-President was dismissed from his position. He had intended to devote much of his time to the cause of Abyei. He even told me that my being assigned full-time to addressing the problems of the area would be a greater service to the country than my foreign service.

"Later, the President assigned the Minister for Public Administration to chair a peace conference to mediate between the Missiriya Arabs and the Ngok Dinka. I was asked to be his deputy. A number of prominent tribal chiefs from the North were asked to be mediators, what is known as *ajaweed*. The conference was to be held in Kadugli, the capital of Kordofan State. The process proved most challenging and precarious.

"As soon as I got to Kadugli, I learned that three of the most articulate and effective leaders of the Ngok Dinka, among the closest associates of my father, were excluded from the delegation because they were considered traitors and aligned with the Arabs. I immediately thought that it was a mistake to exclude them. I sent a message to the Administrator of Abyei, who was waiting for a plane to fly him to the talks, asking him to bring those individuals with him and to use my wanting to meet with them on a separate research project as the reason for my calling them. I then embarked on persuading the Ngok delegation to accept them.

"Persuading the Ngok Dinka to accept those three leaders turned out to be more difficult than I had thought. All of them without exception were adamant that those people had totally sold out and could never be genuine spokesmen for the cause of the Dinka. Our discussion took virtually all night. Only the Administrator took my side. But even that did not help much. In the end, I went to consult our oldest Uncle, who had been my father's Deputy Paramount Chief. As he was suffering from a bad cold, he did not attend the talks. I was delighted and almost surprised that he fully agreed with me and sent his word of support to the still assembled delegation. That sealed the deal.

"The next morning, as the Chairman, the State Governor, and myself visited the Missiriya delegation for a courtesy meeting, they stunned us by revealing that the three Ngok leaders had taken an oath to speak for the Arab position and objected to their joining the Dinka delegation. That's when the Governor sharply criticized them for being unreasonable. How could they demand that the Dinka abandon their people and join the Arabs!?"

"That was the divide-and-rule strategy at work."

"One of the three Dinka elders approached me, obviously distressed. He asked me whether it was legally wrong for a man who takes an oath to speak against his people for rejecting him, to change his mind and join his people when they decide to accept him. He then explained their position to me very candidly and I assured him that there was nothing at all wrong with that. Throughout the talks, they proved to be the best spokesmen for the case of their people."

"You must have felt vindicated and proud!"

"I sure did. I also found myself in the crossfire of all sides. The Arabs suspected me and even challenged my legitimacy as a mediator. One of them went as far as saying, 'If it was not out of respect for the President, we would have objected to having this Tenge with you at the podium.' The Dinka also took me as leaning too much in favor of the Arabs in order to prove my objectivity. One went as far as asking, 'Why are you standing between us and the Arabs? Step aside and leave us to confront each other directly.' The mediators saw themselves as marginalized by the Chairman, implicitly blaming my influence on him. 'What are we here for, if we have no role to play?'"

"You were really caught in between, not a surprising position for a good mediator."

"Two specific issues threatened the process with failure, which I did my best to avert, in the end with success. One was that there was a precedent attributed to my father that a peace agreement between the two communities be based on forgiveness and reconciliation without the conventional blood compensation. Having killed so many people, compensation at the conventional rates would have been exorbitant. Our efforts to persuade them against that position resulted in their offering to pay a very modest amount for what they called a reconciliation fee, which only added to the insult to the Dinka, and frankly to me too. We eventually succeeded in negotiating a much higher level for the so-called reconciliation fee, which was still less than the conventional compensation, but which the Dinka reluctantly accepted after much persuasion.

"The Dinka then insisted that a principle be adopted assuring no blood compensation in the future between the two communities. I thought this unwisely implied that the Dinka planned to attack the

Arabs in the future and expected to inflict heavy casualties on them, for which there would be no compensation. This was not only incriminating, but also grossly presumptuous, for there was no reason for the Dinka to believe that they would be the victors and the Arabs the vanquished in any future conflict. It was with great difficulty that I eventually convinced them against that position. As is always the case in such peace processes, the end result was appreciated by both sides and we then received lavish praise for our efforts."

"Even that could be disingenuous and possibly a matter of courtesy. But it probably meant that you negotiated a solution where there was no clear winner or loser. Or perhaps both sides felt that they won."

"I think both sides were satisfied. That's probably why they were greeting each other with hugs. Even the Ajaweed seemed happy with the outcome. After all, they could claim it as the result of their mediation.

"Meanwhile, the implementation of the Abyei Development Project was now in full swing and I was able to oversee and support it through my position in the government. The project was, however, controversial. Many members of the Abyei elite and Southerners generally saw it as a detraction from the goal of joining the South. The government of Kordofan Province, now State, saw it as an imposition from central government. There were also differences of approach between us and the Harvard Institute. Whereas we wanted a robust development operation, Harvard was committed to experimenting with appropriate technology that required modest foreign input and focused on improving on what already existed.

"I continued to facilitate their activities through my vantage point in the government, but otherwise respected their independence and full freedom, until I felt compelled to be more involved in their operations. Although our different approaches eventually converged, it took time before we could make visible progress on bridging our differences, by which time the country was headed back to war, and the Project was abruptly terminated by the demise of the Addis Accord and the resumption of war."

"Before we get to the demise of the Addis Ababa Agreement, tell us about your contribution as Minister of State for Foreign Affairs. But I assume that this will be a rather lengthy account and suggest that we do that in the next session."

I agreed with the Chairman. As I reflected on our time in Washington, I felt genuinely proud that we had made a difference. And when I say we, I was particularly thinking of the contribution of my wife. I had wondered whether being married to an American would be an asset or a liability in a diplomatic representation in her country. I even began my mission on the controversial note that as an American, my wife would not be entitled to diplomatic status, which included immunity. I argued that diplomatic immunity was not a privilege, but a facilitation of my function. Without protection for my wife, I could not be protected to conduct my diplomatic mission that immunity was supposed to ensure.

"I asked some of my former colleagues from Yale Law School to plead my case. I was one day surprised by the Chief of Protocol to tell me that he had good news for me. They had decided to grant my wife diplomatic status, the first case in their experience.

"My wife proved to be a bridge of which both Sudanese and Americans were very proud. On numerous occasions, I received great praise for her from both sides. I felt very proud of her. I could not have done what I did without her. I saw the success of my mission as a joint achievement. And the evidence of that success would make us number three after Israel and Egypt as recipients of US development assistance. I was tempted to call my wife to share with her these gratifying reflections, but I decided to remain silent as she might wonder what had triggered those thoughts. I only called her for my medicine before retiring for the night.

Session Eleven: Minister of State

The following evening, I was downstairs in the dining room having dinner with my wife. I don't remember where our boys were. It was a quiet and serene setting. We had just watched the news in the living room in front of a flaming fireplace. A spacious hallway separated the living room and the dining room so that we could not continue to enjoy the fire while in the dining room. "Shall I make a plate for you to eat here?" my wife offered. But I decided that we move to the dining room.

My wife was becoming used to my looking distracted and at times introspectively far away. She sat there looking down on the table. A strange silence cast a solemn air at the table. I realized that my wife was trying to read my mind but did not want to ask questions. Then I kept looking at my watch. Again, I realized that she noticed. "Are you getting tired?" she asked a question that was not the one in her mind. She wanted to know why I was looking at my watch. But she realized that it would be getting too close to my secret world to ask the question she really wanted to. I answered the question she did not pose by asking for my pills and getting up to go upstairs to my bedroom.

I began to think about the subject we agreed upon as the topic of the next session—my role as Minister of State for Foreign Affairs. That was a vast topic and I was not sure how I would relate it to the theme of identity which we agreed provided the thread of our conversations.

"Knock, knock," the familiar voice of the Chairman sounded.

"I know who is there, *Raandit*. Welcome*!*"

"I take it you also remember that we are to talk today about your service as Minister of State for Foreign Affairs." The Chairman was generally all business.

"Yes, I do. But how do we begin?"

The Chairman began our session by noting that I was shortchanging myself by calling my service in the United States my most challenging and rewarding. "From what I know, your contribution as Minister of State was equally challenging and you did a lot which I believe must have been also rewarding."

"I appreciate your saying that. And I must confess that I agree with you. And in many ways, the two were closely connected. In fact, I confronted a number of challenging situations of which the outcomes were quite gratifying. I will give you a few examples. And I have to say that our peace agreement continued to be my guiding principle. I could not represent a country that had just peacefully ended its civil war through a negotiated agreement and then contradict that domestic achievement by taking contrary positions regionally and internationally. I wanted to be a bridge builder, not a party to any conflict."

The Chairman commented, "Actually, from what I know, over the years, you acquired a well-deserved reputation for bridge building and reconciliation, at different levels, from local to global. We witnessed this in your efforts to mediate between your Ngok Dinka community and their Missiriya neighbors. You also mediated between conflicting South Sudanese politicians. And I observed this attitude even in your response to interpersonal differences. It is actually a well-known characteristic of which you should be rightly proud.

"But there are times when bridging is not only difficult, but plainly wrong. There are situations that do not lend themselves to compromise. And you are talking to someone who took up arms because the situation had become intolerable. There was no way we could compromise with Islamic fundamentalists."

"But Mr. Chairman, you did compromise, and the mediators who made you compromise were bridge builders!"

"We compromised not because we wanted to, but because we had to. It is not that we welcomed the bridge-building role of the mediators as desirable, but because we could not win decisively to get all we were fighting for and the mediators both persuaded and forced us to compromise. Given the limits of what we could achieve, we saw the agreement as a win-win solution, or, to put it in the opposite, one in which there was neither decisive victor nor vanquished."

"You remind me of what an Ambassador of the United States, who had negotiated the conflict in Bosnia in the former Yugoslavia, said when I cited a piece of advice that Nelson Mandela had given at a small dinner conversation. Mandela said that every human being has something positive that makes him or her human and that to gain cooperation, one must look for that positive to build on. The

Ambassador, with his experience in negotiating the crisis in the former Yugoslavia, responded by complimenting Mandela's virtues, but added that there are people 'who are just bad, bad, bad', and in whom there is nothing good to build upon."

"I am glad he pointed that out. It's a very important point."

"Actually, I do know that my conciliatory approach or bridging reputation is not viewed with favor by everyone. Some people have openly criticized me for that. They see it more as a negative than a virtue. I accept their criticism as a genuine difference in principles."

"I would not go that far. I see it as a virtue, but one that has limits."

"It is quite a challenge to pursue bridging and reconciliation as desirable objectives, but also to know the limits. I think there is also a difference between those who decisively choose to take sides in a conflict where bridging is no longer possible, and those who recognize the impasse, but continue to monitor the situation for bridging opportunities as the conflict progresses. But I think we are getting too deep into these dilemmas. I suggest we go back to lived experience."

"I agree. So please go back to your story."

"I faced the kind of challenge we are talking about soon after I assumed my new position in the Ministry. Following Sudan's President's visit to the United States, I led our delegation to the Ministerial Meeting of the Organization of African Unity, which later became the African Union. By some coincidence, Sudan was elected Chair of the Political Committee. That of course meant that I was in the Chair. That year turned out to be politically charged and potentially explosive. On the agenda were three very sensitive issues: the Comoro Islands, Djibouti, and Western Sahara. These issues made my committee the subject of the most popular attendance by spectators. The room was full and many people peeped in through the windows."

"I suspect that seeing a South Sudanese representing the Sudan must also have been intriguing to Africans. For a long time, African leaders whispered to us that they were appalled by the mistreatment of the Africans by the Arabs in the Sudan, but they were so dogmatically committed to the principle of preserving colonial borders that they could not speak out. President Nyerere was one of those who discreetly argued that Sudan must be an exception to preserving colonial borders. And our friend, the former President of Nigeria, promised that if we captured Juba as the Capital of South Sudan, they would recognize a

Declaration of Independence by our liberation movement. So, what we eventually achieved by armed struggle was what African leaders widely, but quietly wanted."

"It's interesting you say that. Perhaps that was why, beyond that being Sudan's position, I was enthusiastically elected chairman of the Political Committee by the Council of Ministers. And I must say that the way I conducted my chairmanship was also very well received. Our Ambassador, who had been the Deputy Foreign Minister and before that had been the Permanent Representative of the Sudan to the UN, was very complimentary about the way I managed the chairmanship, arguing that I looked surprisingly very experienced and confident for a newly appointed Minister. I think he was insinuating that my UN experience must have been a factor. I doubt that he was alluding to my being a South Sudanese, but of course others might have considered that factor.

"As I recall, the Comoros, about which I had known nothing, involved issues of rebellion and external intervention, which was in the end manageable. Djibouti was a more complex issue, involving its demand for independence, ironically supported by France, the exiting colonial power, with conflicting claims by Ethiopia and Eritrea. As you know, that is where the identities of that region converge. Although very contentious, it was also manageable.

"The most contentious and difficult issue was that of Western Sahara. The question was whether the OAU should recognize the Polisario as the legitimate representative of the Saharawi people. Algeria supported the Polisario, which Morocco and Mauritania opposed. Morocco, supported by Mauritania, claimed that Western Sahara was under the royal sovereignty of the King of Morocco. Algeria advocated the right of self-determination for the people of Western Sahara. As these positions became unbridgeable, a Nigerian Acting Secretary General of the Organization suggested that we put the matter to the vote. I resisted that, because I was certain that it would divide the Organization. I argued that I would not have the Organization divided under Sudan's (that is, my) chairmanship."

"You must also have felt conflicted between supporting the right of the people of Western Sahara to exercise self-determination and the preservation of the unity of Morocco, which Sudan supported. Both principles applied to South Sudan, whose people aspired to exercise self-determination, but compromised to preserve the unity of the country."

"You are absolutely right, but for me the main consideration was to bridge or reconcile the positions in conflict. I told the committee that the issue we were considering was too important to be decided by the committee and suggested that we submit the report of our discussions to the Plenary to make the final decision. When the draft report came for approval, it proved to be very controversial, with contests over such words as 'some', 'several', 'most', and 'majority'. I decided to have a count on each of the disputed estimates. Surprisingly, the numbers of those for and against the recognition of Polisario turned out to be equal.

"During the period of the consideration of the item, I was in close contact with the Ministers of Algeria and Benin, who were the hardliners, in order to moderate their stance. This was seen by Morocco and Mauritania as though I was biased for Polisario. When the issue was tabled for the consideration of the Plenary, they made their allegations against me, but were countered by many committee members who spoke in my defense. I was applying our traditional principle of consensus building, which I had observed my father apply in his leadership style, which required that a judge or a leader in resolving a conflict be seen to side with the party furthest removed from him in order to narrow the gap with the party closest to him. Our policy was closer to Morocco and farther from Algeria. So, I wanted to moderate Algeria's position by engaging him more closely. That was also a way of moderating his position."

"Did you explain what you were doing to your colleagues on the Council?"

"Not really! But I thought it was obvious. Perhaps I should have made it clearer. On the other hand, revealing a strategy might expose it and thereby undermine it. The good thing is that the Chairman of the Plenary was the Foreign Minister of Liberia, who was a friend and with whom I maintained close contact to manage the situation. We scheduled the item for discussion late in the deliberations—as I recall, after an all-night session, at about 5 or 6 am. Earlier that day, it was announced that the Polisario had declared an exercise of self-determination in favor of independence of the Western Sahara.

"At the end of the debate, the Chairman made a ruling that remarkably averted the crisis without a solution. He ruled that the right of self-determination was a universal right to which all peoples were entitled. There was applause. He stated that the people of Western Sahara were entitled to self-determination. Again, there was applause. The people of Western Sahara had indeed exercised their right to self-determination. Surprisingly, again there was applause, by both sides to the dispute. For Morocco, the traditional leaders of Western Sahara had declared their loyalty to the King, which was construed as an exercise of self-determination. For Algeria, the declaration of Polisario earlier that day was an exercise of self-determination. The Chairman then added that recognition of a declaration of self-determination was the sovereign right of every state, not for the organization. That too was applauded. He then concluded that a resolution to that effect would be drafted by the chairman of the committee. Again, this was greeted with a final round of applause. I however excused myself from drafting the resolution, which I passed on to the Secretariat."

"That was quite acrobatic decision making."

"Circumstances conspired in our favor. It was quite a remarkable coincidence of calculation and coincidental developments. Back in the Sudan, the President, who was very happy with the way I had handled the situation, told me that the King of Morocco had telephoned him to complain that I was not following the policy position of my President. I was very reassured when the President commented, 'Can you believe he talked to me as though he knew my Minister better than me?'

"Ironically, the division of the OAU which I had worked so hard to avoid happened two years later when the issue was voted on and the Organization recognized Polisario, and Morocco withdrew from the OAU."

"But you saved the unity of the Organization by denying the people of Western Sahara their rights," the Chairman interjected. "It was therefore a matter of principle to give the people of Western Sahara their rights even at the risk of dividing the Organization. This is an example of a situation in which bridging may be unfair."

"For me, it was a case of balancing idealism with realism. Ironically, I faced the same crisis many years later, in 2013, when I was South Sudan's Permanent Representative to the United Nations and was appointed the Chairman of the Africa Group for the month. The issue was whether the Representative of Polisario, which is a member of the African Union, has the right to attend the meetings of the African Group in New York. Algeria supported their participation, while

Morocco objected. When I took the chairmanship of the Group, the issue had blocked the meetings of the Group for at least two months. I appealed for bridging the conflicting positions of Addis and New York. Again, we were able to achieve a result that allowed the Polisario representative to attend without speaking, which was not really a solution."

"Another instance of what you call balancing idealism with realism," the Chairman remarked. "Perhaps this was a case where compromise or bridging was justified because no real harm was done."

"That's right. Following that trying experience as a newly appointed Minister, I was mandated by the Council of Ministers to visit the three Member States of the East African Community that had been established in 1967 and was being dissolved in 1977 with acrimonious consequences. The immediate problem was the sharing of assets. The operative assumption was that each country would possess what was within the country when the dissolution was declared. But that would have been grossly unfair, as it would favor some over others. The countries involved were Kenya, Uganda, and Tanzania. I don't quite remember what I was supposed to do, but I believe it was an extension of my Chairmanship of the Political Committee of the Council of Ministers and my task was to offer our good offices and try to moderate the crisis.

"My vague recollection of Uganda was the strange combination of Idi Amin's hospitality and his bizarre running of the country. I recall his dismissing those attending our meeting for us to have a one-on-one private talk in which he intimated to me some information to share with my President about some security threats to the regime which I cannot now fully recall and did not give much credence at the time."

"Some of our people who opposed the Addis Ababa Agreement were still in Uganda," the Chairman reflected. "Idi Amin probably wanted to gain favor with the Sudan by exposing their activities to the Sudanese government and even implicating the regional government of South Sudan in order to look credible."

"That was probably the idea and I just ignored him. My visit to Kenya was memorable for a rather disoriented conversation with President Jommo Kenyatta. I met him in his country house quite a distance outside Nairobi. The appointment was scheduled for 10 am and eventually took place at around 12 noon. Kenyatta appeared physically quite fit, smartly dressed in a colorful African shirt, but seemed mentally disoriented. He kept asking me where I was from and repeating, 'All we want is peace'. After a rather lengthy conversation on nothing, he suggested that we go for a walk, during which he demonstrated he was as fit as he looked. Sadly, although it was not obvious in his physical appearance, he was at the tail end of his life and died months after our meeting."

"Sad for a man who otherwise towered as a leader. But those are the unavoidable trials of old age."

"Interestingly enough, I was told that even when he was mentally so compromised, he still ran the country on some 15 to 30 minutes a day when he would be quite alert and focused. No one wanted to be caught on the wrong side during those minutes of mental clarity."

"It's tragic, but that is human nature and the consequence of enduring dictatorship. It is particularly sad that Jommo Kenyatta had been the embodiment of popular democracy. Stepping aside at the right time is wisdom most African leaders lack."

"I take it, that's what you would have done?"

"We will never know. I missed the opportunity."

"But perhaps we can tell from the example of a man who was known to be your model of righteous leadership, Mwalimu Julius Nyerere. In fact, the most rewarding on that mission was my meeting with Nyerere. It took place in his official residence in a tiny office where he sat at a modest desk and I sat in front of him in an even simpler chair. But the conversation was intellectually stimulating and mutually quite enjoyable. Apart from a general discussion of the situation of the Community, I tried to persuade him to mediate between us and Ethiopia over the Eritrean problem. Nyerere was clearly reluctant. Eventually, he concluded by saying, 'The Bible says, "Blessed are the peace makers, for they shall be called the children of God." But I have misgivings on that. If you engage in making peace a habit, you risk wanting conflict to make peace.' A warm relationship was to develop between President Nyerere and me that endured until the end of his life."

"He was a great man in his remarkable simplicity, humility, and modesty, a model of leadership that is rare in Africa—or elsewhere in the world," the Chairman commented. "As you know, I attended high school in Tanzania and also studied in Makerere University, which was then the Center of the Pan-African movement in East Africa. I was particularly inspired by Nyerere's Ujamaa Collective Villages Program, which is often viewed in terms of African socialism, but which is also a practical way of promoting development of African cultural values. I believe it is the combination of these factors that endeared Tanzania, and Nyerere in particular, to the Scandinavian countries as an aid recipient."

"I witnessed that first hand. Tanzania was a country of focus for Scandinavian countries, for which they combined their aid to be more effective. And indeed, Tanzania made very effective use of international development assistance. President Nyerere and I once converged in Stockholm, where he gave a lecture about developments in Africa. During the question-and-answer period, one person asked him whether he regretted applying socialism in Tanzania. With his characteristic humor, he responded, 'Do you in Scandinavia still talk of socialism? I no longer do because I am afraid'. But then he proceeded to show statistically how much Tanzania benefited from his African Socialism and the Scandinavian assistance.

"That is typical Nyerere wit. Combining humor with seriousness was his vintage trademark," the Chairman interjected.

"As I got to know him over the years, another aspect of his personality that I came to admire greatly was his humility. Meeting him and talking with him, you would not know that this rather smallish and humble man was the one with that towering name. You have to be great to be that humble in that prominent position of Head of State. And he did it with a glowing aura of dignity."

"It is obvious that within a short time of your appointment as Minister of State for Foreign Affairs, you were thrust into diplomatic missions that spread widely from Washington to eastern and southern Africa, with, I presume, very diverse issues. Did any particular theme connect the approaches you adopted?" the Chairman wanted to know.

I paused for a moment, in reflection. "I believe what connected them was the sense of pride and confidence I felt in representing a country that had just ended a long racially, culturally, and religiously divisive war. What was more, it was a country that had alienated itself from Black Africa through a distorted self-perception as Arab and with an extremist version of Islam. Being geographically the largest country, with vast natural resources, a million square miles of rich, mostly fertile, arable land, with plentiful rainfall and the reliable flow of Nile waters, and large, but mostly unexplored, mineral wealth and newly discovered oil reserves, Sudan was poised to be continental leader. Articulating the link between these domestic assets as a basis for constructive engagement with the outside world, in Africa and beyond, was an honor and a privilege. Through the peace agreement, we turned a national agenda of devastating war into a strategy that promised equitable development that distributed the peace dividends throughout the country. At least that was our stated policy and aspiration. I was convinced about this agenda, and I believe I was convincing."

"Listening to you now, you convince me!"

"Too late! Unfortunately, all that was eventually to prove more a theory than a reality. And some of us oversold ourselves. I recall that, during President Nimeiri's visit that I organized, he asked me to address a large meeting attended by the whole delegation. I spoke about the domestic basis of our foreign policy and its broader implications in our international relations. My statement was very well received. Not only did many Americans approach me to congratulate me, but my fellow Ministers themselves praised the speech as though it were my own invention. Nimeiri himself kept calling on me in meetings throughout the visit to speak on the same theme. They all liked what I said, but I doubt that they recognized it as authentically representing a well-defined and nationally agreed-upon policy."

"I don't think even the South, whom you were in a sense representing, understood how you were using the Addis Ababa Agreement as the foundation of your diplomatic work. So, you were just a useful tool of the President!"

"As I discovered later, so were we all. I put it metaphorically by comparing the President to a blackboard on which, depending on what was needed at a specific moment, a tactically chosen group would be invited to write their policy agenda to perpetuate the President's rule. When he had exhausted all the groups and he ran out of cards, his rule suddenly came to its inexorable end."

"Before we reach that dead end, I would like to hear more about your experiences in your diplomatic life. I am particularly interested in your Africa experience. After all, we in South Sudan were viewed by our African brothers and sisters as lost, overshadowed by the Arabs. You obviously witnessed a resurgence of the African identity in the Sudanese power structure."

I chuckled. "Right. An experience that stands out vividly in my memory and that also took place not long after my appointment as Minister was the African-American Conference held in Lesotho early in

1977. Flying to Maseru was eye-opening. Although the country is physically located within South Africa, we could not go through Johannesburg because of the Apartheid regime, especially as we had South African freedom fighters with us. We took a chartered plane from Maputo in Mozambique. As we overflew South Africa, with large well-developed plantations, the freedom fighters were visibly nostalgic about their beautiful country, while simultaneously fearing that the apartheid system could do something treacherous to down the plane. As we entered the geographic borders of Lesotho, underdevelopment emerged with a rocky mountainous landscape without any visible evidence of modern farming. The conference was held over the weekend. Ironically, White South Africans flooded our hotel to enjoy interracial entertainment with uninhibited gender companionship that would be illegal in South Africa. It was a remarkable scene to watch."

"Everywhere in the world, racist policies create artificial barriers that block the natural instincts for mixing. Ironically, differences may both generate fear of the unknown and create their own curiosity and attraction. Once the barriers are removed, the trend toward mixing begins. But that's a big topic in itself. Let's go back to your story."

"Sure. The conference itself was quite enjoyable. I was asked to speak on the theme of the changing bases of relations between Africa and America that evolved from the liberation struggle to the ideologically driven superpower global alignments, and to the challenges of partnership for peace, security, and development. My presentation was very well received and helped cultivate many relations that were to continue over the years and facilitate my work in promoting our bilateral relations. One person said she detected the influence of Yale Law School in what I said and the way I spoke. She herself was a Yale graduate. The individuals with whom I established relations included a young Senator, then a member of the Foreign Relations Committee, who requested that we maintain close contacts to assist him in his work. We lost contact until he eventually became Vice President of the United States, when we reconnected. The other was a Black American who was an influential political ally of then President-Elect Jimmy Carter and who became the Permanent Representative to the United Nations, with whom I developed a close official and personal relationship. The third was the President of a major philanthropic organization, who was to be a generous source of funding for my research agenda in several think tanks after I left the government."

"It's quite remarkable how personal relationships can make a difference in shaping one's destiny in life," commented the Chairman in an analytical mode. "Some people consciously keep close contacts with people they meet to call upon for favors at opportune times. Others allow the natural process to make the opportunity offer itself at an appropriate time without deliberately exploiting personal connections."

"I believe in the natural process and find it tasteless to deliberately exploit relationships. I believe that favors come best when they are motivated by conviction that they are deserved unsolicited," I added.

"Those set on exploiting personal relations believe that they are the determining, perhaps the only, factors in whatever one achieves in life. They take every call card or contact as a resource to be tapped at an opportune time. That, of course, is both factually and morally wrong. As to your other experiences, I thought you once told me that you attended the coronation of Jean-Bedel Bokassa as Emperor of the Central African Republic, which he declared an Empire in 1977."

The Chairman reminded me of an almost comic experience. "Yes, it was the most colorful event I ever attended. I accompanied the First Vice-President in attending the coronation. The spectacular ceremony, said to have been patterned after the coronation of Napoleon, cost some $30 million, paid by France. We took with us a herd of sheep as a contribution. As we approached the event, I asked people randomly whether transforming Bokassa from President into Emperor was a reward for past accomplishments or a motivation for future achievements. The answer was usually both.

"The event itself was beyond description. As the First Vice-President got sick, I sat in his place at the ceremony. That placed me close to the Emperor, with the French Minister of International Cooperation between us. In an attempt to engage the Minister in small talk, I asked him whether we were watching phases in the evolution of Africa or pages from the history of France. What I got was a serious response, arguing that the French policy was to support the choice of the African people.

"My sympathy was for a small boy whom Bokassa had chosen among his numerous sons and daughters to be the Crown Prince. The boy clearly looked lost, not comprehending what was happening. As I think back, it now occurs to me that Bokassa probably chose the child because he would not pose a threat to his father's power, as some impatiently ambitious designated successors tend to do."

"It is amazing that it did not occur to him and his French benefactors that he was planting an alien institution in the African body politic, one that was bound to backfire and be rejected," the Chairman observed.

"But isn't that what Africa has done with most, if not all, its institutions of modern governance?" I queried.

"Which is also why they get overthrown or otherwise fail and die a natural death, without tears being shed," added the Chairman. "And, of course, military rule becomes the norm in many African countries. When you were in the government, you had Nimeiri in the Sudan, Sadat in Egypt, Mengistu in Ethiopia, Gadhafi in Libya, Siad Barre in Somalia, in Uganda Idi Amin, and later, Museveni, who seized power by force, and Mobutu in Zaire. Chad had a series of military rulers in rapid succession. Sudan actually stood out in the region as a model for peace because of the Addis Ababa Agreement."

"Unfortunately, Ethiopia had an adversarial relationship with the Sudan because of Sudan's support for the Eritrean separatist movement. Somalia, which was pursuing the unification of greater Somalia in the Ogaden region of Ethiopia, wanted to exploit Sudan's unfriendly relations with Ethiopia. For its part, Sudan, which had become closely aligned with the United States, wanted to woo Somalia away from the East and back toward the West. I was given that assignment.

"During the annual Summits of the OAU heads of state, I had developed rather warm relations with Siad Barre. So I was happy to undertake the mission to engage him, and hopefully persuade him to change his position toward the West and to talk him out of any plans to go to war with Ethiopia. It was my first time in my ministerial position to take the entire plane to myself.

"I was very well received and lavishly entertained by the President and his government. But our talks did not go well. Siad Barre resisted the proposal of shifting positions in the superpower ideological global divide. According to him, nothing could attract him to the West. He said that if he requested support from the East, the process of decision and delivery would be quick. As for the West, the consideration of the request would not only rest with the Executive, but also with the

Congress, with the result uncertain and time-consuming. Ironically, he eventually changed his position in favor of a Western Alliance, but by then he was running out of political life.

"At the time of my mission, Siad Barre's main interest was not only to reaffirm his decision to go to war with Ethiopia, but to persuade us to join him. He said that if we joined forces, it would not take any time to defeat Ethiopia, which he condescendingly and consistently referred to as 'Habash'. Having just ended our own civil war, for which the world, in particular the West, was rewarding us, there was no way we would go to war with Ethiopia. And I had not the slightest doubt that my President shared that position. Somalia went to war with Ethiopia shortly after and not only suffered a stunning defeat, but also the demise of the entire nation."

"It is ironic how naïve leaders can be. To think that he could so easily defeat Ethiopia and that he could count on the Sudan as an ally indicates acute intellectual bankruptcy. He knew that Sudan had just extricated itself out of a long, devastating conflict and was enjoying international popularity for the achievement of peace. How could he expect Sudan to join him in a war whose objective was primarily to pursue Somali national interest, and one that was ill-conceived for that matter?"

"That was the question I myself pondered over and for which I could not find an answer. Of course, his calculation was that Sudan was at odds with Ethiopia over the Eritrean problem and that the combination of the Eritrean liberation movement and the armies of the two countries would overwhelm Ethiopia. But you are right that he did not have an accurate appreciation of the situation. It was naïve at best and intellectual bankruptcy, as you put it, at worst."

"The mistake people make is to think that war is just fighting. It is a rigorous intellectual exercise that involves several phases, planning, execution, and follow-up, all of which involve very serious intellectual challenges. And yet, in a situation of war, decisiveness in decision-making is critical. In the face of imminent danger, you cannot equivocate; you must be prompt in action. That is why military commanders may be better leaders than civilians under critically challenging conditions. Although intellectual depth may not be their trademark, military commanders are tactical, strategic, and decisive. And paradoxically, they fight, but perhaps because they fight, contrary to popular belief, they do not like wars."

"I remember a conversation I had with you about writing books and managing battles. I told you that my wife used to say that when I finished a book and before embarking on another one, I was fidgety. You reacted by saying that you were the same with your battles. That's when I understood a bit more about what going to battle meant in terms of plan, execution, and follow-up.

"By the way, when they introduced military training in secondary schools in 1955–56 for the third and fourth classes in the wake of Egypt's occupation of Halaib, the northern strip of land, I took being a soldier very seriously. In the drills, in the way I stood, walked, and carried myself, I wanted to excel. I got a prize in target shooting. And in the university, where military training was voluntary for students, I enrolled and only withdrew when I felt that the military was taking valuable time from my law studies and I did not know the objective for my military training. It is interesting that, years later, in totally separate settings, I was asked by an African professor of anthropology whether I had a military background. One time it was by a professor who attributed his question to the way I walked. One of my military colleagues in the government told me that the way I carried myself indicated military discipline. In his case, I believe he intended it as a compliment. The case of the professor was probably different, although I did not ask him what prompted his question."

"Now that you remind me about comparing your occupation of writing and my engagement in planning battles, although quite an unexpected comparison, I still believe it. In fact, I experienced both, as I was linked to both professionally. And being a soldier does not necessarily mean being a killer. You will probably not believe it, but I never killed a person."

"But Mr. Chairman, you planned killings and people were killed on your orders, however removed from the scene of killing you might have been. Just because you yourself didn't pull the trigger, responsibility for those killings still lies with you, no?"

"That is, of course, the logic of war. But as I always tell my commanders and soldiers, the ultimate objective is not to kill, but to diminish the capacity of the enemy to fight. The real goal is honorable peace."

We had unexpectedly veered into discussing military matters, about which I knew next to nothing. And our conversation had been long enough. We both felt instinctively that it was perhaps the right point to end the session. "Shall we stop here for the evening?" I posed.

"Obviously we both think so. Since we have not exhausted your work as Minister of State for Foreign Affairs, we should continue with that in our next session."

As we ended the session, I became even more convinced that the Chairman had stimulated me to do what I might never have thought of doing or even had the opportunity to do. I was not writing my memoirs in the conventional sense. Nor was I conceptualizing and preparing a scholarly book. I was conversing with a great leader, a professional soldier, and a scholar, who had also been a friend. He was no longer of the physical plane but was also back to visit me for us to relive our experiences and renew our friendship. And he initiated and maintained that contact with me not to sound the drums of his already well-established glory, but to let my voice be heard and my contribution known. I deeply appreciated it and relished the experience. As exhausted as I felt at the moment, I eagerly anticipated the   next   session.

Session Twelve: Withdrawal

I was recovering well, although, with my right arm still in a sling; there was not much I could do with my right hand. I continued the grueling physiotherapy sessions, which, for reasons I cannot recall, were not fully paid for by the health insurance. The African American therapist was however kind and generous to me and continued to treat me without making demands for payment. But, happily, as my lawyer had negotiated a settlement with the facility where I had accidentally fallen, I was able to pay the therapist for his services.

I also went to the office for some hours each day, mostly to catch up on developments with my lovely young and very efficient assistant. Otherwise I chitchatted with colleagues, received much sympathy, and engaged in intellectual discussions on issues and book plans. After all, writing books was what we were paid to do. Above all, I looked forward to my sessions with the Chairman and eagerly awaited the hours of the evening when he would appear.

That day, I went home and decided to sit with the family at the dinner table. The boys were there. Our boys, whose ages ranged from ten to seventeen, grew up in a close-knit family in which we all sat at the table for meals, often joined by their friends. The youngest always volunteered to say grace, repeating a short prayer which their maternal grandmother said at meals: "Come Lord Jesus be our Guest and bless the food we are about to have." We had a practice of discussing issues at the table. Chairing the discussions rotated among the boys. We always remembered with humor how our third son, at quite a young age, declared, "I want to be the honor," by which he meant that he wanted to chair the discussion. Now the atmosphere was quiet and somber. I knew they were very concerned about my condition, but no one wanted to say anything about it. That deeply saddened me and my attempts to lighten the atmosphere were flat and ineffective.

The truth was that I was thinking of the next session with the Chairman and wondering how I would begin the continuation of my diplomatic experiences. Our eldest son, being himself rather diplomatic, ended the somber situation by saying on behalf of his brothers, "May we be excused?" They were. And they got up and helped clear the table. My wife got up and followed them into the kitchen to do the dishes. She gestured that she understood I wanted to go up to my room.

It was about eight, the time the Chairman would normally appear. I expected to hear his voice any moment. Half an hour later, there was still no sign of the Chairman. I began to count minutes towards nine. Still no Chairman. I began to worry, bordering on panic. Still no Chairman. I called my wife for my pills.

She noticed something rather unusual on my face. "What's the matter, are you alright?"

What could I say? "Nothing is the matter; I am alright." But, of course, I was not.

Here I just left my children deeply concerned about me. And there I was, not knowing what had become of the Chairman. He could be feeling unwell, although I had no idea whether or not dead people have health issues. But what else could have prevented him from turning up as expected? Had I done something that offended him? But then I wondered whether dead people have feelings to be offended. Had I perhaps bored him by speaking too much about myself? But how could that be when all I did was respond to his request. By ten, I gave up. The Chairman was clearly not coming.

I tried to go to sleep, but I could not. I had an episode of seeing the Chairman, excited that he had at last appeared, only to wake up and find out that it had been only a dream of wishful thinking. I went in and out of dozing off, only to wake up to a dream. The next day, I was drowsy with sleeplessness, but could not explain to my wife why I had not slept. I remained in bed all day, trying to make up some sleep, but was still preoccupied with the Chairman.

The joy of having established a new, invigorating relationship with the Chairman turned into doubt and even alienation. Was he really the friend I thought he was? And did he really appear to me or was it all my imagination? Am I perhaps really crazy? Should I fully confess to my wife and seek help? That would clearly take me to the hospital to a ward of the mentally ill, which in the past would have been called a lunatic asylum. No, whatever I have, I cannot be that mad.

Totally exhausted, I eventually fell into a deep slumber. When I woke up, I fell back into my obsession with what could have happened to the Chairman. I began to persuade myself that I had just been in a dream world from which I was beginning to wake up. All those encounters with the Chairman had just been part of wishful thinking, perhaps symptomatic of my missing him. The whole country of the Old Sudan, and Africa, indeed elements from the wider world were all missing his presence, his contributions. But instead of tormenting myself, it was time to forget him.

I went down to the living room. My wife knew that I liked to watch the news with a good fire, and she had asked one of the boys to build one. It was burning beautifully, illuminating the living room with colorful flames. We commented on the news as we watched it. And there was a glow of optimism in the eyes of my wife that I was perhaps getting out of the crisis I had been in. We had dinner, I took my pills and retired to my bedroom in relative normalcy. I went to bed feeling proud that I was indeed succeeding in getting the Chairman off my mind.

Session Thirteen: Return

I had not been sleeping for long when a vaguely familiar mysterious sound woke me up as in a dream. "*Raandit, Raandit, Raandit,* wake up! It is me, your Chairman. Or have you already forgotten me?" I was not sure I heard right, torn between being still half asleep and instinctive resistance to a voice that had just abandoned me. After all, I was succeeding in disengaging myself from the entanglement with the Chairman. But as I became more fully awake, my old excitement about interacting with him rapidly returned.

"*Benydit,* I am so happy to see you, but I was very worried about you," I spoke without thinking about what it meant to worry about him.

"What were you worried about, that I was sick or dying?" the Chairman was obviously joking. "Have you ever heard of someone dying twice?"

"I am sorry I did not put it well. But why did you not turn up as we agreed? I waited for you and wondered what could have happened."

"I wanted to test you, to see how much our conversations mean to you. I now see that they really mean a lot to you."

"I thought that the dead see and know everything. And I see you have already seen how much I was affected by missing you and that I need not tell you now."

"Don't forget that the dead are only human in spirit and not God Almighty or All Knowing. That's why our living say that, when they themselves die, they will inform the already departed of developments in the world they have left behind. They would not need to be told if they were all-knowing. Anyway, are you ready to go back to the agenda for our discussions?"

"Yes, but since you have said you were testing my level of interest, let me test you in turn by asking you what we agreed to discuss in our next session."

"You should not test the dead! Don't forget that our people have a special deference to their dead. Testing is questioning, which brings the dead back to the level of the living. But don't interpret my testing you as disrespect; it is a means of consolidating our relationship. And to demonstrate my respect for you, I respond to your question by saying that we had agreed to continue our conversation on your diplomatic work."

"Thank you, Mr. Chairman. I am not testing you, but I wonder where to begin."

"You were to continue with your experiences as Minister of State."

"Thank you. Okay then. As Minister of State for Foreign Affairs, a major area of my engagement continued to be working very closely with the President in promoting our cooperation with the United States. Continuing to build on the policy implications of the Addis Ababa Agreement, and against the advice of all the organs of the state, the President decided on my recommendation to support the Camp David Accord between Egypt and Israel."

"That's extraordinary! A Southerner shaping such a vitally important policy decision! Few people, if any, would believe it. Tell me how it happened."

"Actually, the process leading to that conclusion was itself quite controversial. We were hosting the annual African-American Conference in which I was playing a leading role. I had been intending to seek permission from the President for me to join my wife in the United States, where she had just given birth to our third son. During one of the sessions, someone came to tell me that the President wanted to see me. I was very curious what the President wanted to see me about. To my pleasant surprise, he told me that he was planning to pay another visit to the United States and wanted me to go ahead to plan the visit.

"I told the President that the assignment could not have been more opportune, as I had planned to request his permission for me to visit the United States to see my newborn son. The President congratulated me and asked whether I needed any help. I realized that he meant financial support. I thanked him and told him that the assignment provided sufficient support.

"The President was accompanied by a high-level delegation that included leading ministers and the second Vice-President, who was also the Minister for Foreign Affairs, a well-known Arabist."

"That itself meant that you were headed for an obvious clash of positions."

"The President was accommodated at Blair House, the official Guest House of the US President. The evening of his arrival, after the Vice-President and the Ministers had left, leaving only our Ambassador and myself with our President, who handed me a piece of paper. It was a statement prepared by his Press Advisor, with the support of the Vice-President, rejecting the Camp David Accords that had just been announced. The President sought my opinion. As I was responding to the President, I passed the paper on to our Ambassador, who read it to himself as I spoke."

"I knew the Ambassador. You will recall that I met him when I went to see you in the Washington Embassy. He was known to be close to the President. So it was smart to have him on your side."

"And indeed he was. I told the President that I did not see how he could reject what was probably the most important achievement of the US President who was his host. The President asked me, 'What do you suggest?' I gave an opinion, which the Ambassador supported. We advised that his response to the media should be that he had just heard the news while he was on his way to the United States, that he had institutions at home that he would instruct to study the situation and offer policy options, and that he would then make his decision based on those options. That became his position.

"In the meeting with the US President, in which I was the interpreter, he repeated several times, 'Mr. President, I need your help.' Our President was politely non-committal. The American President lightheartedly complimented our President for his ministers' level of education. 'You have a very highly educated cabinet, most of them holding PhDs from our universities. You have a more educated cabinet than mine'. I injected in my interpretation, 'That may indeed be the problem of the President'. I don't know what I had in mind in saying that, but it generated laughter."

The Chairman responded, "It certainly makes the case that classroom education or degree certification does not guarantee good leadership. There is also the question of the relevancy of formal education to the needs of the country. For the most part, our education is externally oriented and hardly relevant to the needs of our country. A degree has only paper value if it does not relate to the practical needs in the country. In that sense, American education is more relevant to America than our education is to our country. In fact, our education is more relevant to external interests than it is to our own concerns."

"I couldn't agree with you more. It was during that visit that I had an intriguing discussion with our President about Presidential term limits. It began with incidentally telling the President about a visit I had paid to the Massachusetts Institute of Technology when I was doing my doctorate at the Yale Law School. I was invited by the MIT Center for International Studies. The Director, a man in his 40s, told me that he was leaving his post. I asked why he was retiring at such a young age. His answer was that he had been in the position for four years and that it was time to have someone with fresh ideas. I told the President that the case was a typical example of the American way, which favors renewal toward a better future.

"The President surprised me by saying that he was trying to apply that principle when he told his party that there was a physical and mental limit to what an individual could do. He said he suggested that the President should serve two terms of four years each or one term of six years. I then realized that I had misspoken. I quickly tried to correct my indiscretion by saying that his case was different as he was working to stabilize the country through the revolution. The President then responded by saying that he was persuaded by that argument."

"So, you contributed to making the President believe that he was indispensable!" The Chairman interjected.

"Inadvertently, yes. That second visit also went exceedingly well. The delegation visited California, organized by our flamboyant fun-loving Ambassador who had a flair for the arts and associating with celebrities and intended the trip to be a more relaxed excursion. We had a meeting with the young Mayor of Los Angeles, who later became Governor of California, with whom I struck up a warm interaction and agreed to remain in contact. We also met with a number of prominent media personalities and actors. We were scheduled to go on an ocean boat cruise that would lead us to the home of the famous cowboy actor, John Wayne. As the President was not feeling well, and his Vice-President was not interested in the tour, he asked me to represent him. Although John Wayne was then suffering from cancer, he took us around his beautiful home, where his movies played on screens throughout his spacious house. Guns and other collections of his long acting career decorated the house. I remarked on what a beautiful home he had, to which he responded, 'Yah, it's good living'."

"You really have had wide-ranging experiences around the world. John Wayne is a legendary name that is synonymous with the cowboy movies. Like Elizabeth Taylor, whom you also met so casually in Washington. These are celebrities one does not expect to meet so easily."

"It comes with the professional territory. What is remarkable is that these celebrities are usually impressively simple and humble. In my experience, this is generally true of great men and women. It probably comes with self-confidence and lack of need to show off. It is those who are insecure, however much they achieve, or however high the positions they occupy, who feel the need to project their importance. The result is that they often have the power, but not the recognition or the respect they so desperately need and demand. Some people are very arrogant in power and humble out of power. Sudanese are well known to pull down those who show off in power, and to lift up those fallen from power.

"In other words, they are egalitarian, which is our traditional system, typical of herding cultures. That is what Professor Evans-Pritchard observed among the Nuer when he wrote that no one is allowed to lord it over others."

"Back in the Sudan, in a meeting of the Central Committee of the ruling party, the President announced exactly what he had told me in Washington, that there was a limit to what one person could do, both physically and mentally, and that he was not going to run for another term. The whole house got up, chanting, 'No, No, Mr. President, No!' They stood chanting for quite a while, with the President urging them to be seated.

"As we left the hall, I told a colleague that what the President said was exactly the same thing he had told me in Washington. I added that we were the people who make our leaders turn into dictators. His response was simply, 'Did you really believe what he said?'

"At the end of the President's visit to Washington, as was the case with his earlier visit, he instructed me to remain behind to follow up on his visit. On my return to the Sudan, I found reports from all the institutions from which the President had requested studies opposed to the Camp David Accords. They all recommended rejection in line with the unified Arab position. When I next met the President, he asked whether I had read the reports. I told him that I had and that, as he might suspect, I disagreed with them. And I explained the reasons for my position. He then asked me to prepare a confidential report for him without letting anyone know, even in my ministry.

"I wrote my report by hand, in English, and presented it to the Minister in the Office of the President, who had it typed and translated into Arabic. In the report I began with the positive impact of the Addis Ababa Agreement on our international image as a model of negotiating resolution of conflicts and the wide international support we were receiving on account of that. I said that our foreign policy should be based on our domestic considerations, not positions generated and directed abroad. I discussed the losses the Palestinians had suffered since 1948 through the policies of armed struggle and the wisdom of shifting strategy in favor of a negotiated settlement. I also compared the records of the United States and the Soviet Union in terms of peace efforts in the Middle East."

"This is a concrete example of the different and enriching perspective Southern Sudanese brought to the governance of the Sudan, but which the North never fully appreciated. Because they start from the premise that these people are backward and that, even if educated, they really cannot excel. They saw Southerners as stooges of the West. Only those who closely witness the performance recognize and acknowledge what they see."

"Because of the same racist attitude, I found in England that the British who had been here had a hard time believing that Southerners could become exemplars of education and professional achievement in the modern world. And it was a genuine surprise that was not ill-intentioned.

"I remember my medical doctor brother and I visiting the British director of education in the South, who took us from Abyei to Tonj Primary School in the South. We rang the doorbell and he and his wife opened the door to meet us. They kept us standing at the entrance heaping praise on what we had achieved. They could not believe that those small Dinka children could have attained that level of education in law and medicine and were now doing graduate studies in England. 'You must have very high IQs', the man said. I had had enough of that. 'On the contrary, we would probably fail the IQ test', I said. His wife got the point. 'You are right, the IQ test is culturally biased', she said. They then gestured us into the living room and we were at last seated.

"A more positive version of that was when K.D.D. Henderson, a man who never showed any signs of racism, wrote a raving review of my book, *Tradition and Modernization: A Challenge for Law Among the Dinka*, which he said, apart from one long footnote of academic jargon, was written in the 'Queen's English' and that the book was a testimony to the success of their policy of indirect rule through native administration. I never understood the connection, except, perhaps for the fact that it was about customary law."

"He might have meant that the policy created a conducive environment for the development of the natives in their own context and a constructive transition into the modern world."

"Knowing the man and his great admiration of my grandfather, whom he described as a great leader, and his people as an 'adult race', I think your interpretation is correct.

"Going back to my influence in shaping the Camp David Agreement, if influential decision makers understood that I was behind our President's decision, they would probably have been even more vehement in their opposition, because it would most likely have been seen as antagonistic to their way of running the Sudan as an Arab Muslim country."

"The military is probably an exception, presumably because they see the Blacks as wild warlike tribes who like violence. This can easily be transferred from the spear and arrow to the gun. But of course, this is seen to be the case with the foot soldiers, not at the officers' level, which is understood to require a level of intelligence thought to be lacking in the Blacks. That is why the Blacks from the Nuba Mountains and Darfur were the soldiers in the wars against the South commanded by Arab officers."

"There were, of course, exceptions to this prejudiced view. This was indeed the case in the reaction to my report. The Minister in the President's Office spoke very positively about the report and handed me the original handwritten version and the typescript, explaining that it was a historic document, which I should preserve very carefully. The President called a meeting of the Politburo of the ruling party, the Sudan Socialist Union, and made a statement on his policy decision on Camp David. Several of them came to our house for dinner that night. All of them seemed very impressed by the statement the President had made. At least one of them thought it could not have been written by anyone in the Sudan government. They thought it was written by either the Egyptian or the American intelligence agency. Only my old university colleague, President of the Southern Region, told me that he saw my shadow behind the President as he read his statement. The Leader of the Muslim Brothers was the only one who criticized it as too pragmatic, implying that it did not sufficiently consider Arab political consciousness.

"The President then made a televised policy statement, reading the same statement he had made to the Politburo and which was verbatim the report I had written, with minor changes (deleting some references to him personally). That became our policy on the Camp David Accords, condemned by most in the Arab world, but welcomed and much appreciated in the West—particularly, of course, by the United States. This had a dramatically positive effect on US policy toward the Sudan, making the Sudan third only to Israel and Egypt as a recipient of United States Foreign Assistance."

"I am sure the Arabs in the Sudan, and for that matter throughout the Arab world, would not believe that a Southerner could make such a difference in influencing foreign policy so decisively, both internally and abroad," the Chairman commented, after patiently listening to my long account.

"It's very interesting you say that. Of course, the President and those who were following what we were doing appreciated our work. And others in the Arab world eventually got to know the genesis of Sudan's policy on Camp David. I even got to know that I became quite notorious in some Arab quarters, although appreciated in Egypt. The Prime Minister, who was also my senior Minister of Foreign Affairs, told me, after his visit to a number of Arab countries, that Arab leaders were asking about me. He said this with a sarcastic smile on his face, and I understood exactly what he meant.

"I had an experience on a different issue which also confirms what you are saying. I gave a lecture on our foreign policy at Khartoum University and reported on how our diplomatic efforts in Washington changed US policy towards the Sudan. One lecturer questioned my account by saying that he did not believe that US policy could be so easily influenced by an individual. All I could do was to tell him that I was only giving the facts of my experience. It was for him to believe or not to believe those facts."

"I am sure your being appointed Ambassador to Washington as a Southerner and at that young age was unbelievable to them, let alone making such a significant contribution."

"That is another interesting example. Shortly after my appointment as Ambassador to the United States, I was in the office of an old colleague and friend, who was one of the leading lawyers in the country. A journalist came in and began to talk to him. My friend then asked whether he had met 'our' new Ambassador to Washington. He responded that he had not. Then my friend pointed at me and said, 'Here he is'. The journalist responded, pointing at me, 'This?' I then lightheartedly interjected myself by saying, 'Yes, *this*.' And we all laughed.

"I was sure that it was what the President knew about the progress I was making in reversing the US policy toward the Sudan that made him appoint me Minister of State. In fact, when I was appointed to that position, my contacts in the US State Department literally took that as a promotion in recognition of the work I had done in Washington. They expressed to me their pleasure in seeing accomplishment recognized and rewarded. They could not have been more flattering in their farewell luncheon for me. What was more, the fact that the President authorized me to function simultaneously as Minister and Ambassador in Washington for almost six months gave me an added advantage by alternating my professional identity according to the opportunities in a given situation. That proved very useful in cultivating even closer ties with the United States."

"That's quite an unusual arrangement and a testimony to the trust the President placed in your contribution."

"Incidentally, my connection with our policy on Camp David went back to the visit of Anwar Sadat to Israel. It was of course a dramatic event, and the one that first turned the Arab world against Egypt. Our position was rather balanced between joining the Arab Front and supporting Egypt. I was awakened at midnight with a message that the President wanted to see me. Waiting with the President was the Deputy Minister of Information and our task was to draft and translate our policy position in response to the visit. When he learned that I had been awakened, the President responded with a question that reflected his own sleep habits, 'Why do you sleep so early?' And indeed, he himself was a night owl who once told me that if he slept for more than four hours a night, he would get sick.

"Later, when the Arab world began to react very negatively to our support of Camp David, I witnessed our President explain to the President of Algeria that we were the first in the Arab world to reject the Camp David Accords. I could not believe what I was hearing. But as I reflected, I decided that he must have been talking about our response to Sadat's visit to Israel, about which we had a more ambiguous position.

"In a meeting with Anwar Sadat, which I also witnessed, the Egyptian President asked our President, 'I hope the Arabs are not giving you a hard time for your position in supporting us!?' The President had to acknowledge our difficult position with the Arab countries. And indeed, he began to pull back gradually from his initially unqualified support of Camp David. He even recalled our Ambassador from Cairo for some vaguely worded reasons, and that was actually a positive gesture for the Arabs. The reason he gave was that he needed the Ambassador to take my place as Minister of State, as I was being given another foreign assignment. It was clearly a thinly disguised argument, especially as no ambassadorial appointment was made for Cairo.

"A Congressional delegation led by a Jewish Congressman who was a friend and a close supporter of ours in Washington, asked me after meeting the President, 'As a friend, can you tell me quite frankly whether the President still supports the Camp David Accords?' My response was to candidly admit that the President was under intense pressure from the Arab world and that the best reaction from the United States would be to give him even stronger support to counter Arab pressure. The point was well taken and we remained in America's good graces."

"You were really dealing with a very challenging and precarious position, clearly requiring a delicate diplomatic balance. And I don't mean 'diplomatic' in a professional sense, but more as an exercise of our cultural values in managing human relations, a subject I know you have written about."

"Absolutely! During the years of my service as Minister of State for Foreign Affairs, I continued to confront more challenges, which I managed in a way I believe reflected more my cultural values and upbringing than conventional diplomatic practice.

"The first occurred early in my appointment when I led our delegation to the OAU Council of Ministers in Addis Ababa. I received an urgent message to deliver to the Ethiopian Head of State, then Tafari Benti. It was a strongly worded ultimatum with nine points. Ethiopian fighting planes had violated our air space. The ultimatum stated conditions Ethiopia must immediately meet or face serious consequences, implying a declaration of war. As Minister, I had seen

Ambassadors read their instructions verbatim, some of them very offensive. I decided I would not read my message. Instead, I registered in my mind the nine points and conveyed them in my own constructive manner of speech. The meeting was attended by, I believe, the entire Revolutionary Council, including Mengistu Haile Mariam, who shortly afterwards took over the leadership through a bloody execution-style elimination of virtually all his colleagues. My approach proved very successful, as the Ethiopian government apologized, attributed the violation to the pilot, and undertook to investigate the situation and come up with appropriate remedies. It was quite obvious to me what the reaction would have been had I simply read the ultimatum."

"Especially when you were dealing with a group of hawkish soldiers who would not hesitate to shed blood."

"Exactly! Interestingly enough, Mengistu, who would later eliminate most of his colleagues at that meeting, looked very benign at the time. In fact, he did not speak at all."

"Our people say beware of a person who does not speak. They do not make their case with persuasive words; they fight."

"Worse. They kill. Anyway, my second adventure involved the establishment of diplomatic relations with South Korea. One of the major companies of South Korea was investing heavily in the Sudan and the President wanted to develop closer relations with Seoul. My senior colleague, the Minister of Foreign Affairs, and the entire Foreign Ministry, resisted the idea, since we were supposed to be committed to the non-aligned movement's position in support of North Korea. So, after the President had asked me to pay a good-will visit to South Korea, my senior Minister met with him and reported back to me that they agreed to have our Ambassador in Tokyo visit first to assess the situation, after which a possible visit by me would be considered.

"I met with the Korean economic representative in Khartoum to convey that message and included minutes of that meeting in our daily report to the President. The next morning, I got a call from the President, fuming with anger. He wanted to know what had happened with his instructions about my visiting South Korea myself. Before I could explain, he said that if I did not want to go, he would send another person. I said, 'Mr. President, let me explain.' He responded by saying that there was nothing to explain and slammed the phone. I was tempted to walk over to the Presidential Palace to see him, but I decided to leave him alone to cool down.

"This was Thursday, and Friday was, of course, a holiday. On Saturday, there was to be a presentation of credentials by new ambassadors, which I was to attend. As usual, I went about half an hour before the formalities. As I entered the President's office, I found a very different person from the one who had quarreled with me on Thursday. He was contrastingly warm, friendly, and jocular. He did not even allude to our earlier discussion. I decided to bring it up myself: 'Mr. President, about that issue....' 'What issue?', he interrupted me. I said, 'About South Korea.' He immediately reiterated what he had said, that he had wanted me personally to go, and that he did not even know the Ambassador in Tokyo. If I did not want to go, he would send another person.

"I told the President what my senior Minister had told me and that if I had known that he wanted me personally to be the one to go, there was no way I would refuse. I went on to tell him that sending another person because of my supposed disobedience to his instructions would entail his loss of confidence in me and I would have to resign. I assured him that I would of course go as he had instructed, if he still wanted me to. He still did and I went to South Korea with my wife. We were very well received at the airport, with red carpet and our national anthem. It was a most impressive show.

"After settling into the luxurious hotel accommodation, I was given papers for the program. Among them were documents to be signed establishing diplomatic relations between our two countries. This was of course far beyond the purpose of my mission. I felt the weight and the dilemma of the crisis. To say that I was not mandated to establish diplomatic relations and could therefore not sign would have been to pour cold water on the very warm reception. To sign would have been totally outside my mandate.

"What a dilemma. It was what the Americans say, 'You are damned if you do and damned if you don't'."

"I guess I chose to be damned doing. The ceremony of signing was to take place two days later. I decided on a strategy that would try to bridge the contrasting positions, to hold the stick in the middle, as the Arabs would put it. I sent a message to Khartoum through our Tokyo Embassy telling them what I was confronted with and that if I did not hear from them to the contrary at the time scheduled for the meeting, I would sign.

"Knowing the way the Ministry functioned, my message would be forwarded to the Director of the appropriate Department, who would pass it on to the Undersecretary with comments, and the Undersecretary would forward it to the Minister with his own comments, and the Minister would either discuss the matter with the President directly, or raise it with him in the daily report of the Ministry to the President. Unless the matter was treated with utmost urgency, that would take days, by which time I would have signed and established diplomatic relations with South Korea. I waited nervously. The day came with no response from Khartoum. I signed, still feeling anxious."

"You were either a hero, an adventurer, or a traitor. High stakes alternatives."

"I will leave that for you to judge. The rest of the visit went exceedingly well. But the day after the signing, I was approached by the Koreans with the information that our Foreign Minister, who was attending the General Assembly in New York, had denied the establishment of diplomatic relations, stating that it only concerned economic cooperation. What did that mean, they wondered? I explained that I had just opened a new page in our bilateral relations and that they should not expect our system to be immediately fully in the picture. They seemed content with my response, but I am sure they could not have been fully persuaded, with the Foreign Minister making contradictory statements."

"That was another risk, claiming that your Foreign Minister did not know about a major policy decision you had made and implemented. That's a tough one."

"When I returned to Khartoum, I found a fascinatingly conflicting understanding of what had happened. My colleagues in the Foreign Ministry assumed that the President had directly instructed me to establish diplomatic relations with South Korea without putting the Ministry in the picture. The President himself was pleased with what I had done. Cooperation between the two countries progressed remarkably well from that point on. Many years later, I told the story to the UN Secretary General, who had been South Korea's Foreign Minister, and his response was, 'You did the right thing.'

"I have on occasion told the story to students of political science and asked them what they would have done. This question always generates an interesting discussion, with different responses, but never the one I used. That it turned out to be successful was probably a combination of daring initiative and luck."

"This is really quite a remarkable story of diplomatic adventure," the Chairman commented. "You were clearly between a rock and a hard place."

"As I noted earlier, a friend and colleague, the Nigerian Foreign Minister, wrote a book which he titled *Diplomatic Soldiering*. I guess my adventure would fall into that category. Let me now ask you what you would have done under those circumstances."

"Well, I am a soldier, not a soldiering diplomat. I would probably have wanted clear instructions," the Chairman said. "On the other hand, being a soldier means taking reasonable risks. Whether this was a risk worth taking is probably answered by the end result. As they say, all is well that ends well."

"Another interesting experience I had concerned our negotiations with Ethiopia over Eritrea, which I led. The discussions were hosted by Sierra Leone, with whose Foreign Minister I developed a warm relationship. My approach was to try to reciprocate for the support we had received from Ethiopia in the negotiations that led to the 1972 Addis Ababa Agreement. And my view of a possible resolution of the Eritrean problem was somewhat comparable to my preferred solution to our own situation—full autonomy for Eritrea within Ethiopian Unity. So, I believed we could be of some help. Ethiopia, however, wanted only bilateral relations discussed, with no reference at all to the Eritrean problem. My position was accepted by the mediators as a constructive approach. Many powerful individuals in our government supported full independence for Eritrea. And the Eritrean liberation movement had effectively infiltrated our security system, which also backed the cause of Eritrea. This put me in a very precarious position."

"You seem to have a propensity for getting into difficult situations", the Chairman commented, jokingly.

"Not by choice. It's called destiny," I responded in like manner.

"In both the Bible and the Koran, God, whom we assume controls destiny, is called upon not to impose a burden one has no capacity to carry. You should therefore feel flattered that someone decided that you had the capacity to meet the challenges."

"I don't know whether I had the capacity to carry some of the burdens that were imposed on me. But considering that they seemed to turn out relatively well, I must have had a helping hand from Above.

Often, it was the President's response that was the determining factor between success or failure."

"It's called dictatorship," the Chairman injected, provocatively.

"You would know that better than I do," I retorted. And we laughed.

"I get the jab. But I do not mind. Continue with your story."

"Thanks. So, when I returned to Khartoum after the talks in Freetown, proud of what I had accomplished, and the President directed me to brief my colleagues in the government, the African Diplomatic Corps, and the Eritrean representatives, I was surprised to find a sharply divided opinion. Some of my colleagues, including the Security Chief and my senior Minister, who was also the Vice-President, wondered what was in it for Eritrea. The Eritreans themselves politely thanked me for my efforts but made it clear that the future of Eritrea could only be determined by the Eritreans themselves and not by anyone else. The President of Eritrea would later remind me that we first met in Khartoum when he was 'a fugitive', as he put it. Only President Nimeiri himself seemed unequivocally supportive of what I had accomplished."

After listening to my long narration, the Chairman commented: "Since I was opposed to the arrangement under the Addis Ababa Agreement, which granted autonomy, all I can say is that I would side with the Eritreans. I also would have agreed with their position that the future of Eritrea lay with the Eritreans themselves and not with outside do-gooders. If I may say so, the fact that they achieved their independence means that they knew what they were doing. You almost shortchanged them."

"That was not the first time for me to be wrong. I also underestimated the ability of South Sudan to attain independence. From Ethiopia's point of view, I was perceived as a tough negotiator against their position. Believing that I had outwitted their Foreign Minister, Ethiopia changed the leader of their delegation in the next round of talks. The new leader of their delegation was very close to Mengistu. They totally disowned what we had agreed to in earlier talks. And their new leader expressed the unhappiness of his government that I had travelled in the region to deliver invitations to the OAU Summit that was to be hosted by the Sudan. I told them that I did not want to risk going to Addis Ababa and not be received by the President and that I would go if invited. The leader of the delegation promised to secure an invitation for me.

"Shortly after my return, the invitation came. I went to the President to inform him of the good news. I was surprised by his response. He said that Ethiopia was playing games with us. They had agreed to the visit of our First Vice-President on a date they were to determine and convey to us. For them to invite me when the First Vice-President was waiting was offensive and unacceptable. As for the invitations to the Summit, he said he was extending personal invitations to those toward whom he felt friendly. Mengistu was not one of them. He told me to excuse myself. I tried to persuade him otherwise, but he would not be persuaded. 'Are you trying to change my mind?' he asked rhetorically. 'It is obvious that you do not know the Ethiopians. These are very suspicious and devious people. We Sudanese are very trusting because we live in flat land and see far ahead. The Ethiopians live in mountainous land where vision is blocked by the mountains and one cannot see whether there is danger beyond the mountain. That makes them very suspicious and mistrusting.'"

"That sounds like a clever way to be wrongly insulting. The land of the Dinka is flatter than the North. Would he have accepted that we are more trusting than the Northerners?"

"Probably not. I had just returned to my office when the President called to tell me that he had changed his mind. I thought he was going to give me permission to go to Ethiopia. Instead, he told me to ignore the invitation and not even respond. I found it difficult to do that. I called our Undersecretary, who knew of the invitation, briefed him about the instructions of the President, and told him that I was going to do what I thought was right without involving the President. We therefore sent a polite message to Ethiopia explaining that some exigency had come up that prevented me from going at that point. Nimeiri never learned of what I had done."

"That's another difficult one. I would not want to be in the President's position, kept in the dark by my official, especially after having acted in violation of my instructions. But I understand your moral dilemma and I would say that you probably did the right thing."

"Thank you. Shortly afterwards, the visiting President of Nigeria, who, years later would become my 'Partner for Peace' in our efforts to mediate an end to the second civil war in our country, asked my President to allow me to go to Nigeria for bilateral talks with my

Ethiopian counterparts. The President, probably mindful of how he had prevented me from accepting the Ethiopian invitation, grudgingly agreed, saying that he did not mind, leaving the choice to me. I could tell that he was just being polite to the Nigerian President but was not really comfortable with the idea. I later called him to make sure that he really wanted me to go. He told me that if I wanted, I was free to go, which only confirmed my suspicion that he did not want me to go. I therefore excused myself by giving some contrived reason. The Nigerian President later chastised me jokingly as having disobeyed Presidential orders.

"Which of the two Presidents did he think you disobeyed. I am sure that he was aware of the ambivalence of your own President."

"I think so. And either he or I hinted as much to the other later. At the OAU Summit in Khartoum, Ethiopia was represented by a senior diplomat who was very antagonistic. When the report of the negotiations that Sierra Leone had mediated was presented, his response was to put a very negative "spin" on our position. I obtained permission from the President to speak and gave a full picture of our efforts in trying to find a solution that would reconcile the rights of the Eritreans and the unity of Ethiopia. My presentation was very well received and written messages came to me from the Ministers of Sierra Leone and Liberia, congratulating me and confirming what I had said.

"Then the Ethiopian Ambassador raised his hand to speak. He said he was glad to hear what I said but wondered if it indicated divisions within the Sudanese government on the policy towards Ethiopia. I immediately raised my hand and responded by saying that if we were trying to unite the Ethiopians, should they in turn react by trying to divide our house? The whole Assembly roared with laughter. President Nyerere then spoke to say that the matter should end with my words."

"This is all fascinating and a clear demonstration of your persistent disposition toward building bridges," the Chairman commented. "Although I am not a bridge-builder myself, having fought for my principles, I am inclined to support the positions you took as representing a higher moral ground."

"Thank you. But you fought for principles that also represented a high moral ground. The principle of a New Sudan of full equality without discrimination on the grounds of race, ethnicity, religion, or culture is clearly a very high moral ground. Perhaps the difference is my persistent attempt to build bridges which we talked about earlier.

"Let me relate another drama in that direction. I made a daring attempt to break the impasse with Ethiopia by persuading the President of Sierra Leone, through the Foreign Minister, to invite President Mengistu and my President to Freetown for bilateral talks. They agreed. I attended the meeting with the President while Mengistu was accompanied by his Ambassador to the Sudan. As we waited for Mengistu to enter the room, the President asked me how he should receive him. I advised him to greet him with an embrace—the African way to break the ice. The President did just that and I thought it was a promising start.

"In the discussions, our President was at his best, the best that I ever saw—friendly, flexible, and constructive. He offered to help Ethiopia in addressing the Eritrean problem and asked Mengistu to facilitate Sudan's mediation. Mengistu insisted that he had only been mandated to discuss bilateral relations and not the Eritrean problem. Our President explained very candidly that the Eritreans had infiltrated his security system and that even his own security would be at stake if he disregarded the Eritrean problem. But Mengistu would not budge. The talks failed dismally.

"Ironically, my colleagues in our government were delighted with the failure. The Presidential Press Advisor was to tell me that we had nothing to gain from an agreement with Ethiopia and much to gain from the West through confrontation with Mengistu. I was saddened by such a short-sighted distortion of our value system and national interest in a 'cheap' diplomatic practice."

"I suppose if I were asked where I would have stood, I would have had difficulty responding. All that happened before our rebellion. If it had happened while Mengistu was our host and benefactor, of course we would not have welcomed an agreement between Mengistu and the Sudanese President. In fact, we would have favored conflict between them. Even welcoming conflict to win the favor of the enemies of our enemy as friends is unfortunately part of the game of nations. It is one of the paradoxes of humanity."

"That's why the President, in wanting me to go to Ethiopia as Ambassador, asked me to tell you that although you had a cause in your rebellion, please do not betray your country—an unintended joke, I believe."

"Or just grossly naïve, which is difficult to believe for a general. I think he just thought you would perform a miracle for us. And you might have done, since I would have tried to make you a double agent. And as I told you, although I believe you would have been the exception, double agents are the most dangerous. Please continue with your story."

"I continued to face challenges in managing my working relations with my President. On one occasion, he sent me to Washington to continue our efforts in promoting our bilateral relations, which were already excellent. I had a meeting with a Senator that ended in his adding $30 million to an appropriation bill for assistance to the Sudan. When I later went to thank him, he told me that he was following developments in oil production globally by the hour and that his information was that Sudan possessed large oil reserves, which Chevron and Aramco were not revealing. He argued that it was in the interests of Chevron and Saudi Arabia (through Aramco) to keep Sudan's oil in secret reserve. If they announced the finding of oil in the Sudan, our creditworthiness would peak and the assistance we were receiving from the United States would be peanuts. Furthermore, he advised us to engage our own experts and insist on getting all the information on our oil situation for them to analyze.

"I was quite excited by what I heard and rushed back to report to the President and urge him to ask Chevron to reveal their findings. The President appeared quite skeptical about what I was saying. First, he could not believe that Saudi Arabia would do anything harmful to our national interest. Besides, he said that if the Americans knew that Chevron was hiding the evidence of their findings from us, why did they themselves not confront their company? I told the President that the oil was ours and not America's and that we were being advised in our best interest. I left feeling certain that I had failed to persuade the President.

"I then proceeded to Monrovia, Liberia, for the OAU Ministerial meeting in preparation for the Summit. A few days later, I heard on the BBC that Chevron had announced oil findings in the Sudan. When the President arrived later for the Summit, the first thing he said to me when we met was, "I did what you asked me to do." That was that. Although Chevron continued to play down the quality and quantity of Sudan's oil, we were set on the path of revealing our national wealth, which, as is often the case with the so-called Dutch Disease, would prove a mixed blessing."

"Well, you know my position on that issue," remarked the Chairman. "Of course, I welcomed our having oil, but I wanted to avoid the Dutch Disease and, in fact, wanted oil to cure that disease. That is why I said that we would use oil revenues to fuel the engine of agriculture. That would genuinely have turned the curse into a blessing."

"But initially you were actually opposed to the exploration and exploitation of oil in the South and you threatened to disrupt the work of Chevron."

"That's because I knew that oil revenue would be used to strengthen the Government in their war with us, which it actually did."

"And in our discussion of the issue, you spoke with confidence that you had the capacity to disrupt production."

"It's all a balancing act. Do you intensify the conflict in a theatre where the stakes are even higher and lose even more innocent lives, or compromise tactically? And don't forget, we actually did disrupt oil production by Chevron, and they withdrew because of the loss of the lives of a few men—who were in fact Sudanese, not Americans. Then came in the Chinese, the Malays, and other investors who were less intimidated by the potential loss of lives. And indeed, the production of oil did boost the fighting capacity of the Government, as we had predicted."

"The Liberian Summit itself turned out to be another challenge for me to manage. Sudan had occupied the Chair of the Organization during the year that was ending and was handing over the leadership to Liberia. Our Chairmanship had witnessed the war between Uganda and Tanzania, provoked by Idi Amin, who was universally unpopular. Our President had tried to mediate in the conflict. I had accompanied him to the two countries. The meeting with both Presidents had been quite dramatic. As we flew over the war zone, Idi Amin bragged about his victory, claiming that the speed with which his army had conquered territory was unprecedented in the history of war.

"In Tanzania, we found a very angry man in President Julius Nyerere. Our President had suggested that I interpret into English while he spoke Arabic. I urged him to speak English informally with his brother. But I soon found out that in his anger, Nyerere spoke so eloquently, virtually preaching, that I saw my President pathetically at a disadvantage. At one point, he ineptly said to Nyerere that he thought Africans were prejudiced against Idi Amin because he was a Muslim.

That prompted Nyerere to respond with an air of obvious moral superiority. 'Mr. President,' he began with a tone of false deference, 'do you know that my army chief of staff is a Muslim and I never knew that until a few days ago? In Tanzania, that is never an issue.'"

"That was our New Sudan in operation," the Chairman injected. "Our Chief of Staff too could be a Muslim and I might not know or care."

"So disadvantaged by language and performance was our President that I decided to step in and dialogue with Nyerere directly. Fortunately, I had already interacted with President Nyerere and established cordial relations with him. Equally important, my President seemed to welcome my involvement. Apparently, none of them saw me as overstepping the boundaries of status."

"In Monrovia, the crisis over the OAU approach to the Tanzania-Uganda war surfaced. Tanzania had retaliated against Uganda and was winning. Africa was divided between those who welcomed Amin's demise and those opposed in principle to external intervention. Our President was perceived as biased in favor of Amin as a fellow Muslim and was subjected to intense criticism in the African—and especially Liberian—media. This enraged him to the point of wanting to leave the Summit before formally handing matters over to his successor, which I thought would be disastrous. I pleaded with my senior colleague, the senior Foreign Minister, who was also Vice-President, to do something, but he would not dare confront the President.

"I persuaded the host, President William Tolbert of Liberia, to advise our President against leaving, but he was unrelenting. I went to President Olusegun Obasanjo of Nigeria to intervene. Obasanjo told me not to worry; he would not allow him to leave. Time passed into the night and on to the early hours of the morning in an all-night session. I kept calling the Nigerian Foreign Minister and was told that the President would be coming. Our President, who was a night owl, was still up and I, with some colleagues from our delegation, kept his company. I had the reputation of stimulating substantive conversation with the President during our travels abroad. And the President had a tendency to jokingly ask whether I was planning another book.

"Writing books had become your trademark!" the Chairman remarked.

"Like your planning and fighting in battles, as you yourself made that comparison to me."

"As long as you are not holding it against me by mistaking me for a professional killer.

"No, I am not, since we agree that war is sometimes a necessary evil for achieving virtuous objectives."

"I accept the necessary evil idea as long as it does not make me the devil."

"Our revered freedom fighter a devil!? Of course not. And yet we know that war is bad and must be stopped as soon as a reasonable compromise is struck, which is what I believe you did. Again, we are distracted, though justifiably so.

"Going back to the story at the Summit in Liberia, my conversation with my President continued, as I worried that no one would stop him from leaving the Summit. Then, at about 2 a.m., Obasanjo appeared and we withdrew to leave them alone, but remained within hearing distance. Obasanjo was confidently pressing, while our President resisted. In the end, he argued that he had already given instructions for the plane to be ready early in the morning and that he was expected to be back that day. Obasanjo reacted by posing a provocative question: 'Are you telling me that there is someone else from whom you need approval for your schedule?'

"That probably did it; the President could not entertain the thought of anyone else being in charge over him. He agreed to stay and performed exceptionally well the next day, even on the sensitive issues of human rights. It does not require much imagination to envision what his image and that of the Sudan would have been in Africa and indeed in the world if he had left in anger."

"You were of course part of the system and were correctly protective. If that had happened when we were fighting Khartoum, we would have viewed it a blessing. But all that you have been telling me indicates how much Southerners in the system were doing without the knowledge, far less appreciation, of most Northerners. I should in fact say that most of our people in the South had no idea what you and your Southern colleagues in Khartoum were doing for the country, sometimes in their own name, to counterbalance the Arab-Islamic agenda for the country. Of course, a few of us in the movement became closely associated with what you were doing for us outside the country."

"What is quite striking," I explained, "was the way my approach to our diplomacy was very much shaped by our domestic achievements and policy agenda. The end of the first civil war between the North and the South, which shifted our policy from chronic violence to reconstruction and equitable development, was central to my approach. I was amused when a member of the British House of Lords who had visited the Sudan as State Minister for Foreign Affairs, told me later that throughout our conversation, he understood what I was saying about the North and the South to be referring to the Global North and Global South, only to realize much later that I had been talking about the internal Sudanese division. This indicated both my preoccupation with our domestic situation and the relevancy of that situation at the global level."

"And indeed, the comparison is in place both with respect to identity and related disparity."

"Now that I think back, I find it quite remarkable that both our Arab and African friends often asked me to represent them or be their spokesman. Whatever personal attributes I might have brought into that representative role, I think much had to do with our position at the boundaries of African-Arab identities. I was once told that I was more convincing in promoting the Palestinian cause precisely because I was not an Arab and therefore more objective. My African colleagues also saw being an "African-plus" as an advantage."

"Those are the side benefits of marginalization. Since you are at the margins of the core interests of the groups concerned, you are not a threat. Viewed more positively, you can be a symbol of their own search for a common ground between them without losing faith and a bridge to those outside their circle—as you say, more objective."

"There is something I hesitate to talk about because it was very flattering and may seem self-serving to report, but I also feel that it was too significant to omit. One day, to my utter surprise, I received a copy of a letter by the Chairman of the US Senate Foreign Relations Committee to the Secretary of State, carbon-copying the African-American whom I had first met in the African-American Conference in Lesotho, now the Permanent Representative to the United Nations. In the letter, the Senator said that during the Senate delegation he had led, which had visited a number of countries in Africa, they had been most impressed by the young Minister of State for Foreign Affairs of the Sudan. They strongly recommended that the United States should nominate him to be the next Secretary General of the United Nations. Africa was in line for the next Secretary Generalship. In his response, which was attached, the Secretary of State wrote that I had close relations with their Ambassador in Khartoum and that I was a friend of the United States. Their recommendation was therefore of interest to the State Department and would be given serious consideration.

"The whole idea was a total surprise to me, especially as I could not recall the delegation or the meeting on which they based their judgment. The Americans did not stop at that. Another Congressional Delegation visiting Khartoum raised the proposal with our President, who discussed it with me. I told the President that the idea of becoming Secretary General of the United Nations had never occurred to me. He said that it had obviously occurred to others. He went on to tell me that he was confident we would get the support of Africa and the Arab countries. He urged me to give the matter serious thought.

"The more I thought about the matter, the more I felt that it did not inspire me. For one thing, I was sure that France, one of the Permanent Five on the Security Council, would oppose a candidate who did not speak French. While at the UN as a junior professional, I had wanted to study French, but my Chief of Section, an English lady, flatteringly kept asking me to postpone my enrollment because she needed me. I always regretted not having learned French because it is crucially important in the UN system. But perhaps more important was my own view of the UN Secretariat. I did not think the Organization lived up to the ideals that had inspired me to join in the first place. I was surprised that towering figures in the Secretariat, Directors, Assistant Secretaries General, and Undersecretaries General behaved very humbly toward Representatives of Member States, however junior. Given all the technical know-how which the Secretariat had, we all bowed down with humility in front of government delegates."

"But since you knew the game that was being played and you had your own inner confidence, all that should not have bothered you so much," the Chairman commented.

"That was precisely the view of our seniors. But in my view, there was more to it than that. Interestingly, in a study conducted by Columbia University, senior members of the Secretariat, mostly from the developed Western countries, seemed quite content with this role of quiet leadership behind the scenes. Those of us who were much younger and from the Third World were the ones most discontent with the status quo. Our seniors interpreted our attitude as undue ambition or the desire to be recognized. My own interpretation was different.

Our seniors were members of the developed world, where there were many highly qualified people, and they were quite content to serve modestly behind the scenes. We from the developing world represented a small select group in which our countries had invested much in education and of whom they had high expectations for a leadership role for our countries and people. In fact, I tried to remedy this shortcoming by organizing young scholars in the system to supplement our routine work with seminars and discussion groups on topical policy issues, and I myself also taught a course at New York University. Even this received mixed reactions from the leadership, which demanded undivided attention to the routine secretarial work. With this background, I did not aspire to any position in the Secretariat. The President saw my disinterest and the matter died quietly."

"Few of our people, if any, would understand how you could have downplayed the prospects of such global leadership. I think I do understand your position, but then individual leadership can make a difference in addressing the problem you are describing. The fact that you identified the problem indicates that you could have done something to at least ameliorate it. After all, the image of Dag Hammarskjold is quite different from what you are describing."

"You are quite right. The Egyptian Secretary General, an old friend who was my counterpart as Egypt's Minister of State for Foreign Affairs, and the African friend who replaced him before the end of his full term, represented a more assertive leadership than I witnessed under the Asian Secretary General whose style was quite discreet and humble. In fact, it was the strong assertiveness of the Egyptian that made the United States force him out of office before the end of his term. When I myself rejoined the UN much later at the level of Assistant Secretary General and the Undersecretary, my view of the Organization, ironically, had become more positive. Whether I had grown into the viewpoint of my senior Western colleagues I had criticized because I was myself in a senior position now, or had become wiser with age, I cannot tell. When I met my Egyptian friend in his new position, it crossed my mind to tell him, 'Do you realize that you are sitting in my chair?' Of course, I did not tell him anything."

"I wonder whether he would have believed you or taken it as a fantasy."

"It's interesting you say that. When I was Ambassador in Canada, the US Permanent Representative to the UN, who had been copied on the proposal, came to see me in my house accompanied by a member of his staff, an African American, who had also been in the know. As his boss sat informally on the floor feeling at home, his staff member recalled the proposal laughingly: 'The Senator reported that he had found the right person in Africa to be the next Secretary General'. It was almost like a joke to him."

"To Nimeiri's credit, his response was far more progressive than one would have expected of Northern Sudanese generally at the time. Even his appointing you Ambassador to important posts and then as Minister of State for Foreign Affairs indicated a major change of attitude. But I suggest we stop here and continue with your stories of service in the next session."

"Fair enough, Big Chief. Indeed, I am quite tired. I shall bid you good night, then, and look forward to our next meeting. Until tomorrow?"

Considering the wide range of issues the Chairman and I covered after our resumption of our conversations, I became increasingly appreciative of his visits. I continued to be convinced that I would never have documented all that I was telling him. And in fact, although we had known each other well, it was now obvious that there was much we did not know about what we had done before we became friends or had been doing even when we were friends. And there was a lot more to say, which is why I was glad that our sessions were continuing.

"Until tomorrow. Good night." And with that, the Chairman vanished into the thin air whence he had appeared, leaving me in solitude in my room. I slept peacefully and painlessly.

Session Fourteen: Ambivalence

I awoke the next morning feeling refreshed. On mornings after my visits with the Chairman, I felt oddly clear-headed about my thoughts and service, despite the heavy medications I was still taking. I was glad that the Chairman showed interest in my account of my role in foreign service, as that was the main area of my national service. What I felt particularly good about was that our conversations were reassuring me that I had indeed made significant difference in the service of the country. Even more gratifying was that this service was appreciated, at least by those who were closely following what I was doing. The most influential Minister of Foreign Affairs who had known me since our days together in the UN was particularly supportive. And so was the President, quite independently. The confidence I felt and projected about the support of the leadership made me credible and effective in my representative role, regionally and internationally.

After the session following the return of the Chairman, my wife saw that my spirits were higher. But she had no idea why that was so. Given the generally mysterious way I was behaving and the concern of the family about the state of my wellbeing, any sign of improvement in my condition was a source of relief. But their uncertainty and therefore anxiety persisted. As much as I'd have liked to ease their anxiety, I could not tell them, or her, about my late-night visits with the disembodied Chairman!

Later that night, fortunately, the Chairman arrived at about the time he had done before his withdrawal. "*Raandit,* I hope I am more or less on time and not giving you cause for concern as I had done," the Chairman greeted me apologetically.

I smiled in reassurance. "I am always glad to see you."

"You will recall that we agreed in our last session that we would continue with your recollections of service, both abroad and at home."

I felt amused that he said "you will recall..." as I could think of little else throughout my days. I couldn't suppress a small smile of amusement mixed with flattery that he had not only returned but wanted me to continue recounting my experiences.

"As you can tell, I am delighted to see you again. But are you sure you want to hear more about my diplomatic service? I thought I was already risking too much self-praise."

"Come on, *Raandit,* I thought we had long gone beyond those sensitivities. If you were engaged in too much self-praise, what would stop me from letting you know? Those who know you actually believe that your problem is the reverse—too much humility—although that too is appreciated."

"Thank you for your kind words. But remember, I am not narrating these experiences for you personally: They are for a wider audience with little knowledge of me and my character."

"Let me therefore lead our discussion. Can you tell me about the time you wanted to resign and were persuaded by the President to retract your resignation?"

I paused with a small smile. That was an interesting event and I was pleased the Chairman had asked me to tell him about it. "That was after eight years in the Foreign Service. I told the President that I was advised by my eye doctor to attend to the acute glaucoma that had afflicted me since high school. My doctor thought I had to give greater priority to taking care of my eyes. The President argued that I could go abroad for treatment as often as the doctors advised. I thought that would not be practical. He and I had a very good working relationship. Some people complained to me that I was not being promoted to senior Minister of Foreign Affairs because of prejudice over not being Arab or Muslim. Personally, that did not bother me. I knew the President respected my role and nearly always took my advice. Twice, he intimated to me to expect to be appointed senior Minister in the next reshuffle. Once, he asked me to polish up my Arabic in preparation for becoming the senior Minister. When it did not happen, I realized that Arabic and perhaps Arabness in general might be a consideration. But it still did not bother me. Once in New York, I was told he had spoken disparagingly about his pan-Arabist senior Minister and added, 'I have my own Foreign Minister', referring to me. His reluctance to let me go was further evidence of how well we were working together, often to the obvious resentment of the senior Minister. In the end, he persuaded me to accept the position of

Ambassador to Canada with my ministerial status. 'You can then combine your work with writing books', he said."

"That must have been a mixed assignment. Although it was good to be favored over your senior minister, that was setting you up for a conflict with him. And there was no way he could not know the situation. But of course, there was nothing you could do about it, except to demonstrate your loyalty to your superior."

"That was precisely what I tried to do, but it was obvious that I could not fully assure the minister of my loyalty. There were in fact situations where I defended him against hostile decisions by the President, sometimes successfully and at times without effect. And when I failed, he assumed that I had engineered the negative decision. I once asked a colleague who was a close friend of his what he, my senior minister, thought about our working relationship. With a sense of humor that made me laugh, he said, 'Why don't you spare me from this question?' The answer was, of course, obvious: my senior colleague did not look with favor upon our working relationship. He must have been happy to see me leave for Canada."

"Presumably, so were you."

"I suppose so, though I was ambivalent since I was enjoying my ministerial work. The years in Canada were, however, uneventful, both positively and negatively. The transition back to being Ambassador after having been Minister was quite trying. The fact that I still retained my ministerial position was only reflected in my income. Otherwise, it looked like stepping down. In fact, the governor of one province asked me why, after having served as Ambassador in Washington and as Minister of State for Foreign Affairs, I was serving as Ambassador to Canada? He asked more specifically, jokingly undiplomatic, whether that was a demotion? Of course, I could not go into the details of the situation. Nor could I fully rid myself of the insecurity I felt."

"I can understand the ambivalence you felt, but I would have thought by that time you would have developed an inner self-confidence based on your accomplishments that should have placed you above those insecurities."

"The issue was not really within me, but with the protocol practices that should come with status. But you are right that inner confidence should make one rise above those considerations. Whether one's contribution is fully understood and appreciated is a different matter. The answer is mistily uncertain and sometimes paradoxical.

"An example in this connection was the tragic demise of the Ministers of Foreign Affairs of Liberia and Ghana in military coups in their countries in 1980. I had worked very closely with them as fellow members of a core group of ministers, which included those of Kenya, of Gambia, and of Sierra Leone among others who were mostly of the same mind and made decisions in close consultation. We became close friends. I was also quite impressed by President Tolbert of Liberia, even though we heard rumors about major discontents beneath the seeming stability of the system. Their brutal killing was a source of great grief for me and an indication that hardly any country in Africa can be said to be immune to potential coups."

"Coups are impositions of crude force and are therefore inherently unstable," the Chairman pointed out. "But they are evidence of serious illness in the body politic that needs to be diagnosed and cured of its root cause. That is why we were strongly opposed to military coups as a solution to the problems of the Sudan. If you make people understand the real cause of the problems, the demand for reform can be a natural course of events at the popular level. Reform can thus come from the people and not as an imposition by the elite."

"It is a genuine dilemma because the strategic options for change are limited and not easily implementable. After all, you took up arms to draw attention to the problem, if not to impose a military solution."

"I think you get the point. I know the line is thin in popular perception, but it is important."

"I get the point, as you put it. Thank you. Anyway, despite my engagement outside the country, I continued to follow developments inside the country and specifically in my area of Abyei. Tensions between the North and the South were mounting and the situation in Abyei was becoming increasingly explosive. I received a letter from one of my brothers explaining the situation and urging me to do something even though I was abroad. I responded with a complaint that I had done my best in my attempt to alleviate the situation, but my initiative had not been supported by many in the family. I therefore wanted to pull back and let others try alternative approaches. But I could not really distance myself from the problems facing my people.

"Shortly after my arrival in Canada, I returned to Khartoum for consultations. I received another letter from a cousin informing me about the suffering of our people who were being subjugated. He used the Arabic word *muthahdeen,* plural for *muthahd,* which I have translated as subjugated but implies a combination of domination, denigration, and humiliation. He said that people were hopeful that together with the President, we could perhaps do something to alleviate the situation. The letter was in Arabic, brief but powerful, and very moving. I immediately requested an appointment to see the President. I described the situation as effectively as I could and then handed the letter to him. He read the letter with obvious but unvoiced emotions. His utterance after reading the letter was, 'I will not allow any Sudanese to be subjugated,' using the Arabic verb *uthahd*. He then said we could go on discussing all day; the question was what he should *do*. He asked whether forming a high-level committee to study the situation and make recommendations to the President would help. I said that it would at least tell the people that the President cared."

"But you know the popular saying that the best way to kill anything is to form a committee for it."

"I know, but then, to every rule there is an exception. I hoped this would be one. Anyway, the President decided to appoint the Minister of State for local government to chair the committee and we immediately worked on forming its composition. Prominent national personalities, including the Deputy Chief Justice, tribal leaders, and representatives of the government of South Sudan and Kordofan, were included. Before the announcement was made, I was requested by individuals to brief the youth of Abyei, including university students. To my astonishment, one of my brothers advised me against doing anything on Abyei, as that was bound to be misunderstood as our family again asserting its traditional authority over the area. I felt deeply hurt that, instead of appreciation, my motives were being questioned and criticized. I decided to go to the house of the President's legal advisor, who was drafting the decree, and tried to stop him. He was flabbergasted by my attitude. He said that the news from Abyei had been very disturbing to them and that they had been trying to do something, but without success. If my intervention had made a difference, how could I allow myself to change my position because of the views of children? We agreed to move forward with the plan."

"That was wise. That's what leadership is all about."

"Thank you. Within days, people began to react to the decision and more names were proposed and added to the committee. Among those added was the Paramount Chief of the Missiriya. The work of the committee soon turned into a discussion of the status of Abyei between the North and the South. Representatives of the Southern Region in the committee demanded the implementation of the provisions of the Addis Ababa Agreement pertaining to Abyei, while the representatives of Kordofan, among whom was a regional minister from the Nuba who was more Arab than the Arabs, asserted that Abyei was uncompromisingly part of the North. Interestingly enough, his attitude demonstrated that the greater the proximity to the dominator and the longer the duration of domination, the greater the humiliating impact. That minister told me that he did not understand why the Dinka were so keen on their Dinka identity. He said that although he was Nuba, his wife was Arab and most of his support was from the Arabs. It reminded me of what British administrators had written in comparing the Dinka and Nuba relations with the Arabs, one, asserting equality and even superiority, while the other seemed to admit of subordination. The committee became polarized in a way that overshadowed the objective which the President and I had in mind."

"But what you and the President had in mind was a band-aid approach that would have sidestepped the political cause of the people of Abyei," the Chairman noted questioningly. "And yet the people needed some immediate relief. I admit it was a dilemma."

"You are right. My main concern was how to ease the suffering of our people in the interim, not to address their long-term political grievances. The reality obviously turned out to be different: neither objective was achieved, and the stakes were raised."

"Our committee went to Abyei for popular consultations. What I witnessed confirmed all that I had heard about the oppression of the Dinka. In a meeting of the committee with the Paramount Chief and the Chiefs of the nine sub-tribes of the Ngok Dinka, a statement was read by an Arab from the Missiriya who represented the area in the national parliament, written in classical Arabic, stating that the land the Ngok Dinka occupied was the land of the Arabs who had welcomed the Dinka to settle as their guests. The document was signed by all the nine Ngok Dinka leaders. I could not believe what I was witnessing."

"Did they know what they had signed?"

"That's the point. I asked that the document be translated into Dinka. One of the powerful Ngok local figures who was known to be allied with the Arabs was a man who had been a sectional chief and a close associate of my father, although their relationship was very ambivalent. Father would imprison him and then release him and bring him again close to him. He was one of the people Father had told me would be a source of problems for the area. After Father's death, he became a security agent of the government forces in the area and was eventually appointed to a position of power in the tribe. When I asked for the document to be translated into Dinka, he jumped up and shouted out loud in Arabic, 'It should not be translated.'"

"He exposed himself, not even cleverly."

"Absolutely. And he had the reputation of being clever. I gave my reasons for wanting it translated and the Chairman ruled in my favor. After it was translated, all nine Chiefs, one by one, distanced themselves from the document. They said they thought they had signed a document that called for peace, reconciliation, and cooperation. One of them asked, 'Can we bring peace between us by deceit?' The same Arab stooge had asked the Chairman in what capacity I was on their committee, that of a minister in the government in Khartoum or the leader of the government in the forest that was abducting and killing people? The Chairman ruled him out of order and defended me as a national leader and a statesman.

"After the meeting I approached the elder and said to him, 'Uncle, as I grew up and saw you with my father, I took you as one of the noblemen of our tribe about whom we were very proud. Has our land become so destroyed that even people like you have descended to this humiliating level?' I felt amused by his candid response, although I did not show it. '*Mading*, the land is destroyed.'"

"It is terrible the way oppression demeans people into such indignity. He obviously knew that what he was doing was absolutely wrong. He was stooping to save his neck and gain some favors. He must have realized, or should have realized, that in the long run this would not endure and that justice would eventually prevail."

"That's true, but in a very complex situation, right and wrong become confused and confusing. While our meeting was going on in Abyei, word reached me that a number of members of the liberation movement from Abyei had come from the South and had been arrested. I immediately informed the committee and, after some internal discussion, orders were given for their release. They were released and advised to go back to the South. Ironically, the same Elder who was an informant of the security forces in the area, and who had behaved so abominably in the meeting with the huge committee, advised them to leave in the middle of the night before their expected departure because he was aware of plans to have them ambushed and murdered. They left and shortly after they crossed the borders of South Sudan, soldiers who had chased after them arrived and were stopped by the South Sudan contingent in the area. The liberation movement members were spared—barely."

"This shows that even spies seldom totally abandon their innate loyalty to their primary identity group."

"Tragically, although assassinations are unknown to our people, this man was later killed at night with his wife and the assassins were never found or identified."

"That's sad," the Chairman paused and reflected. "So how did your committee discharge its delicate mission?"

"Our committee eventually presented the President with its report, which made recommendations suggesting alternatives that raised the stakes in the South-North conflict over Abyei, far above the security and administrative reforms the President and I had envisaged. From the way the President thanked the committee members and even said that he had wondered how best to reward them, whether materially or symbolically, I could tell that he was not happy with what we had done. When the Deputy Chief Justice told him that he and I hoped to write a book about the experience, the President reacted favorably, but I knew it was fake."

"That confirms that he had intended the Committee as a delay tactic to buy time away from solving the problem."

"You are right. After waiting for a while without action by the President, I went to see him. I told him that people were asking me what had become of our work and whether the President was going to take action. The President responded by telling me to go back to my duty station and that he would act at an appropriate time. He assured me that he would meet the demands of the Ngok Dinka. He wanted every Sudanese to be free and to fully enjoy the dignity and rights of citizenship. After all, he had given the people of the South their freedom, why not the people of Abyei? It all sounded too good to be true. But then the President surprised me by the reason he gave for waiting. 'If I take a decision now, people will say you have become the President'. Unbelievable!"

"In a way, it should not be surprising because it indicates that he realized the legitimacy of your leadership for your people, for serving their interests, whereas he was the personification of their oppression, and therefore not their legitimate leader. But of course, he exaggerated his fears. In fact, they were fake."

"I thought he was on the verge of a ridiculous paranoia, if he really meant or believed what he said. Anyway, I went back to Canada, but returned to the Sudan a few months later to attend the meeting of the Central Committee of the ruling Sudan Socialist Union. I found the country close to turmoil. South Sudan was acutely divided between the Dinka and the Equatorians in what became known as Kokoro. Prominent leaders of South Sudan, mostly Dinka, were under detention. The situation in Abyei had markedly deteriorated. A rebellion, led by one of our brothers in Abyei, was rapidly spreading over the South and presaged a resumption of the North-South civil war. Over a dozen Ngok Dinka leaders, among them members of my immediate family, were rounded up throughout the country and locked up in several prisons and detention centers in Khartoum.

"In the meeting of the Central Committee itself, the governors of Bahr el Ghazal and Kordofan States attributed the increasing tensions and local rebellions to the Ngok Dinka, and particularly members of my large yet prominent family. I wanted to speak, but was advised by the Chairman, the First Vice-President who was also the Head of National Security, against speaking. However, after the meeting, I approached him and proposed a two-prong initiative to address the disunity in the South and the tensions in Abyei. On Abyei, I argued that we had no power over those who had already taken up arms, but that the best way to neutralize them was to reach agreement and cooperate with the leaders of the community, most of whom were now under detention. He agreed in principle, subject to the approval of the President.

"The Vice-President soon reported the President's approval of the initiative on the South, and even agreed that the mediation be led by the Former First Vice-President, who was highly respected by the Southerners. I secured the consent of the leaders of the major factions in the South. The Former First Vice-President agreed to lead the mediation effort, provided he received written approval from the President. His suspicion was that the President was not really interested in solving the problem of disunity among Southerners. He was right; the President never gave a written approval."

"He had in fact orchestrated the whole thing, which he then attributed to the Southern opposition to the regional government."

"Absolutely. I knew that much from my own private conversations with him. The President's response to my proposal on Abyei remained pending. For weeks, I kept going to the office of the First Vice-President only to be told to come back the next day. Meanwhile, the First Vice-President, also in his capacity as the Security Chief, was making much-publicized statements that the detainees would be charged with high treason, a crime obviously punishable by death. In the end, I gave up trying to meet with him and began to write a report documenting my efforts and failure. Under the circumstances, I considered my remaining in the government untenable and must therefore resign. I was writing the conclusion to my report when I received a message from the Office of the First Vice-President that he wanted to see me immediately."

"That was quite a political adventure. It's possible that you yourself could have been suspected of being an accomplice in the alleged crime."

"That's very interesting you say that. The South Sudanese Vice-President, who was championing the division of the South, advised me to keep out of anything to do with the detainees, both from the South and from Abyei. In fact, he advised me to get out of the country as soon as possible. He argued that people knew my position from my writings, but that I could get implicated in what my relatives were alleged to have done. Nevertheless, he was one of the people I eventually persuaded to consent to my initiative to resolve the differences among the South Sudanese leaders.

"The First Vice-President received me very warmly and with obvious excitement. He apologized for the length of time it had taken without an official response to my proposal because he was waiting for the President's approval. He said the President had given his full approval and handed me a document to that effect in the President's own handwriting. 'He is a sensible man; he will not do anything harmful to the interest of the country. Let's support his initiative'. The First Vice-President then proceeded to heap praise upon me, describing me as having been endowed by God with wisdom. It was an astonishing contrast to the man who had evaded meeting me for so long."

"It was a government run by fear of the President. If he supported you, that gave you power with confidence. If he did not show you support or had misgivings, you felt paralyzed."

"Absolutely! My initiative was not fully supported by the Ngok Dinka community. While most of my family members supported me, there was opposition among many, including some family members, for reasons ranging from personal prejudices to extreme positions of principle. I remember an argument with a cousin, a judge about to leave for his new post in the South, who opposed the initiative on political grounds. He took the arrest and detention of the Ngok leaders as part of the struggle. And even if they were to be tried and found guilty of treason and executed, that would be part of the struggle. They would be martyrs. That judge soon joined the struggle and became one of the leaders of the movement to the end."

"He was of course right as a matter of principle, but saving the lives even of rebels did not mean betraying the cause. That was blind extremism."

"The process of the talks itself was remarkable. All the detainees would be taken to the impressive conference room of the security building every morning, dressed in neat clothes, with no evidence of their detention. At the end of the day, they would be returned to their prisons or detention centers where conditions were appalling, with the detainees sleeping on the floor in congested cells."

"Two security officers attended the opening session, to the obvious distress of the detainees. When I asked which language should be used, they all said Dinka. I responded that there should be Arabic translation so that the security observers should understand what was being said. The officers apologetically said that they would be there for only a few minutes and would leave. Once the proceedings began, however, they became so engrossed in what was said that they remained there throughout the process. The Dinka too began to appreciate that their grievances were being heard, so much so that when the officers were late on one occasion, the detainees wondered why they were not there. One of them was to tell me later that he had learned a lot more from those talks than he learned from graduate school. The Ngok Dinka grievances were registered where it mattered the most."

"It is surprising how people fail to see the obvious, that the presence of those officers offered an opportunity for them to present their grievances to the authorities. This is the insecurity and suspicion of domination that creates a weakening vicious cycle. It's good you corrected it."

"Indeed. My approach was to start from the premise that I did not know what they had done and were being accused of, but that it had to do with the contest over Abyei. The government's stated demand was that we must bring back our brother who was leading the local rebellion that was spreading insecurity to the South. My response was that the best way to counter his rebellion was for the government to cooperate with those inside. To our people, I reiterated my position that we were confronting serious obstacles to the goal of rejoining the South and that we should fall back on the President's policy of a special autonomous status for Abyei and stabilization of the area through the delivery of social services and economic development. The proposal was very controversial and took months of intensive debate. In the end, it was conditionally accepted, in that the people of Abyei reserved the right to join the South should they conclude that their rights of citizenship were not being respected in the North.

"Another very delicate balance between principle and pragmatism. It must have been a tough call."

"It was, but I felt convinced that I was doing the right thing to get our people out of the dangerous position of life and death. The process ended with their release, which became a spectacular event that was heavily covered by the media. It was like a second Addis Ababa Accord. I hosted a luncheon for the released, to which the Missiriya leaders were invited. The Missiriya leaders also hosted a major dinner event in the famous officers' club, which was also covered by the media. From being threatened with prosecution for treason, the released were now being described by the First Vice-President as Ambassadors of Peace. The President himself was very pleased with the outcome. He was to compare that outcome with the earlier work of our committee on Abyei, saying, 'The report of your committee was bad' and at last revealing what I had suspected to be his position all along."

"It showed that what he considered good was what pleased him; anything he did not like must be bad."

"But there were to be a number of unexpected reactions from critics. One was from a cousin who said to our medical brother—who was among those released and was in fact the leader of the group—in my presence, 'That you would come out of prison alive is something I never expected, given the way you were arming people to murder innocent persons in the forest.' I could not believe my ears.

"A second incident was with a leading politician who was a friend of my doctor brother. He and another friend invited my brother and me for dinner, presumably in honor of their released friend. After we had eaten and had some drinks, he surprised me by asking who had authorized me to intervene on behalf of the detainees. What mandate did I have to do that? Or was it because I felt it was my obligation as the son of the Chief? I felt infuriated and let him know. I told him that if he was one of those who must be given a paid position to be of service to his people, I was not one of them. I said I did not need to be given a position and a mandate to take initiatives I considered to be in the interest of my people. I deeply regretted having eaten his food and wished I could have vomited it out. We immediately left. He had probably had too much to drink. The next day, he came and sincerely apologized. I accepted his apology."

"These are of course painful incidents, but they should not be entirely surprising. Quite apart from the deep animosity toward the North, our people are motivated by different considerations with vested interests. You know our people are fiercely competitive and any ideas or action to which they are not a party and for which they cannot claim credit is inherently suspect. Once you understand and accept that, nothing should surprise or shock you. In other words, you must develop a thick skin."

"I guess you are right. But worse, the third incident was even more negatively consequential. To my astonishment, a combined team of Ngok Dinka and Missiriya arrived in Khartoum to convey to the government their opposition to what we had done. I visited them in their hotel and, while they greeted me with courtesy, one of them, the son of the elder who had been hostile in the consultation meeting in Abyei, ignored my presence as he remained seated, watching the television. I recognized that immediately and reciprocated by also ignoring him. I tried to reach out to the Deputy Paramount Chief of the Missiriya, but he politely declined to see me, giving the sensitivity of the situation as his excuse. They met the First Vice-President. An in-law of mine from Abyei who had defected from the liberation movement and became a government informant reported to me what had transpired. According to him, the response of the Vice-President was that the whole process was their setup to expose me and that they would now move to get me. Although my immediate relatives who heard this became very worried, I was not concerned because I did not really believe his story."

"Those are the double agents who can be more dangerous than regular spies," the Chairman commented, repeating his familiar line about double agents.

"Actually, what I later learned was that the First Vice-President rebuked them. He told them that he could not understand why they would object to a solution that not only freed their people but also offered a solution to the problems of the area. Another exaggerated version was that he threatened to have them arrested instead."

"Probably another double agent reporting to you."

"Probably. To complicate the situation even further, the Governor of Kordofan, who had been in the United States during these developments, returned and sided with the rejectionist group. When I met him and briefed him, expecting him to thank us for what we had done, I was flabbergasted to hear his objection on no other ground than that those who had been detained were his political opponents, while the rejectionists were his supporters. I was enraged and let him know my outrage. I told him that I had expected gratitude from him, but that I now knew where the responsibilities for the problems of the area lay. I said that I was going to leave the country but would let my views on the situation be known to the national leadership. Some of my people who heard me were reported to have said that whenever they saw me angry, they rejoiced. I never fully understood their reasoning."

"They either wanted you to rebel or to deter the enemy by your anger. As I always said, our mobilization of Southerners was a constructive harvesting and management of anger."

"As it was, the governor softened his position and became more conciliatory. He suggested that we hold a public meeting to forge a consensus in the community. At first, he was threatening in his tone, which provoked an angry reaction from the audience. One of our brothers who was a student at the University of Khartoum surprised everybody when he got up and told the governor that if his attitude represented the position of the government, then 'some of us will join our brother in the rebellion'. Taken off-guard by that rebellious response, the governor turned to our medical brother, who was sitting next to him on his left side while I sat on his right, and asked him who the speaker was? Our brother's response was, 'I think he is one of the university students.' The governor suddenly moderated his tone and became more constructive and even suggested that the process of consensus building be extended to the communities in the home area. I then left for the United States with a deep sense of accomplishment and satisfaction."

"It is interesting that the threat of rebellion by your brother from the university and denial of him by your medical brother seemed to have a positive synthesis. I wonder how the governor would have reacted if he had known that the student was your brother. Might that have aggravated his negative view of the family as a potential source of more rebels?"

"Possibly! It was an arduous mission, one of the most daunting tasks I have ever undertaken. Later on, some of those detainees would casually state that they were released in May 1983 without any indication of what it took to get them released. Some of them make reference to my intervention, but not to the challenging negotiations. I still look back on that event as one of the achievements I am most proud of because I believed I saved the lives of people who very likely would have otherwise been killed."

"And rightly so. As a future rebel myself, I don't know which side I would have taken under the circumstances. At least you saved lives for another rebellion, as many members of your family later became among our best freedom fighters."

"No comment, as we would say in diplomacy." I chuckled. "Anyway, for austerity reasons, the Embassy in Canada was among the missions to be closed. I went back to Canada to close the Embassy. The President first wanted me to go to the UN as Permanent Representative. The 1983 outbreak of your liberation movement took place while I was still in Khartoum. As I was closing the Embassy in Canada, my Egyptian colleague, with whom I had confidentially shared my expectation for the new posting, urged me to return to the Sudan quickly because, as he put it, decisions in our part of the world change very quickly, depending on the last person to talk to the leader. He was prophetic. Literally several days before I returned to take up my new assignment to the UN, the President decided to send me to Ethiopia as Ambassador, ostensibly to confront you.

"I discussed the situation very candidly with the President. I gave him two reasons why the assignment was not a good idea. First, I told him that he and Mengistu did not see eye-to-eye on major policy issues.

How would I relate to Mengistu as his representative? Second, our brothers in the South had just rebelled for a cause. What would I tell them? The President's response was remarkably simplistic. I should tell Mengistu that although they differed on matters of ideology and policy, they should not allow themselves to be exploited by the superpowers. As for our rebel brothers, I should tell them that while they had rebelled for a cause, they should not betray their country. In the end, I said that I would go, if that was his considered decision."

"I am sure that's not what you would have said to us."

"I could not believe the simplicity of the President's instructions. Many relatives and friends strongly objected to my accepting the assignment, some concerned about my own security, others on political grounds. But I decided to keep my word to the President. I then returned to the US to prepare for taking up my new post. My wife said she would respect my decision. But as I drove to the Kennedy Airport in New York to fly back home, I changed my mind and decided to let the President know that I would not go to Addis. I called my wife and informed her and she supported my new decision just as she had supported my decision to accept the appointment. I wrote my letter of resignation at the airport. In the letter, I said that both for the reasons I had tried to explain to him and for other personal reasons, I would not be able to take the assignment. I said I was not looking for another assignment, but only hoped for his understanding and that our cordial personal relations would continue. I also assured him that whatever I did and wherever I lived I would always serve the interests of my country."

"That was a bridging noble position. I wonder whether he could understand the nuances of your difficult position?"

"As soon as I arrived in Khartoum, I took the letter to the President's office and gave it to the Secretary to deliver to him. He asked whether I wanted an appointment and I said it would not be necessary. The President left the next day and, according to his Secretary, seemed saddened by my letter and mumbled to himself something like, 'We must give him what he wants.' I got a call from the Minister of Foreign Affairs and was asked to meet. He told me that the President had instructed him to find out where I might like to be posted and that they would grant my wish. I repeated to him that I did not want another post, only understanding and support in case I sought an appointment in an international organization. That's how I left the foreign service. But my cordial relations with Nimeiri continued to the end of his life."

"This is quite a story of service. For me, as I told you when we first met in Addis Ababa and you told me the story, I would have welcomed your coming as Ambassador to Ethiopia and seeing how together we would have managed the situation to our benefit."

"I am afraid I would not have been comfortable with divided loyalty and certainly would not have been of much benefit to either side. And my divided loyalty was all connected with the acutely divisive war and peace in the South," I added. I then reminded the Chairman of his position when the Addis Ababa Agreement was concluded in 1972. "I heard that you were one of the rebel officers who were opposed to the deal. Much was of course done during the ten years of the Addis Ababa Agreement. But in the end, it was undone. In retrospect, how would you evaluate the experience under the Agreement?"

"Yes, I was against the Agreement because I did not think it had addressed the root causes of the problem of the Sudan that was responsible for the war. I even wrote a letter on January 24, 1972, documenting the reason for my opposition. As I mentioned earlier, that was when I first introduced the vision of a united new Sudan. I identified the central problem of the war as the dominance of Arab nationalism. I argued that any country with multiple nationalities, but dominated by one of the nationalities economically, politically, and therefore socially and culturally is inherently unstable and bound to erupt in warfare. I categorically called for an end to Arab nationalism as the basis for our domestic and foreign policy. I saw the evolution of the united New Sudan over ten years. Five years of two separate armies and five years of a careful integration of the two armies into the army of the United New Sudan. And of course, the failure of the Addis Agreement was inherent in its limitations. It did not envision or develop the framework for a new united Sudan of full equality."

I agreed with the Chairman and recalled an incident that revealed to me that the government had in fact intended the Addis Agreement only as a tactic for defeating the movement. "I attended a meeting in which the President revealed his original intentions about the Addis Ababa Agreement. He had just decreed applying the system of regionalism in the South to the whole country. This was very controversial in the North. People feared that it would be a source of divisiveness that might lead to the fragmentation of the country. The

143

President formed a committee under the chairmanship of his Vice-President, who was also the President of the Southern Region.

"One day, the President walked into the meeting of the committee and made a statement. He wondered why people were afraid of regionalism. With an air of confidence, he said, 'The truth be told to God, when we accepted the Addis Ababa Agreement, we did not intend it to last; we wanted to use it for two or three years and then tear it up. The South would have put down their arms and would have no power to fight. But we have found that it works and is succeeding. So, why are people afraid of applying it to the North?'

"I could not believe my ears. Had I indeed heard him correctly? I later asked my colleagues, including those Northerners who had participated in the Addis Ababa negotiations, about the President's statement. Probably embarrassed, they simply dismissed it as nonsensical and not seriously meant. But it was indicative of the inclination of the North to sign and dishonor agreements."

"In my January 24, 1972 letter, I argued that a united New Sudan was only possible through action and not through paper declarations, resolutions, or machiavellian scheming. I was not even concerned about the Addis Ababa Agreement being dishonored. I just thought it was a bad agreement."

"But you eventually accepted it and were absorbed into the Sudanese army?" I posed a challenging question.

His response alluded to what would eventually become the key factor in his leading another rebellion. "Yes, I did, but with lingering doubts that would eventually be revealed in my leading a liberation movement that aimed at addressing the root causes of the Sudanese problem. I resisted its being called the Problem of the South; it was the Problem of the Sudan."

"Another experience I had with the President that was quite revealing had to do with what was known in the South as Kokoro—division of the region into ethnically based sub-regions. The President and I were in Dar es Salaam in connection with his mediating role between Uganda and Tanzania, in his capacity as OAU Chairman of the year. He and I sat alone in the evening outside the Guest House under a clear sky. We were discussing the situation in the country. The President focused on the developments in the South where people were asserting their genuine autonomy and making demands for equitable sharing of resources with the center.

"The President saw that as a challenge to him personally. 'With all I have done for them, they are being ungrateful', he said to me. 'Can you believe that they are criticizing the President personally? I am going to lift my hands off their Region and see how they will manage without my support'. I told him that he shouldn't do that. After all, the solution of the southern problem was probably his greatest achievement. How could he allow that to fail by denying the South his support?'

"The President then introduced the issue of division: 'Let me tell you something confidentially,' he began with a deceptive tone of sincerity. 'There is a proposal from a southern leader who is alleging Dinka domination and wants the south to be divided into ethnically based regions. I am resisting that. Do the Dinka even realize that I am protecting the unity of their Region?'

"That's what I meant when I opposed the Addis Ababa Agreement. It reflected good sounding words on paper not backed by the right and sustainable actions."

"Exactly. About two months later, he introduced the division proposal to the Central Committee of the ruling party. He called it 'only a suggestion' by a Southern leader, whom he named, which he was simply tabling for discussion. That triggered a heated and acutely divisive debate in the south whose implications would affect the regions for a long time and linger on to this day."

"All these are indications of the fundamental flaws of the Addis Ababa Agreement."

I agreed that these instances indicated a deep lack of commitment to the Agreement and that it was indeed destined to fail in the end. "When the President eventually decided to impose Sharia on the country and divided the south into three regions, thereby unilaterally abrogating the Addis Ababa Agreement, he declared that the Agreement was not the Koran or the Bible, that it was created by him and his southern counterpart, and that they had the right to change it.

"As you know, the Minister of Foreign Affairs, one of the individuals pivotal in negotiating the Agreement, confronted the President on his decision, arguing that it was illegal. I was to learn later that the President asked him whether he knew the south better than his southern partner to the Addis Ababa Agreement. The Minister told him that on that issue, he certainly did from a legal perspective. That was to be the breaking point between the two previously very close partners."

"That probably contributed to the Minister eventually joining our movement—one of the prominent Northerners to do so."

I shrugged slightly.

"You remind me of an anecdote. In a meeting with the former Nigerian President who became my Partner for Peace, he said to the President that since our famous former foreign minister is a Northerner and yet now is in the Southern-based rebel movement, could he not be a bridge builder between them? Almost interrupting the Nigerian leader, the President said, 'We Sudanese are very forgiving people. We fight, but once we agree, we forgive. The one person who will never be forgiven is this individual. I understand why the Southerners are fighting, but why would an Arab join African rebels against his own Arab people? Does he want the Africans to throw the Arabs into the sea?' I could not believe my ears! How was it possible for the leader of an African country to share such a racist view with Black Africans? I never understood. But of course, in due course that individual was indeed forgiven and even became advisor to the government in Khartoum."

"Are you sure he was forgiven? Or merely contained!?"

"That I do not know. What I do know is that more negative developments took place before the reconciliation. I was to learn later that the Minister was nominated for the position of Deputy Secretary General of the United Nations and was assured of support by the Africans and the Arabs, but our government—unbelievably—opposed his nomination. What would have been a great honor for the country was scuttled for reasons of political differences on Southern policy. It shows how pivotal South Sudan was, not only to the political instability of the country, but also to the dynamics of interpersonal political stands among public figures."

"That's why we thought it was wrong to call it a southern problem; it was indeed a Sudanese problem."

"Ironically, the leader of the Muslim Brothers, as Legal Advisor to the President, was to tell me quite categorically that the President's decision was clearly illegal. He had been Attorney General and had been the driving force behind the Islamization agenda that was undermining the Addis Ababa Agreement. One of the ironies of the Sudanese situation was that the Brother was to tell me that he did not understand why the President kept assigning him to those important positions when they both knew that they were on opposite sides politically? He said that they both probably realized that they were playing strategic games. The President on his part told me that the Muslim Brother was the most dangerous person politically. The Muslim Brother himself did not tell me whether or not he gave the President his legal opinion on the issue of abrogating the Addis Agreement and how the President reacted."

"To the contrary, he was probably happy that the President did what they would have wanted to do but could not. It is the same as the military imposing Islamic law on the country, which the Muslim Brothers could not do politically."

Our discussion then shifted to the Chairman's original opposition to the Addis Ababa Agreement. "I got to know later that your opposition to the Agreement would turn into a blessing in disguise for you personally. To move you away from agitating against the Agreement in the integrated national army, you were sent to the United States to a Staff College for military studies. And you were again later sent to the United States to do a Ph.D. in agricultural economics."

"Yes, that happened, for reasons I did not probe into, but believed it was divine intervention on my behalf."

"No comment," I responded, evasively. I recalled to the Chairman that their rebel Commander-in-Chief later confirmed to me very clearly that it was done to keep him at a distance, but also to give him an opportunity. Ironically, it was a punishment that proved a reward. Perhaps the Chairman was right, and it was a divine scheme.

The Chairman responded in a way that indicated a shrewd understanding of the situation. "I somehow knew that it was intended as a preventive punishment. I don't think they realized that it would be a blessing in disguise. Had they realized that, I doubt that they would have chosen that form of punishment. But if they later claimed that they intended to offer me the opportunity, then I accept it as a gain for us together."

Our session had been very long and, although I did not know how the Chairman felt, I thought it was time to end. The Chairman might have no longer been subject to human-type exhaustion but, in my fragile state, I certainly was. I was actually impressed that we had covered so much ground and that the Chairman had been so engaged, showing no sign of boredom. Of course, I had no idea about how the dead feel, whether they get bored or not. Although it was my story that was being told, I was again afraid that I had overplayed my card. But if I had, the Chairman did not show any signs.

I decided to raise the issue directly with the Chairman, "*Benydit,* can you do me a favor!?"

The Chairman seemed to look at me with curiosity about what I had in mind.

"Could you tell me if I bore you with my recounting experiences? After all, you probably talk to many people about their own experiences, as indicated to me earlier, and that would be far too much to listen."

"Come on, *Raandit,* how many times would you want to be reassured? After all, what makes you think that I get bored? I should not tell you more about me or the dead for that matter which you probably will not understand. All I need to say is stop worrying about it. I have my own built-in protection mechanisms that would not allow that. Besides, by now you must know that you enjoy a favored position in my scheme of things."

"I thank you *Benydit.* I will bear that in mind and not ask you again."

"Good!" the Chairman concluded, with obvious satisfaction.

As our session was ending, I suggested that our next session turn to our later reunion and discussion of the role of the Chairman in the renewal of the liberation struggle.

"That sounds good. Good night and sleep well."

I also bade him good night, not knowing what that meant to a dead man.

Session Fifteen: Reconnection

My last conversation with the Chairman had been reassuring. I now had no doubt that he welcomed our sessions and that I did not risk boring him or losing his interest: quite the contrary. For whatever reason, he seemed genuinely interested and engaged. My only challenge now was selectivity, deciding what was important enough to cover.

I began the conversation by recalling the visit the Chairman and his family made to us when I was Ambassador to Canada. "I was very happy when you and your family visited me in Canada. Since your defection to the rebel movement and your post-war absorption into the Sudanese Army, we had lost touch. I believe I ran into you once or twice at a friend's house. So, I looked forward to renewing our relationship."

"I remember that visit very well. You were a very gracious host."

I recounted some aspects of the visit. "Unfortunately, my wife was visiting her family and was out of the country at the time. But we had good domestic support. What I particularly remember about that visit was a dinner I gave in your honor and during which I was not such a good host, as I raised some tough questions that must have given you a rather hard time."

The Chairman's response was gracious: "I don't remember you ever giving me a hard time."

I continued with my recollections about the dinner discussion: "My questions related to the political developments in the country at the time. And I addressed you more as an intellectual and a friend than as an officer in the army. And yet, it was in your military capacity that I addressed my main question to you. And that is where I was perhaps not sufficiently considerate of the sensitivity of your position.

"The regime in Khartoum was then in the process of undoing the Addis Ababa Agreement by introducing Islamic Sharia as the law of the land, to be applied throughout the whole country. Although I was representing the government, I saw that decision as a dangerous violation of the Agreement, one that could trigger a return to war. I asked you then what you, the South Sudanese in the army, thought about that. You were ironically more diplomatic than I was. Your answer was, 'That is for you politicians.' I thought you had been co-opted into submitting to the will of our oppressors. That is why I was totally surprised when you led the rebellion against the regime."

The Chairman responded: "I remember your raising that point when we met in Addis Ababa after our rebellion. You said to me then that I had fooled you by not revealing to you my plan to rebel. I also remember telling you that my plan was a top secret that I did not share even with my wife."

"As you will recall, shortly after your rebellion in 1983, the President changed his decision to appoint me Sudan's Permanent Representative to the United Nations and asked me to be Ambassador to Addis Ababa. He claimed that Addis Ababa, being the seat of the Organization of African Unity, was more important to us than the United Nations. But I knew that his real objective was for me to confront you.

"I told the President that I had two concerns about the assignment. One was that he and Mengistu, the Ethiopian leader, did not see eye to eye. What would I tell him? The other was that our Southern brothers had just rebelled for a cause. What would I also tell them?

"With a simplicity I still find astonishing, the President's answer to my questions was almost dismissive. On Ethiopia, I was to tell their Leader that even though the two of them differed on policy matters, they should not allow themselves to be exploited by the superpowers. And, as for the Southern rebels, I was to tell you that even though you were fighting for a cause, you should not betray your country.

"Obviously, I was not persuaded by his answers. And although my wife graciously said she would support whatever decision I made, my extended family and my friends and colleagues did not think I should accept. That is when I resigned from the Foreign Service."

With his characteristic sense of humor, the Chairman recalled what he had said to me when I first reported my decision to him: "As I told you when you first told me your decision, I thought you should have accepted and been Ambassador for both of us."

I then recalled something else he had told me: "But you also told me in connection with one of our diplomats, whom you thought was a double agent between you and the government, that the most dangerous are the double agents. In fact, you repeated that in our last conversation."

With humorous courtesy, he said, "You would have been an exception."

"Thanks for the confidence," I responded and went on to recall an account of my visit with him after his successful rebellion. "My first visit to you in Addis was quite an introduction to your movement. It was of course organized by my cousin, who was the manager of your office. Going to you was quite an experience. I did not really know what to expect of a man who had been a friend but was now a rebel leader. I anxiously waited in the sitting room with a number of your commanders. One of them had just joined the movement. I told him that he was being missed in Khartoum and that a number of Northern leaders had told me that he had been playing an important role inside the country. For reasons I still do not quite understand, he seemed irritated by what I had said. 'Why would they miss me?' he asked with obvious agitation. As I reflected later, I began to think that he thought I was insinuating that he had a hidden agenda with Northerners."

I proceeded to recount my recollections about my meeting with the rebel commanders: "One of the things that struck me most was the way your commanders joked about their war experiences, battles fought, behavior of frightened soldiers, scenes that could make some people cry, but which they described with roaring laughter. I thought to myself that war must be a transformative life adventure. I did not know whether to sympathize with them or to be critical of them."

"War is bad. Civilians think soldiers like war. They don't. It confronts you with existential choices, kill or be killed. That is traumatic. Even when you have escaped imminent death and you have killed, you are deeply wounded and haunted by the experience. In the modern world, they have methods for treating the wounds of trauma. For us, you suffer and perhaps soothe the memories with cathartic laughter that could easily have been cries or silent tears."

I was deeply moved by what the Chairman said. My account then went to the highlight of my meeting the Chairman: "I was eventually escorted to your room. Just outside the room were armed guards. They inspected me thoroughly and took my wallet for safekeeping. When I entered your room and you greeted me very warmly, I said that I was glad you were well protected. You asked whether I had been inspected.

I answered affirmatively, but stressed that far from being offended, I appreciated your being well protected."

Details of my conversation with him kept flowing. "We had a good chat and caught up. That's when I told you that you had fooled me into thinking that you had been co-opted by the establishment and were no longer a revolutionary. That was also when I spoke to you about a friend of mine who had complained to me that he had written to you twice and had received no response. I advised you that there was no need to alienate your people who are predisposed to support you and risk pushing them into joining your enemies.

"You explained to me that it was not your intention to disregard him and that it was the pressure of the war that had distracted you. You said you would respond to him, which you did. Interestingly enough, over time, he became even closer to you than I was. He became the contact point for keeping me informed of the developments at the war front."

The Chairman responded rather apologetically. "That was quite ironic, since my relationship with you was longer and deeper than my relationship with him, which indeed soured later."

"It's interesting you say that. When my friend later became your most venomous critic, I reminded him of the time I mediated between the two of you and how he became closer to you than I was. His explanation was that my relationship with you was friendship, while his relationship to you was motivated by getting closer to you to steer you away from your New Sudan Vision."

I could tell from what the Chairman said in response that he was somewhat jarred by my friend's believing that he would steer him away from the principal goal of his struggle. "That sounds very presumptuous! How could he expect to steer me away from the most fundamental principle of my movement?"

"Your conflict began in the late 1980s during the famine that hit our part of the country the hardest. The world accused and condemned both the Government and your movement for using food as a weapon of war. In one-way or another, many of us did. We also urged the international community to respond by urgently delivering humanitarian assistance. I wrote an article in the Brookings Review which included a sentence that a prominent Senator cited in a statement to the Congress. It said, 'It's not the dead who suffer; it is those who cause their death and those who watch them die'. My friend focused his attack on your movement and particularly yourself for not caring for the people."

"I remember his ferocious attacks against us. But I did not care to respond."

"You will recall I tried to mediate between you. I remember when he was visiting Washington and was with me in my office, I dialed you and told each one of you that I had a surprise for you and passed the phone on to you. Remarkably, you were so cordial that no one would believe you were quarreling. You told me that you had no reason for not talking to him since you held nothing against him."

"And that was the truth," the Chairman commented.

We then moved on to discuss the ideological objectives of the movement: "This brings me to an issue I consider the most important one in our conversations, and that is the Vision of New Sudan which was the centerpiece of your struggle."

"Of course, this is a vision which I know you and I shared. I am deeply concerned about what has become of it. And I know that your friend was one of its initial supporters and later turned against our position. I know that he became one of our most bitter opponents. Perhaps we should talk about this in our next session."

It was interesting that the Chairman should introduce the most important subject for his liberation movement when we were ending the session. Perhaps that was precisely because of the importance of the subject, which should be the central topic of our sessions. I also welcomed that because this was one of the areas where our positions converged, even though I was not a member of the movement. I therefore looked forward to the next session to talk about that.

Session Sixteen: Vision

It was time for me to go to the surgeon for post-operation checkup. The operation was healing well and physical therapy, though a very painful exercise, was showing positive results. Despite the progress, I was still in pain. So, I asked the surgeon to renew the prescription for the painkiller. The prescription was renewed.

I stopped by the office briefly for a show of face and a follow-up on developments. The fact that I could not use my right hand was a handicap for the essentials of office work. So, I just chatted with my assistant and dropped into the offices of my colleagues for greetings.

Back in the house, the day passed quite smoothly. My wife sat working at her desk and went out for chores. I sat in the living room watching the television for news. In the evening we all sat at the table for dinner. The table was nicely decorated with flowers and candlelight. My wife's always-excellent food was laid out. The usual brief grace was said by our youngest son. The atmosphere was serene with light conversation. Concern about me was still on the faces of the family but was subdued. They realized that I was unwell, but not out of control.

As the evening passed, I was eager to go into my isolation in my room for the expected resumption of conversation with my secret guest. After some anxious moments of waiting, the now familiar gestures came and the voice announced his arrival.

"*Raandit*, greetings. I hope you had a good day."

"Welcome! Glad to have you. Yes, I had a relatively good day, all things considered."

"Relative to what? And what are the 'all things'?"

"*Benydit,* you ask difficult questions about issues for which you know the answers. Anyway, I know you are kidding. So, let's get to work."

"I didn't think what we are doing is work. I thought it was a pleasant game. And the ball is with you."

"It certainly is pleasant, but I would not call it a game?"

"Are you contradicting the Chairman, a dead man? But I forgive you. Let's begin the session with a question from me. What did people really understand by the New Sudan Vision?"

"Thank you for the forgiveness with no wrong done. All the same accepted and appreciated."

I knew that the question was rhetorical because the Chairman knew the answer. Nor was he really testing his own memory of the objectives of their own struggle. The motive behind the question was implicit in the question itself. Did people really understand what the concept meant and what it hoped to achieve?

My answer was elaborate and frank. "To tell you the truth, most people did not really know what it meant, and if they did, they thought it was either a pragmatic tactical ploy for more realistic objectives or else just utopian wishful thinking. Some Southerners who understood it as representing a more serious commitment to unity disapproved of it for precisely that reason. A few Southerners and Northerners understood it and agreed with it. There were also those who understood it and rejected it out of fear that it would destroy the status quo to their disadvantage."

I then focused on the different perspectives and interests involved in the reactions of various groups. "Of course, no reasonable person would object to the principles of equality and non-discrimination on the grounds of race, ethnicity, religion, culture, or gender, except those who use these as bases for domination and oppression. To the extent that the Vision of the New Sudan implied preserving the unity of the old Sudan on new bases, South Sudanese mostly opposed it partly because they were deeply against any form of unity with the North and partly because they did not believe that full equality in one Sudan was possible.

"The popular response among your soldiers when asked what they thought about the objectives of the war in the context of unity in a New Sudan was 'We know what we are fighting for'. The implication was that, while their Chairman spoke about unity for his own calculated reasons, which they accepted, they knew that they were fighting for the independence of the South. The dominant Arab Muslim North on the other hand rejected the vision of the New Sudan as repugnant to their existential interests and indeed as naïve because they were sure it could not be achieved.

"What I found fascinating about your January 1972 letter on the Addis Ababa negotiations is that it was far more complex in its vision than people generally seem to understand from it. People believe that you were against the agreement because it aimed at a solution for South Sudan when your objective was unity in a New Sudan. In my reading of the letter, you seemed to emphasize maintaining the army of the South, the Anyanya, as a strong force to defend an autonomous Southern Sudan against the central government. You were against the absorption of this force and wanted the two armies to remain separate for at least five years, after which the merger of the two could be carefully carried out over another five years. Your vision of the country was a federal arrangement between the North and the South from which either side retained the option to secede. What was clear was that you wanted the dominance of Arab Nationalism in the Sudan to end.

"Co-existence on equal basis with partition as an option was central to your initial proposal. Later, it seems that your vision evolved into a New United Sudan of full equality free from the dominance of Arab Nationalism. This is why the popular perception that you were committed to unqualified unity is obviously an oversimplification."

"I think you read my letter correctly. It is also true that our political thinking evolved and became more focused over time. Although the options of unity, co-existence, and partition were always in our equation, they became more clarified as our movement became more genuinely national."

"My other observation from your letter is your persistent perception and presentation of the government as weak and your movement as strong and growing stronger. Your view of the enemy as weak and your force as strong was consistent throughout the duration of the war. Were you always convinced about this or was it a strategy or tactic to boost the morale of your army?"

"I can frankly say that it was both. You have to have faith in your strength to confront an even stronger force. And you can't convince your fighting force if you yourself as their commander are not convinced. Whether this conviction is real or constructed is less important than the subjective faith in your strength. Of course, we were weaker than the army of the government, but we had the strength of our cause and our commitment to our liberation."

"Was the unity of the country that you so forcefully articulated and advocated intended as a means to an end or the end itself?"

"Our preference for unity always involved separation as a fallback option, which we knew was the popular aspiration of Southerners. The question was always how to achieve it, and we believed that raising the objective of the struggle to the liberation of the whole country could make it more feasible to liberate the South. It should however not mean abandoning the greater objective of liberating the whole country from the domination of one identity group, if only as an ongoing goal to be pursued by others with a more direct interest in the outcome."

"But you can now see that the complexity of your strategy could not be easily understood by ordinary Southerners. I even wonder whether it was fully understood by your comrades-in-arms."

"What Southerners did not realize fully is that the world is against breaking up countries," the Chairman injected. "This is quite apart from the African commitment to preserving colonial borders. What made the independence of the South acceptable is that our noble objective of promoting equality in a united New Sudan was rejected by the North, which made them look unreasonable. The independence of the South was essentially due to the failure of the North to justify and sustain the unity of the country. In that sense, we were both idealistic and pragmatic."

I then resumed: "I remember a conversation I had with the lead negotiator for the government. I told him that you really believed in the unity of the country. His reaction was, 'We prefer the position of your separatist friend to the unity of the Chairman.'"

"And he was right," the Chairman commented. "The separation of the South would leave them free to preserve their Arab-Islamic dominance, as it did. The unity we wanted would have fundamentally transformed the system and forced them and their divisive agenda out of power."

"But that too would have been ironic and paradoxical, since the vision of the New Sudan as an ideal was inclusive of all and not to exclude any group."

"But you cannot be inclusive with those whose objective is the monopoly of power based on an excluding ideology. The formula for their inclusion is their reform and transformation, which inherently means excluding to include, a paradox as you say."

"I think I understand," I said, although I was not sure I understood how that paradox could work in practice. I then introduced the issue of his own ambitions for power, as the opponents of the New Sudan

Vision saw it. "The general feeling in the North, shared by many in the South, was that you were too ambitious to be the President of the Sudan. I remember telling some Northerners that you were realistic and pragmatic enough to know that Northerners would never accept a non-Arab and non-Muslim as the President of the country. I said you would probably support as President a Northerner who shared your vision for the country. Your reaction to me was, 'Why are you denying me the Presidency?' And yet, I was right that Northerners generally could not fathom the idea of a South Sudanese as President. My friend told me what I actually also heard a Northern Sudanese, who was otherwise a liberal, say in reaction to the belief that you wanted to be the ruler of the Sudan, 'Whom is he coming to rule?'"

The Chairman was clearly indignant. "In our New Sudan, it would no longer be for them to decide who should rule or be the President."

"But that is precisely why it was very difficult to achieve the New Sudan Vision," I said and then recounted experiences I had had with Northerners about the prospects of transforming the country to reflect its racial, ethnic, and cultural diversity. "I recall a conversation I had with a group of Sudanese diplomats in Khartoum. It was a dinner conversation. I was advocating a system that would be based on the racial, cultural, and religious pluralism of the Sudan instead of the Arab-Islamic agenda that had dominated the country. One of the people at the dinner was a person who looked very sickly and in fact died shortly after. As the dinner was about to end, he said to me that the vision I was advocating was unrealistic because Arabism and Islam were too deeply entrenched in the North to be transformed into something different."

I reiterated to the Chairman my original argument about the difficulties of realizing the New Sudan Vision. "That is why separation was more acceptable to the dominant Arab-Islamic elite than the transformation of the system.

"I remember raising the question to you in our Washington house over dinner whether the New Sudan Vision should be pursued to the end and at all costs, even at the risk of the extermination of our people, or whether it should be phased to allow our people to have a break and re-gather their strength for a later round in the struggle? You responded with the question of whether people should remain second-class citizens to avoid extermination. You also asked why people should allow themselves to be exterminated. I could of course have argued that people do not allow themselves to be exterminated; they get exterminated because they have no capacity to protect themselves. But I chose not to pursue my point. I remember sharing with President Carter my discussion with you and he seemed to take your side. 'I know what he means,' he said.

"But, of course, as you made clear in your January 1972 letter, you did not rule out alternative solutions to the goal of unity in a New Sudan. I remember your telling me that separation would essentially come as a fallback solution and as the pragmatic preference of the North."

"Which," he rejoined, "was the number one preference of the South, as you know."

"Yes," I agreed, "but a preference which they had no real means of achieving without the North conceding it in their own interest, if you know what I mean."

"I certainly do," the Chairman affirmed. "I have often said to people that although I knew you well, I could not swear whether you were an unequivocal unionist or a separatist. I believe you saw the two as closely interconnected. I remember you saying that even if the goal of the South was separation, only by transforming Khartoum on the principles of the New Sudan could the independence of the South be guaranteed. But you also said that if the South succeeded in transforming the system in Khartoum in their own image, then why separate?

"You are also known to have said that both the separatists and the unionists in the South had a mutual interest in fighting together for the liberation of the South. After reaching the border between the North and the South, the separatists could stop while those interested in liberating the whole country could continue. But then you added a rhetorical question about whether you would continue alone if your fighting men stopped at the border?"

That triggered a memory in me: "I recall you also said that achieving the independence of the South would require effective force. 'We will squeeze them until they literally vomit us out,' you said."

"And that is exactly what happened," affirmed the Chairman. "That is what I call the pragmatic preference of the North. And while it was the first preference of the South, it was not our best possible outcome as a movement because it would leave some important issues unresolved. For one thing, quite apart from leaving Abyei in limbo, it left out the people of the marginalized areas of the Nuba Mountains and Southern Blue Nile who had been inspired by the vision of the New Sudan to join our struggle. The people of Darfur were also prompted by our vision to rebel. Even the Beja and the Nubians in the far North shared our vision. Now they are left to struggle alone in a system that treats them as second-class citizens. For another thing, even the independence of the South is not secure from the divisive interference of the North, as the South has already experienced."

So, quite apart from the New Sudan being a shared aspiration with the marginalized groups in the North, it is in the long-term interest of the South. I recalled what the Chairman said to me about the contribution of these Northern groups to the struggle. "I remember you telling me that we could not have achieved the goals of our struggle without the alliance with the Nuba and the Angassana, which is why you did not want the resolution of their problems to be deferred in the peace talks."

"That's right," he reaffirmed.

"I really believed that your movement had succeeded in stimulating a process of transformation from which the Sudan could not pull back. I used to say that Sudan would never be the same again. And much of that had to do with the extent to which you had inspired the marginalized non-Arabs of the North and even the liberally minded 'Arabs' to embrace the goal of transforming the system."

I recounted to the Chairman the way I felt about the independence of the South: "I attended the Independence Celebrations. The jubilation of the people of the South, who stood in the blazing sun, was an exhilarating enjoyment of their hard-won freedom, supported by the international community. But I also thought of the allies we had left behind in the Old Sudan. I was therefore pleased when the President of our new country said in his independence speech that South Sudan would not abandon them, and that we would continue to support them through peaceful means. In that respect, I felt that the independence of the South was a monumental achievement, but it was also an unfinished job for those who had fought with the Southerners for a shared vision."

"That was good that the President publicly committed to supporting their cause through peaceful means. But once the South became independent, the international community would discourage any involvement in the internal affairs of another independent country.

Efforts by South Sudan to help them would be very much constrained."

I agreed and elaborated: "If post-conflict relations between the two countries were cordial, South Sudan could help mediate a peaceful resolution of the problems of those areas. After all, I don't think they want to break away. All they want is the right to govern themselves free from Arab domination from the center and have a fair share of the national power and wealth."

The Chairman qualified what I said: "It sounds simple, but I wonder whether it is. If they still believe in our New Sudan Vision, that would require a major transformation that is fundamentally threatening to the entire system that is based on identity differentiation and discrimination."

"You are probably right. I visited the Nuba Mountains and Blue Nile before the referendum in the South," I resumed. "They could not believe that South Sudan would vote for independence. 'The South is our older brother; how can an older brother abandon his younger brother in danger?' they asked. 'We are members of the movement and our people are in its leadership. Our people have died in the struggle and within the borders of South Sudan. How can the South leave us?' But should the South become independent, they still hoped it would continue to support their struggle. Even then, I realized that, should the independent South support their struggle, Sudan would work to undermine the independence of the South. That is what has happened."

The Chairman recalled how he insisted on having the cause of these groups treated equally with that of the South in the negotiations. "I remember the American mediators and even some of our members in the negotiations trying to persuade me to postpone the issues of Abyei and the two areas of the North to be discussed later and to focus instead on resolving the problem of the South first. I told them that if we postponed the Abyei issue, we would never resolve it. I also told them that the two areas were part and parcel of our struggle and should not be left behind. But this is now all history."

"All the same, the achievement of independence for the South was almost a miracle," I recalled, going back to our earlier theme. "I never really believed it could happen. As you know, I strongly advocated self-determination, but, to be honest, that was not because I wanted the South to secede. I wanted it to be a pressure on the North by impressing upon them that unless they accepted the principles of the New Sudan Vision, the country risked being partitioned. I always stipulated three options: unity within a framework of full equality; co-existence in a framework of unity in diversity; or outright partition. I did not fully realize that the rulers in Khartoum would indeed prefer partition."

"That was too subtle, or should I say too clever? The trouble with that approach, if I may say, is that it underestimates the cleverness of the opposing side. You must always give due recognition to the intelligence of your opponent, never underestimate the enemy."

"Advice taken, but too late for the purpose. On the other hand, isn't that what you meant when you proposed in your 1972 letter a five-year co-existence of the two armies, followed by another five-year process of merging the armies, and establishing a federal framework with option of secession?"

"To some extent, yes. But I was straightforward about those alternatives. I did not use the option of secession as a means of inducing the North to accept the option of a New United Sudan."

"I see," I said, although I recalled a conversation I had had with the Chairman of the Referendum Committee, a professor of law from the North who taught me and later became a colleague and a friend. "He was being blamed by Northerners for facilitating the independence of the South. He told them that they should instead be grateful to him because he did what he knew they wanted.

"And he was right, even though it was very brave of him to fulfill their unstated wishes, which he knew they were ambivalent about and would almost certainly deny, as they have indeed done.

"I recall other occasions when I strongly defended both self-determination and unity. I remember an event at the Carter Center in which President Jimmy Carter met with a group of experts on the Sudan whom I had recommended to advise him on his mediation efforts. We met alone in the morning and then with him over lunch. Almost interrupting the report on our earlier meeting, he placed the blame for the war on the rebel movement and argued against self-determination. He said that he had been to Khartoum and had seen Christians go to church. There was therefore freedom of religion in the Sudan. He added that no one wanted the Sudan to be divided. Although I was polite, I felt enraged by what he said."

I described to the Chairman my reaction to President Carter, conveyed with controlled rage: "I could not resist challenging him. How could he say that there was freedom of religion just because he saw people going to church in a country that declared itself Arab and Islamic Sharia as the law of the land in the whole country? I also told the President that if he wanted the Sudan to remain united, the best way was not to say that no one wanted the country divided, but to tell the North that unless they created the appropriate conditions for unity, their country was in danger of being partitioned. President Carter responded by saying that he entirely agreed with me. How could he agree with me in light of what he had just said? He went on to say that he did not care whether the Sudan was united or divided. That sounded more like a reaction of indignation than a genuine opinion."

The Chairman commented: "It's difficult to blame a person like President Carter. He had a lot of idealistic and noble objectives but was not sufficiently informed about the situation and the high stakes he was dealing with."

"Actually, that meeting was an attempt to correct an earlier adventure by him. I got a call from his advisors in Nairobi to tell me that the President was undertaking a mediation initiative with the parties to the Sudanese conflict and wanted advice from me, specifically on the individuals involved. I asked whether that was his own initiative or at the request of the parties? The advisor did not know exactly but thought that it had been requested by the parties. Later I understood from you that you had actually advised him against it, as the positions were far apart and would only put his own integrity at risk. The President of the Sudan also told me that President Carter had offered to mediate and he could not reject his offer. When he failed to find a solution, he was outraged that they asked for his mediation when they were not ready to agree. That was when I advised his mediation team to better prepare the President with expert advice the next time he contemplated a peace initiative. That was why they convened that meeting."

"That's exactly what I mean by good intentions without adequate knowledge."

I recounted to the Chairman another situation where I was faced with the same challenge. "You remember that I was confronted with the same dilemma in the Task Force organized by the Center for Strategic and International Studies in July 2000 to develop a coherent

US policy to end Sudan's war, to guide the incoming administration. At the suggestion of the funding institution, I co-chaired the task force with an American from the Center. The task force was comprised of fifty individuals who were knowledgeable on the Sudan."

I told of the challenge I faced in the task force: "Virtually all of them were against self-determination for the South and the division of the country. They did not even see the US playing a leading role for peace in the Sudan. For them, the Sudan had no strategic interest for the US. The only importance of the Sudan was its support for terrorism, its destabilization of friendly neighbors in the region, and the humanitarian situation caused by the war. In their opinion, if George W. Bush became President, he would have no interest in world affairs, far less in the Sudan. They thought that efforts to end the war in the Sudan should be left to Europe, with the US supporting from a distance."

"That was simply not true. It was just a way of evading responsibility, which they should have known. They also probably didn't know the world expected the sole superpower to shoulder it."

"That was precisely the premise of my argument. Playing my cards carefully to avoid being seen as abusing my position as Co-Chairman, I made a contrasting case for US leadership in the search for peace in the Sudan. I reversed the three priority areas identified by the task force. Sudan's involvement in terrorism was based on the fact that the government viewed the Christian West as supporting the cause of the South. They therefore saw the Islamic terrorist organizations in the Middle East as allies on the principle that the enemies of my enemies are my friends. It is for the same reasons that Sudan was destabilizing the countries of the region, which they viewed as sympathetic to the cause of the South. The humanitarian crisis in the country was also caused by the war. My conclusion was that, by ending the war, we would stop Sudan's involvement in terrorism, its destabilization of the region, and the humanitarian crisis."

"That was well put. But that was from the perspective of the US. What about the Sudanese perspective, the cause of the conflict and how to resolve it?"

"Bear with me. My story is not yet over. Much more is coming. As for the strategic importance of the Sudan, I made the point that Sudan was the meeting ground of the great religions of the world, Christianity and Islam, and of the two regions, Africa and the Middle East. It could be a point of reconciliation or conflict, with far-reaching implications. As the sole superpower, the United States could not afford to be indifferent to an area of such global strategic importance. It must instead take the lead in ending the war."

"I am still waiting for the Sudanese perspective."

"Here it is. I argued that the best way of promoting unity was to use self-determination as a threat to pressure the regime to create conditions conducive to unity. To ensure unity in some form, I argued that we must try to reconcile two seemingly irreconcilable realities, the Arab-Islamic Vision of the North and the African Secular Vision of the South. That was the root of the 'One country, two Systems' formula which the task force recommended for the interim period. The task force also strongly recommended that the US play a leadership role in the mediation to end the war."

"That was a strategic formula that was eventually widely accepted and became very influential in the negotiations."

"Northerners generally took it as a clever separatist ploy. I met Nimeiri when he was visiting Washington while our report was very much in the news. He said to me, 'I hear that you have become a separatist.' I asked him what I had done to become a separatist. He mentioned my advocating two systems. I asked him whether the arrangement he had established under the Addis Ababa Agreement was not 'one country, two systems.' He suddenly changed, 'You are absolutely right.' That ended the matter. But I was to keep hearing from the Sudanese later that our 'One Country, Two Systems' formula became a basis for the separation. What was intended to be a basis for unity in a way reinforced separatism."

"Not only that, but 'One Country, Two Systems' implied uniformity or consensus within the two systems. You were living under an Islamic system to which not all Sudanese adhered. As for the South, you now see how torn apart it is by tribalism."

"You are absolutely right. I remember giving a talk at Khartoum University and a Nuba Professor asked me where we would place the Nuba in our One-Country-Two-Systems formula? That's when I thought of changing the equation to 'One Country, *Multiple* Systems', which would give all the five regions of the Sudan—South, North, West, East, and Center—the right of self-rule within the framework of national unity. But it was too late. We had already succeeded in selling the formula of 'One Country, Two Systems'.

"Of course, President Bush won the election and became surprisingly active on the global scene—and in ending the Sudanese war. Our Task Force Report and its 'One Country, Two Systems' formula became the cornerstone of US policy to end the war in the Sudan.

"I know you were initially opposed to the Task Force; I believe based on the advice of some of our friends who saw my co-chair as more friendly to the Khartoum government and less sympathetic to the cause of the South. In fact, our friends advised me against accepting the position of co-chair or even involving myself in the work of a task force, which they boycotted. But quite apart from the fact that the funders made my co-chairing the task force a condition for their funding, I feared that, if I did not participate in it, the organizers would seek alternative sources of funding and we would not have the opportunity to influence the process."

"It is true that I was opposed to the Task Force initially for the reasons you gave. But I also told our friends that I was encouraged by your participation because I was sure you would influence the process and the outcome in our favor. I remember referring to the formula of 'One Country, Two Systems' in a meeting you were chairing, and you responded by saying that I had endorsed your formula. I told you that my formula was different from that intended by your co-chair, whose real intentions were, I believed, disguised in the progressive-looking proposal of your task force.

"Quite apart from what I feared was your colleague's hidden agenda, the reason I did not like your version is because I saw it as an alternative to the New Sudan Framework. For me, and I know for you too, the 'One Country, Two Systems' formula was the second-best option. It was an alternative to the failure to achieve the New Sudan goal. To make it a permanent alternative was defeatist. As it turned out, even that formula was abandoned in favor of Southern independence."

I agreed with the Chairman. "You are right. People of course want clear-cut solutions, black-and-white. But, to tell you the truth, 'One Country, Two Systems' for me was an interim grey-area arrangement for preserving the unity of the country, but it also set in motion a process of interaction across the dividing line that could in due course evolve into the New Sudan."

The Chairman had quite a different take on the situation. "That too was too clever and tenuous. It would not be understandable to most people. And if they understood it, that would also bring to the forefront the divisive issues that favored separation."

I told the Chairman how I discovered the similarity of our views on the formula of 'One Country, Two Systems', although I did not articulate it in those terms. I remembered forming circles in my two hands by connecting the thumbs and the index fingers and crossing the two circles to form two entities with a shared area at the intersection. That to me was the North and South, separate but intersecting. I learned later that the model I had formed with my fingers was the Chairman's second of six models. The first model was the New Sudan in which the shared space in the middle of the intersecting circles would expand to cover the whole country. The third model was the Islamic State, which he argued had failed. The fourth model was an indigenous African State, which he termed hypothetical. The fifth model was the total partition of the country along the North-South dualism.

The Chairman continued his comment on the developments leading to the independence of the South. "Ironically, the United States itself, though initially against partitioning the country, became the leading supporter of Southern independence. Most Southerners, of course, also wanted it as their first option. But we in the movement, especially I personally, considered it the last option, a fallback position. I realized that you shared my position on the options, perhaps more than most of my colleagues in the movement. You remember when you told me that some people saw you as the theoretician of our movement? I told you that, while I personally liked the ideas in your writings, I did not know whether the movement generally would consider them as representative of their position. Part of the reason was, of course, because most of them did not read your works and knew of your ideas only through distorted hearsay."

I agreed with the Chairman and even reminded him of a discussion we had had on a related issue. "I remember asking you why it was that when you spoke of unity in a New Sudan, your position was applauded as heroic, and when I expressed similar views, Southerners criticized me? I asked you what the difference was other than that you carried a gun and I did not? Your answer was that people believed in what they saw as practical. If one voiced a vision that they did not believe was backed with force, they would not believe it. The fact that you were leading an armed struggle for the vision of the New Sudan made it more believable than the fact that I was merely advocating it."

I asked the Chairman to explain something that had always baffled me in his intellectual articulation of his vision for the unity of the Sudan: "I have never really understood why you always referred to diversity, which you classified into historical and contemporary elements of diversity. How can such deeply rooted diversity be a basis for unity? Is this not a contradiction or at least a paradox?"

"You are correct that it sounds paradoxical. What I meant was that we go back a long way in our history, where we are known as one entity composed of diversities. That identity is mentioned in the Bible and has remained through various historical phases to this day. In other words, diversity has been a characteristic that did not divide us in the past and should therefore not divide us now. Diversity has been an enriching factor in our unity and should be recognized as such. I hope I have clarified the issue."

"Yes, to an extent, but you still need to explain how you can reconcile this concept of diversified unity with the call for self-determination based on diversity."

"Calling for self-determination with a view to the independence of the South is sloganeering without substance, not only because diversity should not in itself be a basis for separation, but also because crying for self-determination does not bring it about. That is why your group of the so-called Concerned Southerners calling for self-determination was a distraction that threatened to play into the game of the North. How could they attain self-determination simply by calling for it? In the end, they would compromise with the North in favor of their continued dominance. Recognizing diversity as a feature of our unity that needed to be managed more constructively was more challenging, but equally rewarding. That was why I opposed the initiative of your group."

"That's very interesting. In a way, it jives with my guiding principle of optimistically seeking opportunities in crises or turning a negative into a positive. Instead of diversity being a source of division, you turned it into an asset for unity."

"You got it well."

"I know you thought that some of us were actually agents of the Northern political parties. I must confess that as I shuttled between you and the group, you made me believe for a while that I was playing a constructive role. When you made your opposition unequivocally clear and I decided to resign because I did not want to be involved in an initiative that threatened to divide the South, I suddenly turned into a bitter enemy of our group. This was particularly the case because the funders withdrew their support, which was based on my involvement. It took quite a while before I could restore a semblance of normal relations with the members of the group."

The Chairman explained his position at the time. "I wanted the decision to be entirely yours, but I was of course very pleased with the decision you made. Although it might have seemed to you to be a small issue, it was in fact a significant support for the movement, since the initiative of your group would have caused a major division in the South."

"As you will remember, the anger of the group with me was compounded by the fact that I also stopped their plans to create an alternative forum involving Sudan's government and the movement, with the support of Nigeria. The President of Nigeria, who was a friend, had apparently agreed to fund their planned conference, but asked his people to coordinate with me, which they failed to do. When he learned about this, he ordered them not to proceed with the plans without fully coordinating with me. The more I learned about the plan, the more I became convinced that it was in fact aimed at undermining the policy stance of the movement on the New Sudan agenda in favor of a clear commitment to the principle of self-determination. I told the President that, as planned, the project would divide the South and that we should start afresh to ensure the participation of the movement. As both you and the government were also opposed to the conference, the President stopped funding the project. That became another bone of contention between me and the group."

"Again, let me reiterate that I did not want to influence you on either your resignation from the group or your opposition to the alternative plan for a conference," the Chairman recalled. "But as I told you at the time, you made the right decision, which was very helpful to the movement. Actually, you did many things for the movement which only a few South Sudanese know. But, as you know, I personally followed closely all that you did for our cause, especially since you involved me directly in most of what you did. But perhaps we should talk about this in our next session."

I agreed. We ended the session on an issue that was very important to the unity of South Sudan, about which Southerners generally knew nothing. I remembered that it took a long time for my colleagues who felt let down by my decision to get over their anger and resume their normal relations with me. Many years later, one of them who had sympathized with my decision was to show me the letter of my resignation, which confirmed the historic importance of the decision. I retired for the night, again appreciating the importance of my conversations with the Chairman and grateful for the opportunity he had granted me.

Session Seventeen: Trepidations

It was almost two months now since the operation. I went back to the surgeon to assess the progress of the recovery. The surgeon was very pleased with the progress. But when I asked for the renewal of the prescription for the painkiller, he became suspicious. He agreed to give me a prescription for the last time and suggested that I consult with my physician.

I tried to procrastinate about going to the doctor. After all, what could a physician do about talking with the dead? Or, for that matter, about talking to one's self? Or worse, about madness? But my wife insisted that he was our physician and the least he could do was to recommend a more appropriate course of action. So, we went.

The doctor was a very pleasant, polite, middle-aged man. He received us warmly and respectfully. The surgeon must have been his friend and must have given him some details of my condition. But in the usual manner of the doctors, he wanted to hear all about it from the patient personally.

"So, tell me why you are here? Your surgeon mentioned something about a prescription drug that he thought you might need but did not think the operation still justifies his prescribing the medicine."

I told him all about the accident, the operation, and the treatment that followed, including the therapy that was still on-going and very painful. That's why I still needed the painkiller.

"But the intense level of pain that justified the prescription in the first place is much reduced?" he made a questioning statement.

I agreed but confessed that I had been receiving a visitor from the other side in the evenings and that taking the medicine had become a necessary stimulant for my conversation with the Chairman. Without it, I didn't think the conversations would continue.

My wife's jaw dropped and her eyebrows shot up before she consciously put her face back to neutral. I saw the dawning of understanding in her eyes. Suddenly, she knew everything.

The doctor attempted to mask his surprise and decided to get to the point. "I am going to suggest something, but please do not misunderstand me. I will give you a one-time prescription that is not renewable. I think you need to see a psychiatrist. I am not saying that you have a mental illness. I just think that there is an interesting interaction between the medication and your literary creativity that stimulates the conversation you have with your dead leader and friend. But this is beyond my qualification. I think a psychiatrist can help you. And I know just the right person for you."

Of course, I had no choice but to accept his decision. Besides, my wife seemed satisfied with his approach.

The appointment with the psychiatrist took some time to arrange. Meanwhile, I continued with the medication prescribed by the physician and my conversations with the Chairman continued.

In our next discussion, the Chairman appeared and sounded a bit distant. "*Benydit,* you sound quite subdued. Are you well?"

"After all this time with you, how can you still ask such a question? How can you ask a dead man whether he is well?"

"How then do I ask about the condition I see you in?"

The Chairman surprised me by saying; "I see you have been discussing our conversations with doctors. Did I not warn you about that? Now you are being referred to a psychiatrist. What does that mean?"

I was taken aback. "First of all, how did you know all this?"

"I told you that the dead know things through mysterious ways that you will not understand, and even I cannot explain."

"But since you seem to be following everything and to be very knowledgeable about everything, what is the point of our discussing all these issues that you must know anyway?"

"Remember that my reason for initiating these conversations was not so much to get me informed as it was to recollect and record our experiences for you to pass on to inform others as you see fit. And also for the sake of history and posterity. So, let me reverse myself and advise you not to worry about seeing the doctors. After all, you have not been accused of madness. Besides, they are professionals whose code of ethics respects confidentiality. They may even have some useful advice to give you. So, let's continue with our conversations."

The Chairman then went straight to the issue of the role I had played in support of the cause of South Sudan. "How did you get involved with the cause of the South in the first place?" he asked, to get us back where we had ended in our last conversation.

"Is there a Southerner who has not been involved in the cause of the South? My political consciousness began, I believe, around 1951 in what was then called Rumbek Junior Secondary School. It was really intermediate school but was affiliated with the first secondary school in South Sudan, which was Rumbek Senior Secondary School.

"Political consciousness was just emerging in the South, and it was closely associated with developments in Northern Sudan and Egypt. My brother and our young uncle, being from the Ngok Dinka area bordering the North, and administered as part of Northern Sudan, were far more informed in politics than even the older students at the senior secondary level."

"How did you get to study in the South when your area of Abyei was part of the North?" the Chairman asked.

"It was a rather exceptional situation. We started schooling in Abyei Elementary School in 1943. It was the first school to be opened in the Ngok Dinka area. In those days, our people were opposed to sending their children to school because they thought it would not only alienate them from their society but would also corrupt them morally. Father, who was a strong supporter of education, sent all his sons to school, unfortunately not the girls, and urged his chiefs to do the same.

"Our school in Abyei was modeled after the South Sudan Educational System. The language of instruction was Dinka, then English, and, in religious terms, although Abyei Elementary was a government school, we fell within the Catholic sphere of influence. After four years, we were supposed to continue our schooling in Kwajok Missionary School, but an English Director of Education in Bahr el Ghazal persuaded our father to have us transferred to Tonj Primary School, which was intended for the sons of chiefs and government officials. I remember a line that children used to chant at Tonj:

Tonj School boys
Sons of Chiefs
You will be the Kings of Sudan.

"After completing the sixth year at Tonj, we joined Rumbek Junior Secondary School in 1951. In fact, the year Father toured the South before deciding whether to remain in the North or join the South, we travelled with him until Tonj. Although we were just children, Father consulted us on the matter and we agreed with his inclination to remain in the North for the same reasons he considered. We also naïvely believed that the British wanted the Ngok Dinka to join the South to have a clear racial division with the North to justify partitioning the country. The British, so we thought, would then grant the North independence and continue their colonial domination of the South. Although my brother does not remember this, we definitely favored the independence of a unified country, inspired by Egyptian nationalism, as the most reliable way of ending colonial rule. So, you can see the roots of the New Sudan Vision in us that far back."

"I can understand why your brother does not remember your supporting your father's decision to remain in the North. Given the current political climate, it could indeed be a case of selective opportune memory or forgetfulness."

"I think it is more appropriate to acknowledge the historical facts and evaluate them in their historical context. That is actually applicable to some of the critical decisions our forefathers made as leaders of a difficult and volatile border area."

"South Sudan was barely politically conscious, and their awakening was associated with developments in the North," the Chairman commented.

"And in Egypt, where the revolution of Mohamed Najeeb, whose mother was said to be Sudanese, was in the limelight. Jamal Abdel Nasir had not yet taken over. Focus was still on Najeeb. This was 1952. I remember reading a magazine, with a photo of Najeeb on the cover, with an article titled, 'How I Seized Power'. I still remember the key introductory paragraph:

'Naturally, we hoped to win the day, but it was also possible that we would find ourselves in prison or in front of a firing squad. My wife was well aware of this, but she was not afraid. On the contrary, she urged me, 'Mohamed, it is time to do something for the country. And God will be your Aid'."

"So you were really a revolutionary at an early age?"

"I guess you could say that. We fully identified with the North as the front lines of the anti-colonial national struggle. The threat of Northern domination was then still vague and distant. Our response to those colleagues who voiced concern about Northern domination was that, while the British were too powerful for us to resist, Northern Sudanese were not that much more powerful than us. We would be able to resist their domination. That is how immature and naïve we were," I concluded.

"Actually, you were quite advanced for your age," the Chairman commented. "And I believe that had to do with your proximity to the North. The South was still at the pre-nationalist stage of development."

"I know I am recounting what you already know, but you encouraged me to put on record our experiences for a wider audience and perhaps future generations," I said.

"Absolutely. Don't feel inhibited by the thought that you are educating me. You are recording for history. And the more the better."

"Our Junior Secondary School was transferred to Tonj in 1953 to establish Tonj Intermediate School. After a year at Tonj Intermediate, where my brother and I were among those promoted to jump a year and, having passed the exam for entrance to the secondary school level, we were transferred from the South in 1954 to continue our studies in the North. Our father had always wanted us to transfer to the North, but we preferred to wait until the secondary school level, when English, rather than Arabic, would be the medium of instruction. The outgoing British District Commissioner facilitated the transfer. He would later write proudly that our transfer was the last thing he did before leaving the country.

"Southern political consciousness became more awakened as the British rule was coming to an end. The Sudanization of senior positions previously held by the British indicated that Northerners were taking over from the British as the colonial rulers of the South. No post previously occupied by the British went to a South Sudanese. The 1955 mutiny in Torit had broken out and, although it had been aborted with British disciplinary intervention, it had triggered a rebellion in the South that would escalate into the 17-year civil war."

I really felt self-conscious about repeating what was common knowledge, but I wanted to present a logical and comprehensive sequence of political developments. "Our political awareness more or less matured in the secondary school. Students in the North were divided into the left-wing democrats, many of whom were communists; the right-wing Islamists, mostly Muslim Brothers, and the Independents, who were considered non-political. Of course, we could not be Islamists, far less Muslim Brothers, nor could we join the apparently indifferent Independents. So, we became democrats and bordered on becoming communists. We were avid readers of the communist literature and participated in cell unit discussion groups. I still remember verses we used to chant in praise of Stalin:

Stalin never died
The Great Stalin
He never died;
He only moved from the Kremlin
To come and live in our hearts
The hearts of the struggling masses."

"It seems as though you had been captured by the communists," remarked the Chairman. "You were more communist than I was later alleged to be. In the South, Christian Missionaries had succeeded in reversing the Marxist slogan by labeling Communism, instead of religion, as the opium of the people."

The Chairman's comment was quite a challenge. Of course, I felt no affinity with socialism, let alone communism, but the historical association was glaring in my report. I had to explain the riddle to the Chairman without denying the past.

"What attracted us to the left was that the democrats, in particular the communists, whose political party was known as the Anti-Imperialist Front, were the most sympathetic to the cause of the South, and advocated autonomy for Southern Sudan," I elaborated. "Otherwise, Northern students were more generally committed to the cause of the Arab world than to addressing the grievances of South Sudan. They went on strikes and staged demonstrations in solidarity with the Algerian struggle against French rule and in protest to the 1956 joint attack on Egypt by Britain, France, and Israel. In contrast, they did nothing to protest the government's burning of villages in the South. Only the communists joined the students of Rumbek Secondary School, then relocated in Khartoum, in their demonstrations against the government's Southern policy."

The Chairman injected a thought that had never occurred to me. "It seems that your expectations of the Northerners ironically reflected your close association with them. It would never have occurred to most Southerners to expect Northerners to stand up in support of the cause of the South."

Despite the perspective offered by the Chairman, which underscored the anomaly of our situation, I felt quite satisfied that I had clarified our ideological past by linking it with the struggle for our Southern Sudanese cause. I indeed felt proud that our commitment to the cause from which some Southerners try to delink Abyei went that far back into our youth. I elaborated.

"What you are saying brings to mind what I recently learned from a fellow student from Khor Taqqat, who would rise in Sudanese politics and the Islamic movement. He said that, to the Northern Sudanese students at the time, what was happening in South Sudan was very far from their consciousness. South Sudan was so remote from them that, although they were saddened by the 1955 massacres of Northerners in the South, it was not really comprehensible to them."

"It is a situation where you can either blame them because they should have known better, or understand that they did not know rather than being morally indifferent," the Chairman reflected. "Jesus asked his Father to forgive his wrongdoers for they knew not what they were doing."

"You are reflecting the forgiveness of Jesus Christ. That at least explains why none of our colleagues showed any anger or bitterness against or over what was going on in the South, despite the tragic news from the South and the mournful Koranic verses that were being chanted to accompany the news."

"Please do not compare me to Jesus Christ. I am already afraid that our conversations, if known, might be misconstrued as my having risen from the dead."

"I don't think there is that risk. The likely risk is that I not be believed—or be believed mad. But I must say that your comments make me better understand our experience in Khor Taqqat School. Remarkably, we never feared any retaliation from our fellow students and nothing remotely hostile was displayed toward us by any student. I remember only one student remarking very casually, almost jokingly, 'What are your people doing to our people in the South?' There was no anger or bitterness in his remark. And I don't think I even responded."

"There is always a positive side, even in a tragic situation. That was a positive experience that must have registered in your consciousness, even though you were not aware of that at the time. It could even have contributed to your bonds with the North without your knowing."

"That's a very interesting point. I must reflect further on it." I then focused on the way we responded to the Northern attitude toward the political oppression in the South. "We threatened to not join our Northern colleagues in one of their strikes as a protest to their indifference. Our colleagues attributed that to the directives of the Committee of the National Students' Union. They sympathized with our position but argued that two wrongs did not make a right and that they would take our complaint to the National Committee."

I then recounted how our experience in the secondary school in the North influenced our political action in the university. "As a reaction against the attitude of Northern students to the cause of the South, the three of us, my brother and our young uncle, both of whom became medical doctors, and myself, having just entered the University of Khartoum, organized the Students' Welfare Front, which was in fact a Southern Sudanese party with a disguised name, on the advice of my senior colleague in the Faculty of Law. My secondary school colleagues, democrats and communists, who had taken Southern Sudanese membership in their party for granted, were very disappointed with us, especially with me personally.

"Despite our initiatives to organize our South Sudanese colleagues, our position in the politics of South Sudan remained somewhat nebulous, being from the ambiguous area of Abyei between the North and the South. Southern Sudanese students nominated me to be their representative in the Students' Union, but I declined because I did not feel that I would be an authentic representative. I did, however, represent the position of the South on several other issues about which I felt no ambivalence or reservation."

"That's precisely what I am trying to say, that Southerners would not believe that you played that role," the Chairman interjected.

"But Southerners know that the citizens of Abyei played a heroic role in the two civil wars in the South and were highly acclaimed as very brave fighters for the cause of the South!" I noted.

"You are absolutely right. And I am a good witness of that side of the story of Abyei. It's a good example to bring up. But I think being a freedom fighter is a distinct demonstration that leaves no room for doubts, at least among the comrades-in-arms. This is different from civilian politics, especially in the isolated world of academia."

"Interestingly, I continued to be active in promoting the cause of the South, even though I never officially joined the rebel movement. My roommate was a Northern colleague from the secondary school. And many of my friends were Northerners, some of them Muslim Brothers. Perhaps because of my association with Northerners, I was very open with them in my discussions of the Southern problem. Southerners, on the other hand, feared that such openness was politically dangerous.

"My argument was that discussing with Northerners would make the cause of the South better known to them and perhaps win supporters. I did not then know the wisdom of Nelson Mandela that I learned from him many years later, that in every human being by virtue of his or her humanity, there is a goodness that can be tapped and used for fostering cooperation. That principle was essentially what I was pursuing. To the contrary, some of my South Sudanese colleagues even feared talking to me openly because they felt that I was too close to Northerners and might reveal sensitive information to them that could be politically dangerous. In fact, I once overheard a senior student advise a junior student against being too open with me. All this did not in any way affect my commitment to the cause."

It suddenly dawned on me that I had been talking without any reaction from the Chairman. "Are you still with me *Benydit?*" I asked.

"Yes. As I told you, I want this to be also a narration of your own experiences. And I am genuinely interested in listening to your story. What you said about the attitude of your Southern Sudanese colleagues is generally true of the oppressed. It is the paradox of domination. The oppressor succeeds in frightening the oppressed so much that they do not explain their grievances. Instead, they resort to secretive means of pursuing their cause, which ends up in using unlawful means that generate even more oppressive measures. Oppression becomes a self-fulfilling prophecy."

The Chairman then decided that it was perhaps a good point to stop the session. "Let us continue from this point in our next session."

I was very pleased with the session. I felt that, for the first time since our conversations started, we had discussed issues that were at the center of the Chairman's ideological and political agenda. It once again confirmed the fact that, although I was never a member of his liberation movement, we were very much of the same mind and shared the same vision for our country, and indeed humanity. I became even more excited about our project and looked forward to the next session.

Session Eighteen: Psychiatry

It was at last time for the appointment with the psychiatrist. I agreed for my wife to attend with me. We found the psychiatrist to be a very congenial, gray-haired, rather elderly man, but otherwise an energetic and lively person. He approached us warmly, almost as though he already knew us. In the characteristic fashion of doctors, he requested me to tell my story fully, which I did. Then he asked some pointed questions.

"When the Chairman comes to you, do you see him looking as you used to know him?"

I explained what I had already discussed with the ghost of the Chairman; his appearance was always rather vague and mysterious; his shape fuzzy and ill-defined; but his voice was always clear and recognizable.

The psychiatrist probed even deeper. "But is the conversation truly a two-way exchange in which you see the figure of the Chairman? In other words, do you actually see his lips move and hear words coming out of his mouth?"

I really could not answer his question with any certainty. I confessed that I could not tell.

"Which of you do you think shows more interest in your conversations, he or you?" The psychiatrist asked another question I had never really thought about. It did, however, occur to me that I always seemed to speak more than he did. But I had always assumed that I was expected to be the one telling the story. I explained that much in my answer to the psychiatrist.

"But you were supposed to discuss your shared experiences? You were to hear his message to pass on as you saw fit and to record your own story as well? He particularly emphasized that your people did not know much of what you did for the country. Is it possible that the real intention of the Chairman was to provide you with an opportunity to have your story known more than that his message be heard? After all, he is far too well known for him to be as concerned about his story being heard as he is about the contribution of his friend to the cause of the nation being better known and acknowledged."

It all sounded very interesting and quite plausible. But I really couldn't give an opinion that would not endorse the interpretation of the psychiatrist, which would seem self-serving.

My wife asked to speak. "Sure," the psychiatrist responded enthusiastically, as though he expected her to provide useful insights. "My husband's symptoms of talking to himself, sometimes laughing out loud, make me wonder whether he could be suffering from a bipolar disorder or even schizophrenia. I have read much in the hope of finding some diagnostic interpretation of his condition. I realize that my reading is that of a lay person, but I also know people with similar symptoms who are diagnosed as having mental disorder. Some of them are adults in their middle age."

The doctor seemed impressed by my wife's comments. But he corrected her with professional knowledge, moderated by personal courtesy. "You make good points, but you know our profession is progressively refining its understanding of the mind. There are diverse behavior patterns that we used to label collectively as mental illnesses. We are now realizing that the characteristics of the mind are quite complex and varied. What some people might call mental illness may well be distinctive qualities of a rare positive mental makeup. You certainly know of outstanding names of individuals who founded world religions and who heard voices and received messages to pass on to humanity. And I am not even talking of the many individuals who have enriched humanity with artistic spiritual, moral, and even political contributions who might be labeled as unbalanced and perhaps mentally challenged. So, I wouldn't be concerned about what you have read."

He then turned to me and said, "Let me now speak to you very frankly and tell you what I think. After all, that's why you are here. I believe you have a strong urge to let your people know how much you have done for them. You are convinced that they do not know. It is also obvious that if the Chairman was alive, your close association with him and the way you used to work together would have made your role obvious for all to see. His death and absence have obscured your contribution, except for a few people who know you and your relationship with the Chairman well. The fact that these people sometimes point out how unfair it is to you that only a few people are aware of what you have done for the country registers deep in your consciousness. So, you really want to tell your own story, and the appearance of the ghost of your friend, the Chairman, and his request that you register your joint story of achievement, offer you the opportunity to do what you would want to do anyway but lack the right opportunity to do. The Chairman is in fact offering himself, through your imagination of him, to be your conduit for reaching out to a wider audience."

I truly found what the psychiatrist said quite fascinating. But what did it all mean for the way I should manage the situation? And above all, was he going to give me the prescription I needed and wanted?

The psychiatrist then came with his conclusion and response to my request for the prescription. "You clearly need to continue your conversations with the Chairman, which I believe is good for you. But you have become addicted to the medicine, which is not good for you. I am going to strike a balance in the middle by reducing the dosage, the strength of the medicine, but encourage you to orientate yourself to stimulate an atmosphere conducive to pursuing your conversations. With the help of the reduced dosage, you can deliberately decide that both you and your deceased friend, the Chairman, need a joint account of what you both did to be recorded. Do it as an almost conscious decision to record your experiences. I would even suggest that you gradually wean yourself off the medicine and continue to create the climate conducive to continuing your conversations. If this proves difficult, come back and we can consider other approaches."

I found the discussion with the psychiatrist quite illuminating and, although I could not tell how well it would work, at least I was told that I was not crazy and that what I was doing was willful and worthwhile.

But what did all this really mean? If our conversations were really of my own doing to serve my own purpose, why did I need the Chairman? After all, I had already written books, why would I not have just sat down to write my own account of my experiences, including joint activities with the Chairman? There was, it seemed to me, still an element of mental disorder or instability in the situation.

But, rationally, it was obvious that I could not have told the story on my own the way the Chairman and I jointly constructed the story telling. And as the psychiatrist explained, mental conditions are complex and various forms and degrees of disorder are part of normalcy and might even stimulate creativity, sometimes with great results. I was not dreaming of great results, but we were telling a significant story that might otherwise not have been told, at least not in the same manner. I decided to console myself that we were doing something clearly worthwhile.

Session Nineteen: Politics

After I took the reduced dosage of the medicine, the experience appeared more natural than it had previously felt. I now realized more fully that I had a vested interest in the process rather than attributing everything to the Chairman's agenda for the transmission of our joint message.

My wife was very impressed that I was coping well with the reduced dosage, which she attributed to a strong will. She was persuaded that I had become addicted to the medication and kicking the habit was no mean feat. She was very complimentary. And she seemed to share her excitement with the boys, who also looked relieved. There was certainly some brightness in the house.

I now realized that the conversations with the Chairman were really my agenda. Even the timing of the sessions now seemed to be determined by me. And the more I felt in control of the process, the more I hoped to steer the substance to the Chairman's agenda. I was becoming increasingly less egocentric or self-serving. But the Chairman still wanted to focus on my experiences, which he felt strongly were less known by our people. Or was I still torn between self-interest and altruism?

At our next session, the Chairman opened the conversation with the issue of the South Sudanese fear of discussing their own grievances with Northerners, which we had touched upon in our last session. He saw it as the defeatist psychology of the oppressed, being so afraid that they do not dare explain their cause to the oppressor. This, of course, contrasted with my openness with Northerners about the cause of the South. Southerners, on the other hand, saw this as exposing one's self to the oppressor.

I told the Chairman that there had indeed been times when I clearly did things that exposed me to the oppressor. I recalled one such occasion. "What Southerners do not know is that, after a visit to Europe, I brought back into the country the first constitution of the Sudan African National Union, then still known by the acronym of

SACNU, as named when it was formed by the leaders in exile, with the help of our young uncle who was studying medicine in Italy. It was he who requested me to take the constitution to members of the underground Southern Sudanese movement in Khartoum. Deeply worried that I would be in serious, even deadly trouble if the document were discovered, I inserted it into the lining of my overcoat and nervously went through customs undetected. I handed it over to one of the leaders of the underground movement."

"That was quite a risk to take," the Chairman commented. "You were really laying down your life. Had they searched your coat and felt something hidden inside, that would have been a treasonous act. The punishment could have been life imprisonment or death."

"Ironically, later, in London, where I had gone to pursue post-graduate studies after appointment to the teaching staff of the Faculty of Law, I was accused of masterminding and leading the Southern Sudanese rebel movement in the whole of Europe, even though I was not a member of any political party or movement. I was going through a traumatic battle with glaucoma, whose symptoms had first appeared when I was in high school, but which was only detected in my last year in the university. I had an operation in both eyes in Berlin that was supposed to have succeeded, only for the condition to resurface in London less than a year later, threatening blindness, which I feared was imminent. As a result, I was severely demoralized and hardly attended to my studies except for a therapeutic focus on customary law and other literary materials that brought back some cathartic memories of home. My performance in African Law was so advanced, thanks to the fieldwork I had already done as an undergraduate at Khartoum University, that even masters and doctoral students consulted me on their projects.

"I was surprised and elated when my professor of African Law, based on materials from my field research during my Khartoum University years, proposed that I proceed with a doctoral program which he would supervise if my university back home approved. I was excited and wrote proudly requesting the approval. Sooner than expected, I received a letter, which I thought was a positive response to my request, but to my shock turned out to be an order for me to return to the Sudan immediately. That plunged me even deeper into an acute crisis."

"When a whole identity group is suspect, it is difficult to apportion individual responsibility. It is as though the whole group is presumed guilty until proven innocent. So you can understand why Southerners prefer to be in the shadows," the Chairman rationalized.

"And yet the principle that there are some fair-minded people even among a prejudiced group remains valid. I soon received a letter from a classmate and friend, who was practicing law, giving me the details of the allegations against me for supposedly masterminding and leading the South Sudanese movement in Europe. The source was the military attaché in London. The crisis was eventually resolved by the intervention of prominent Northern Sudanese personalities, among them the legendary Speaker of Parliament who played a leading role in the 1947 Juba Conference in which Southern Sudanese are understood to have endorsed unity with the North, the famous editor of the *El Ayam* daily newspaper, and the former Academic Secretary in the University of Khartoum who was then on a course in Oxford. The Sudanese Students' Union in the United Kingdom also supported me. A colleague, a graduate student at Oxford University and a Muslim Brother, wrote a letter to another colleague in London University, which was made public, in which he noted that my mistreatment indicated the gravity of injustice in South Sudan.

"The fact that I was so unjustly treated, but that prominent Northern Sudanese and fellow students supported me, showed the complexity of the situation in the country and my own personal position in the conflict. I later learned that my father had interceded with the President, who actually gave me that information. That too added yet another dimension to my personal standpoint."

"It is frankly quite remarkable and exceptional for a South Sudanese to get that kind of support from the North on an issue involving the conflict in the South. It makes your position quite exceptional, despite your sharing the characteristic persecution familiar to South Sudanese."

"Actually, to be more accurate, there were people even among the students in London who accused me of treason. And that accusation would be repeated over the years by Northern Sudanese who built on hearsay. I recall a fellow student coming to my place and, on hearing of the allegations against me, decided to call the military attaché, whom he said was an old school classmate and a friend. I wanted to withdraw to give them privacy, but he insisted that I listen. The gist of the conversation was the military attaché asserting his allegations against me, describing me as 'hating' Northerners, while the student with me argued that his friend did not know the person he was talking about. He almost concluded that it was a case of mistaken identity.

"Eventually, the military attaché called for us to meet, which we did. He explained in great detail the erroneous grounds on which he had based his accusatory reports. He stated that he had not expected the drastic response from Khartoum and that he thought they would wait until I was back in the country and then take their action against me. He pledged to correct the situation. He proposed to arrange a meeting with the President, who was expected to pay an official visit to the United Kingdom.

"While the preparations for the President's visit to London were underway and the Embassy was organizing my meeting with him, Scotland Yard was busy looking for me to assure that I did not pose a threat to the visiting President and would not do anything that would embarrass Her Majesty's government. I first met with the colorful Minister of Education, a military man. After a brief lighthearted conversation about their recent visit to China, where they had been paradoxically impressed by the communist system they fought at home, he said to me, 'You seem like such a nice young man, why did you do all this?' I asked what I had done. He explained the allegations, which I refuted. I told him that while I disagreed with their Southern policy, I was not part of any organized opposition. He said that as a military officer, what concerned him the most was to have his orders obeyed. I should have obeyed his orders and gone back to defend myself in court. When I told him that I was not a soldier, his response was, 'Don't you know that every young Sudanese is a recruit?' We had a pleasant chat."

"That is also a characteristic of the Sudanese. There is always a gap between polite appearance and vicious animosity," the Chairman commented.

"Then," I resumed, "he said he would take me to meet the President and that all I needed to tell the President was that I did not do what I was accused of. He advised me not to talk about my disagreement with their Southern policy. The President received me warmly and only referred lightly to the allegations against me, which I duly refuted. He said my father had contacted him to bring my case to his attention. He spoke very warmly about my father, whom he described as a patriot, and said I resembled him in the way I carried myself and talked. He said we should forget whatever had happened and directed that I discuss the details with the Minister. I thought the Minister and the President both acknowledged that I had been wrongly accused, but I was to learn later that the President went and told my father that they had *forgiven* me in deference to him."

"As is the case of the paradoxical politeness and viciousness, there is nothing surprising about that double talk," the Chairman commented. "In a way, it is typical of their misrepresentation of facts to serve their purpose. I think, in this case, it was both a way of acknowledging that you were wrong, while also making your father feel good that his word was respected and that his intervention had benefited his son."

"That meeting in 1963 was not my first with the President. I first met him in 1961 in Germany where I led a delegation of Khartoum University students on a program of exchange with German universities. The occasion of my travel to Germany revealed to me for the first time the political prejudice against Southerners. I was first issued a passport that made it valid only for the Arab Republic of Egypt. Then, when the university wrote to the authorities that I was going to Germany on an exchange program, they revised the passport to say, 'Also valid for West Germany.' I then went to see the Minister in the Presidency then known as 'The Lord Chamberlain' in the British tradition, who was a friend of my father, with whom I had first met him, to explain to him that I would be visiting my brother in Italy. He called the Minister of Interior to plead my case for a more open passport. He argued that if a son of a patriotic Chief like my father could not be trusted, how were Southerners expected to be loyal citizens? The passport was again changed to 'And also valid for all countries'. I still have that passport for the records."

"It certainly is concrete evidence of the prejudice against Southerners. The assumption was that you would become a rebel or propagate against the government. They forgot that you had a vested interest in your studies back at home. On the other hand, many Southerners left their studies at home to join the rebellion."

"At that time, the rebellion in the South had not yet gained momentum. Our program in Germany involved working in factories for about a month before traveling around the country. We were working at Siemens in Berlin when the President visited. His delegation was scheduled to visit Siemens and the leadership asked us to receive the President. The students of Khartoum University were opposed to the military rule. So, our team did not want to receive the President. I pleaded with them that whatever our internal differences, the President was our national symbol abroad. We must honor him as such. It took a lot of persuasion and even an offer of an incentive of a day off for them to agree.

"I was of course at the head of the reception line when the President came with his delegation. After having moved on as we received the rest of the delegation, the President returned to greet me again. It seemed that his accompanying Lord Chamberlain, who had facilitated my passport, had told him about me and my father. So, the President warmly mentioned my father and what a patriotic leader he was. As he moved on, the Foreign Minister, who had the reputation of being eccentric, obviously surprised by the President's attitude toward me, turned to one of my colleagues and asked, 'Is this Samuel with you?' 'Samuel' was the condescending generic name for any South Sudanese who was assumed to be Christian. My colleague informed him that I was their leader."

"They must have felt that you deserved what you got by persuading them to honor people who did not deserve it."

"That's exactly what happened. They mocked me, '*tas-tahal*', which means 'You deserve what you got'. They even began to call me 'Samuel'. I was of course furious and was tempted to write to him to say, 'If you, the Minister, can behave that way, what can we expect from the man in the street?' My colleagues persuaded me against that on the ground that he was a known eccentric."

"They were right. You would have lowered yourself to their level. Besides, you would have betrayed your colleague for sharing with you what was not intended for you to hear."

"Interestingly enough, while I was interviewing Sudanese leaders on a book I was writing on the human factor in British Colonial Administration, I wanted to interview him but was afraid to approach him because of his reputation for eccentricity. A prominent tribal chief and national figure told me that they were friends and took me to him without appointment. He accepted to be interviewed, but only after an eccentric jab at me. 'You Sudanese are hopeless. Even when a man is made an Ambassador, he walks in without an appointment?' But this was said as a friendly jab and our interview went very well. I refrained from reminding him of our earlier encounter."

"It probably would not have meant anything to him, if at all he remembered."

"Actually, I had long learned to accept it with a sense of humor in the wider context of our relations with the Northerners and in which I knew I occupied a very ambivalent position. The fact that I vigorously and openly advocated the cause of the South among Northern Sudanese colleagues was a matter of concern to my Southern Sudanese compatriots, who were afraid that such openness might reveal too much information and preferred to operate clandestinely among Northerners. It was too risky. While in London, one of my colleagues once introduced a fellow South Sudanese to his Northern colleague as a Zairean to hide the connection.

"When one of our rebel leaders visited London, he met with us, Southern students. In a subsequent discussion with our Northern colleagues, one of them asked whether we had met him. I answered that we had. A fellow Southerner, who had been in the discussion, later reprimanded me for admitting to having met a man condemned to death in absentia. My response was that if we had denied meeting a leader of our cause, we would either not be believed, or if we were believed, we would not be respected."

"On another occasion, Bishop Edward Baroni of Bahr el Ghazal, who was on his way to the United States, was met by my Southern Sudanese colleagues at the airport and I was not told about it. My cousin, who had defected from the air force and whom I helped to have reinstated, was living with me. He was invited to join the group. Probably out of family solidarity or guilt consciousness, he eventually confided in me and told me about their meeting. When I later raised the issue with my colleagues, they quite candidly told me that I was too close to Northerners and that people's lives were at risk. When I think how much you eventually inspired so many Northerners to stand side by side with Southerners in the struggle, it makes me appreciate even more what a difference you made in the minds of Southerners."

"Discrimination and domination create gulfs that are difficult to bridge. Fear of persecution is probably the most lethal tool the oppressor uses. It limits the moral power of the oppressed to make their cause known and to appeal to the better side of humanity in the oppressors. They remain ignorant and more easily in denial of the evil deeds they perpetrate. Correction becomes even more elusive. Actually, I don't think we ever talked about that phase of your political activity. And I believe that most South Sudanese probably know nothing about all this."

"My role in South Sudanese politics has always been something of an enigma. South Sudanese colleagues in the United Kingdom were critical of me for not formally joining the rebel movement. This is why it was ironic that the regime accused me of masterminding and leading the rebel movement in Europe. And this is why I believe my South Sudanese colleagues in England secretly welcomed my persecution, as they expected it to radicalize me against the government. They even asked me to lead a demonstration against the visiting President, since I had nothing to lose, while they remained aloof to protect themselves. What they did not seem to realize was that my approach to the cause of the South was based either on principle or expediency, not angry emotions."

"I think it was your role in the United States, especially after you left the diplomatic service, that helped our movement the most and we followed it closely. Of course, we were also aware of your work as Ambassador to a number of countries and as Minister of State for Foreign Affairs. We also saw how effectively you used the Addis Ababa Peace Agreement as the centerpiece in Sudan's foreign policy and a basis for promoting the Sudan internationally. But it is what you did after you left the government that was of direct interest to us in the movement."

"After I turned down the assignment as Ambassador to Ethiopia and resigned from the government, I went back to the United States. As I flew from Khartoum via Amsterdam, I asked myself whether I was turning my back on my country? The answer was of course a resounding No. What then would I do? I had no plans or any idea what I would do. Although my wife supported my decision to resign, with a family of four young children and a wife who had given up her career to raise those children, I would later conclude that I had made the right, but reckless, decision."

I then recounted the story of my writing political fictions. "I decided during the flight to Amsterdam that the first thing I would do was to put in fictional form some of the ideas about the crisis of national identity in our country that I had written in scholarly works. I wanted the message to reach the hearts and minds of the Sudanese people at the popular level.

"As soon as I landed in Amsterdam, I bought two writing pads. And throughout most of my flight to New York, I began writing. From time to time, the Englishman sitting next to me would ask a question. I would briefly answer him and go back to my writing. About forty minutes before landing in New York he spoke in very determined voice, 'I really must interrupt you; who are you and what are you writing about?' That was when I stopped writing and we talked until we landed."

"That's amazing. How did you conceive what you were writing within such a short span of time?"

"I really don't know. To this day, I cannot explain how it happened. It was as though someone was dictating to me and I was simply writing it down. For the weeks and months that followed, I continued to write. When we went for our annual camping on a lake with members of my wife's extended family, she told me that people were always free to do what they wanted and that I could write if I wanted to. I continued to write. At one point, one of our sons entered our tent and found me writing. 'Dad, you are working! I am going to tell on you!' he said. I laughed and went with him to join the group.

"That was my first novel, *Seed of Redemption,* in which the hero is the descendent of a woman captured into slavery while pregnant, and for whom the spiritual leaders of his family prayed and ordained that she would bear the fruit of her people's redemption."

"What about your second novel?"

"That was *Cry of the Owl,* which was translated into Arabic as *Taa'ir El Shoum, Bird of Doom.* As you know, among the Dinka, when an owl cries or makes sounds sitting on your hut or a tree near the vicinity of your home, it is considered a warning that some disaster is about to strike you or your family. The source of the impending misfortune must then be spiritually diagnosed and appropriate measures taken to avert the crisis. The powerful and direct Arabic translation is more pessimistic than the original title. The owl only alerts to danger and is not itself a source of danger. That is why the image of the owl among the Dinka borders between being evil and wise. The West focuses on its wisdom.

"I don't know much Arabic, but the Arabic translation of the English title is more awesome. It immediately conveys the magnitude of the crisis, which the English title does not."

"You are quite right. Actually, I got to like the Arabic title as much as the English. The novel is about two individuals who represent the extreme polar points in the crisis of national identity that divided the country between the Arab Muslim North and the African secular South. Acutely divided as they were by this identity cleavage; they discover at the end of the novel that they are in fact blood brothers.

"The transitional government had made overtures to reach out to you to discuss what they defined as the problem of the South. You dismissed their revolution as a continuation of the former military rule. You also maintained that you were not dealing with the problem of the South, but the problem of the Sudan. By the time I visited the Sudan in 1986 toward the end of the one-year transitional period, attempts to dialogue with the regime had ended.

"The Transitional President was a known Islamist. He surprised me by saying that he had just dreamt about me before learning that I was in the country."

"You must have represented something that was worrying him," the Chairman interjected.

"Then he should have dreamt about you," I responded.

"That would have been a nightmare."

"Yes, I was obviously less threatening. Anyway, he spoke very favorably of the leader of the Muslim Brotherhood in the Sudan. He said that contrary to what people thought, that Muslim Brotherhood leader was more tolerant of religious diversity than the sectarian leaders. Whatever those leaders might say about abolishing Sharia, they would never do it. In fact, no Muslim leader would dare abolish Sharia," he stated affirmatively.

"Was it not you who told me that the ousted leader was saying that if he went back to becoming President, he would abolish Sharia?" the Chairman recalled.

"That's right. It was in Washington. I had organized a luncheon for him at the Brookings Institution where I was a Senior Fellow in charge of the African Studies Program. My idea was to give him a platform to reflect on his experience and draw lessons that might offer guidance on how to respond to the crisis of governance in the country. Instead, he spent his time condemning the leader of the Muslim Brotherhood, whom he had involved in his government as attorney general and then as legal adviser in the presidency. The former President was clearly advocating his own return to power. He said that, since it was he who had introduced Sharia, he would abolish it as soon as he got back into the leadership. He was asked whether he regretted anything he did as President? His only regret was including that Muslim Brother in his government. That meeting convinced me that the President never had a vision for the country, he only used people to help him stay in power."

"I take it you now agree that we were right in trying to oust him!?", the Chairman posed a rhetorical question.

"I don't want to go that far *Benydit*. Don't forget, I was in his Government and we had an excellent working relationship."

"But that was when you thought he was genuine about the Addis Ababa Agreement? That was what made you join?"

"True! But whatever his motives, as long as the agreement lasted, it served our purpose. And when it was abrogated, I resigned."

"Point taken! That's why we never held it against you, working with him. Please continue with your visit to Khartoum."

"Among the people I met in Khartoum was the man who was both the leader of the largest political party in the country and the spiritual leader of his sect. The other man I met was his brother-in-law, who was the leader of the Muslim Brotherhood. The campaign for the elections was intensely underway. I cannot believe how these two men, who are in fact brothers-in-law, spoke so viciously about one another to me, an outsider. As you know, the Leader of the Muslim Brotherhood was married to the sister of the leader of the largest political party, who was one of two female classmates in the Faculty of Law. The Muslim Brother was our lecturer."

"Yes, I remember your saying that you helped her catch up when she joined your class months after the classes had begun, and which apparently offended another Muslim Brother. I assume that was before she married your Muslim Brother lecturer."

"Yes. And she interrupted her studies after they married, for him to continue his graduate studies in France. He then returned and taught for a while before becoming a full-time politician. And his wife went back to complete her studies in the Faculty of Law."

"What was it like to be a classmate with a Muslim Sister?"

"That's very interesting you ask that. She and another girl from a prominent Northern Sudanese family joined the Faculty about two months after the semester had started. We had been alerted to girls joining the class by our teacher, the Muslim Brother. He was in effect jokingly alluding to the impact the girls would have on the class. I was the first person the girls encountered when they came to the Faculty. And they soon turned to me to help them catch up. This involved giving them my notes and at times dictating the notes to them myself."

"It's ironic that he would joke about the effect of the girls on the class when you would expect that, as a Muslim leader, he would be discreet about that and in fact want the male and female students to keep a distance," the Chairman commented.

"It's something of a paradox. Although they were together, it was a very self-conscious togetherness." I resumed my recollections. "One day, a well-known Muslim Brother in the Second Class entered the room to find me dictating my notes to the sister of the leading sect and the largest political party. He asked her in Arabic what was going on. She explained that she was copying my notes. He wondered why she did not get the notes directly from the teacher, the Brother. She wondered why she needed the teacher when she could get them from a classmate. She was clearly uncomfortable with his line of questioning and he detected it. He did not know that I knew Arabic and that I understood all that he was saying. When he learned later that I knew Arabic, he worked hard to win me, obviously to compensate for his earlier behavior. He eventually became a friend."

"The Dinka believe that, among children, a fight usually ends up in friendship," the Chairman noted.

"Actually, I know that from other personal experiences. I also had another encounter with a Muslim Brother who became a lifelong friend. He saw me reading the Arabic side of the notice board and approached me. 'Can you read Arabic?' he asked. Before I could respond, another colleague who was standing by and knew me injected, 'He is a graduate of Khor Taqqat Secondary School', which implied that I of course knew Arabic. Shortly after, he invited me to have tea with him and a friendship grew."

"That really is ironic that Muslim Brothers would approach you somewhat condescendingly and end up your friends," the Chairman remarked.

"What is even more ironic is that a Muslim Brother nominated me for the executive committee of the Law Society and other Muslim Brothers voted for me while my communist friends did not. My roommate, who was a communist, apologized that he had to tow the party line.

"But my relations with our teacher, the leader of the Muslim Brotherhood, were quite contentious for reasons that were never clear to me. I always participated actively in class discussions and liked asking questions. Most of my teachers liked that and even encouraged it. But I suspect that my Muslim Brother teacher did not. I once asked a question about something I genuinely wanted to know, but inadvertently offended him. That day, there was an attempted coup and our teacher took much of the constitution class time to discuss that incident. After some time, I asked whether that was the lecture of the day or an informal conversation. The class laughed. That surprised me since my reason for asking was because I wondered whether I should have been taking notes.

"My teacher paused, looking at me quite angrily without saying anything. Then he resumed his discussion of the political climate for some time. Finally, he cynically turned to me and stated, 'And now, with your permission, may I begin the lecture of the day?' Without a word, I nodded. After the lecture, he asked me to go with him to his office. I went. But we were not alone, as other students also followed. Then he said to me lightheartedly, 'Just because there is a rebellion in the air, you also want to rebel?!' I explained that I sincerely wanted to know because I wanted to take notes if that was the lecture. He said I should have known how the other students would take it. 'Did you not see how they laughed?' I told him I was myself surprised by that."

"You really got his pride hurt. Are you sure the girl he was to marry did not figure in his emotional reaction?"

"In retrospect, that was probably a factor. At the time, I did not even know what was brewing between them. On another occasion, during a symposium, we were discussing parliamentary system and comparing the bicameral to mono-cameral systems. He spoke in favor of one, I believe the bicameral system, without discussing both comparatively. I asked whether we should not discuss the merits and demerits of the two systems before giving our preference. He responded by saying that the issue was like religion: You are either a believer or you are not. One of the Muslim Brothers who was close to

199

him, the very one who had asked whether I could read Arabic and became a friend, supported my argument. I myself chose to be silent throughout the rest of the session. Whenever he asked me a question, I simply responded by saying that I did not know. I was clearly in a quarreling mood."

"You were quite a fighter against your teacher. That was quite daring of you, considering that he had power over you!"

"As you know, pride and a sense of dignity are among the values deeply ingrained in a person from early childhood in our culture. They cannot be compromised for demeaning utilitarian considerations. Short of walking out, I was prepared for any further action from him," I elaborated.

"I didn't realize you were a soldier at heart," the Chairman remarked.

"Not a soldier, just a proud Dinka."

"How about a proud South Sudanese or African!?" the Chairman corrected me.

"That would be even better, if we were there," I conceded.

"But who will take you there but you?" he probed, rhetorically.

"We should and will together. But let me go back to the story of my relations with my Islamist teacher. His rather adversarial attitude toward me came across very vividly one afternoon as a number of us, his students, including my Muslim Brother friend, sat with him in the Students' Club. One of the students asked him who had won the prize of the first in the class? Without even a gesture toward me, he said 'It had been given' to me. The students began to congratulate me. I had already received the news from one of my European professors, who had congratulated me. But not a word of congratulation came from my Muslim Brother Lecturer, even as the students congratulated me in his company."

"But you must know that what you were experiencing was a minor indication of the monumental national problem that our liberation movement later fought to correct," the Chairman commented.

"I suppose it was both indicative of the national question and personal. Years later, my Muslim Brother friend, who was also close to our teacher, told me that he once asked him what his problem with me was. His answer was that I acted as though I was a lecturer myself and not a student, an accusation I could not in the least understand, as I do not recall ever being insubordinate to any of my lecturers. I certainly never felt what he was accusing me of."

"That clearly confirms that you were a hidden competitor to him in front of his future wife, at least intellectually, especially given the fact that you seemed close to her in the way you helped her catch up. He might even have seen in you a future political thinker who would pose a challenge to his own vision for the nation. But perhaps we are giving him too much credit for foresight."

"It certainly now makes more sense than it did at the time. Interestingly enough, that female colleague told me that it was surprising that my brother was the first student she got to know in her previous Faculty and I the first she got to know in the Faculty of Law. My brother and I actually joked that his loss was my gain. So, in the world of the Muslims, with their sensitivity to any form of gender relations, however innocent, who knows how all that came across?

"Actually, as I noted earlier, there were two girls. One was the sister of the leader of the religious sect and the largest party. The other was the daughter of a prominent lawyer, whose mixed Egyptian Sudanese family was quite liberal. Although I worked with them both at the beginning to help them catch up, it was the daughter of the lawyer with whom I became close. Our friendship in fact drew much attention in the university and beyond. It was clearly an anomaly in the conservative Muslim Arab environment and the North-South divide of our time. After meeting her, my father later asked me whether we were just colleagues or were more than that. I told him that we were colleagues and friends and even if there was more to the relationship than that, she was a Muslim. To my surprise my father asked me, 'And what are you?' I could not believe that my father who gave his consent for us to be baptized as Christians when we were still children would ask that question."

"For them, getting converted to Christianity was just a means to education," the Chairman commented. "They did not consider it binding in a way that would inhibit other aspirations. Besides, since conversion was a flexible means to education, it should be flexible enough to allow the pursuit of other objectives. It's quite a liberal outlook."

"That's exactly right. Going back to my relations with my Muslim Brother lecturer, I was to discover that the world does indeed go around and that our paths would cross in a more positive way. On graduation, I was appointed on the teaching staff of the Faculty and my Muslim Brother lecturer and I became colleagues. And many years later, we again became colleagues in the government, he initially the Attorney General and I Minister of State for Foreign Affairs. And as I noted earlier, he became Advisor to the President and was critical, at least to me privately, of the President's division of the South in violation of the Addis Ababa Agreement. In fact, we became relatively close. One of the diplomats who worked closely with him was to tell me that he spoke highly of me. Perhaps his wife ironically eventually influenced his opinion about me."

"It is quite possible that the qualities he saw in you early that made you come across as a competitor became qualities he admired and led him to accept you as a colleague he respected. That is why you must avoid writing a person off on the basis of specific time-bound events. There is always room and time for change, perhaps in both directions."

"That's for sure. Going back to my visit to Khartoum many years later after the regime's overthrow, the first thing that struck me was how the whole nation was in denial of the former President as the one solely responsible for the crises of governance in the country. It was as though all those who had worked with him were only functionaries or tools of his dictates. Speaking for myself and for a number of colleagues in government, we served him as a leader who had brought peace to the country and unified our people beyond the North-South divide. To say that we were all simply tools of his dictatorial will was insulting to the nation as a whole.

"It reminded me of what I found in Ghana after the overthrow of Nkrumah. I was attending a UN conference in Accra in 1968 and I occupied an office full of files of complaint against Nkrumah. It was astonishing how that African hero was denied by virtually everyone and vilified as the devil incarnate. I was also reminded of my first visit to Germany in 1961, where I also found the nation in denial of Adolf Hitler, said to not even be a German, but an Austrian, and considered solely responsible for what the Nazis did to Germany and indeed the world. I said then, and continue to say now, that unless we identify in society and within ourselves the objective factors that produce a Hitler, we will not be able to prevent the rise of such a monster in our midst."

"That's too refined and forgiving an approach, which is far above the moral order of most people. Scapegoating is much easier. It was because of our own conviction about the shared responsibility that we rejected the military takeover as a continuation of another military regime, even as a transition to the so-called democracy which was a continuation of the Arab domination."

"Going back again to my visit to Khartoum in 1986, my first meeting, as I said earlier, was with the sectarian leader/politician, the former Prime Minister. He told me that the country was threatened by two evils: racism, for which he ironically blamed you, and religious bigotry, for which he blamed his brother-in-law, the leader of the Muslim Brotherhood (my former teacher) and his group. Referring to the Brotherhood, he said, 'That is why I do not miss any opportunity to hit them like a snake'. As he said this, he raised his hand to gesture striking with a stick."

The Chairman commented: "It sounds like the common saying that the best defence is offence, calling the fighter against racism the racist. It's ironic."

"The sectarian leader/politician asked me to join forces with him and gave me a document in which he outlined his policy, to study and then give him my response. In that document, he stated his case against your movement and argued that you were confronting the Arab-Islamic power that was far mightier than them and which they could never defeat. He also considered your movement a predominantly Dinka movement. He said they would be confronted by the alliance of all the other tribes, who are the overwhelming majority, and which they could not defeat. In a way, this has indeed become a self-fulfilling prophecy or is the outcome of their divisive design, as the South has become divided by a complex of identity conflicts that seem to pit the Dinka against an alliance of other ethnic groups."

"Yes, but what he missed or deliberately ignored is that the movement had inspired and mobilized the vast majority of the marginalized peoples of the country who could have overwhelmed the group he assumed to be unbeatable. I think it is fair to say that the identity politics of the Sudan will continue to play out with an uncertain final outcome."

"I agree entirely. My written response to the document of the sectarian/political leader was polite, but unequivocally critical. I said that it was divisive of both the country and the South, and although I did not tell him explicitly, it was clear that there was no way I could join him on that platform.

"The Muslim Brother was equally vicious in his attack on his brother in law. 'I hate to say this,' he began apologetically, 'but whatever he does is selfishly in his own personal interest. He believes that he is the only one qualified to lead his religious sect and the country. I consider myself dispensable and can be succeeded in the leadership of the Brotherhood by anyone else, but not him.' He went on to say that the sectarian leader had betrayed them on several occasions by making secret deals with the former President. Apparently, the sectarian politician had approached them to enter into an alliance with him, but he said that, if they agreed, they would insist that the terms be put in writing.

"Although the sectarian leader won the elections and became Prime Minister, the Brotherhood did surprisingly well, winning a third position in votes. This made them a power to be reckoned with. And their power intimidated the Prime Minister into dishonoring the promise he had made to suspend the application of Sharia.

"When I met the Prime Minister, the issue of my first novel came up. I had been told that he had publicly made critical comments on the book. After discussing the political situation, I alluded to his comments. He was surprisingly complimentary, saying how much he appreciated my addressing the issue of identity and encouraged me to continue to do so. He said that his only complaint about the novel was that instead of remaining with the fictional theme, the story shifted to politics, which he considered divisive.

"The Prime Minister went on to make the case against his political adversaries. 'I have no problem of identity,' he said. 'I know I am an Arab and a Muslim. But I also know that there are other identities in the Sudan. Who is a better leader for the country: the one who recognizes the diversity of the country or the one who denies it?' Of course, it was a rhetorical question which did not need an answer."

"So, he was offering us a choice between two evils, being dominated or only accommodated. It never occurred to him that we could have a better alternative for us to choose from."

"This is the same leader who reportedly said that there was a price to every Southern politician. The main problem with North Sudanese is that they never believed that South Sudanese had a culture, which of course means lacking social and moral values. They also took Southerners as utterly corrupt for reasons of both poverty and greed. All this is compounded by the fact that the poorly educated, who were the first generation of politicians, were alienated from their social and cultural context, which placed them in a void of cultural values without the constraints of their traditions or the norms of the modern context. These are challenges that still confront South Sudanese today."

The Chairman indicated that we were entering a complex area of state and nation building that went beyond our immediate agenda for the evening. "I think we have had enough exchange of views for tonight. And I would like us to discuss your efforts for the peace process with the former President of Nigeria, whom we got to know as your Partner for Peace, which I believe was the title of the book in which you documented your efforts."

We agreed that our next session should cover that issue. After taking my pills, I lay reflecting on the discussion we had just had. I realized that the Chairman was indeed one of the very few South Sudanese, in fact Sudanese generally, who knew our efforts for peace and made a significant contribution to the agreement that eventually ended the last war that had devastated the country from 1983 to 2005. I looked forward to the next session.

Session Twenty: Mediation

As I waited for the Chairman to emerge, I wondered how I would approach the issue of our efforts for peace. The challenge was to recount the facts without self-promotion. That would not be an easy balance.

"Good evening, *Raandit*," the Chairman greeted me, announcing his arrival. "I am eager to hear about your efforts for peace. As I recall, you and your Peace Partner, the Former President, spent quite some time shuttling between us and Khartoum, mediating for peace. How did that come about?"

"Let me begin by saying that I really appreciate your giving me the opportunity to share my experience on this issue," I began.

"Documenting what actually happened ought to be in our mutual interest. I am not at all doing you a personal favor," the Chairman reacted.

"You remember I said that my resignation was the right but reckless decision in view of my family needs for income. Well, within two weeks of my resignation from the government, opportunities began to open up for me. One of those was an invitation by the International Center for Scholars in Washington to be a visiting scholar, to work on a project of my choice. That was when I finished the biography of my father. I was then appointed as the first Distinguished Fellow of a philanthropic fund enabling me to give lectures and seminars to the staff and members of the board. The President was one of those I got to know in the African-American conference in Lesotho in 1976. After two years in that position, I was invited back to the International Center for Scholars, this time in the staff position of a Senior Research Associate. That is when I began to work more directly on the Sudan Peace Process."

"How did your Partner for Peace come into the picture?", the Chairman asked.

"When I went back to the International Center for Scholars, I organized a conference on ending the conflict in the Sudan. All the political parties in the Sudan were invited. All of them, except for the Islamic Front, which transformed itself into the Islamic Charter Front, attended. The Islamic Front sent their charter. I also invited my Peace Partner and a former African American Ambassador to the UN as Senior Statesmen to offer advice.

"My Peace Partner was in Asia as our meeting was about to convene. His wife had just been killed and I called him to express my condolences and to tell him that I fully appreciated that under the circumstances, he would of course not attend. He surprised me by saying that he would attend the opening part of the conference, then rush back home for the funeral of his wife. That was a demonstration of his true loyalty to the African Mother Continent. In fact, in explaining his decision to me, he said, 'As I once told you, I will always respond to any call for the service of Africa.'

"That Conference resulted in the book, *The Search for Peace and Unity in the Sudan*, which I co-edited with the Director of the Center. Ironically, a friend of mine, who would later become a close associate of the Islamic regime in Khartoum, strongly objected to my including the Islamic charter in the book as a promotion of the Islamic agenda. It was one of the areas where he and I sharply disagreed.

"Shortly after the book was published, I got a phone call from my Peace Partner, asking about a follow-up to the conference. When I told him that the book was out, he said we should not let it gather dust on the shelves, but should instead use it as a basis for a peace initiative to end the war. That is how we began our shuttle diplomacy."

"I recall your visits to us in Addis Ababa. That is how your Peace Partner became a good friend and a strong supporter of our movement, especially after he returned to power as the elected President of his country."

"I worked with him very closely, both when he was a member of the Inter-Action Council of Former Heads of State and Government and when he was back as the elected President. Through him I became one of the resource persons that assisted the Inter-Action Council. That was how I joined his delegation with the Former Prime Minister of the United Kingdom on a visit to South Africa as a follow-up to the mission of the Commonwealth Eminent Persons to engage the government of De Klerk on the release of Nelson Mandela, then still in prison. That was my first time visiting South Africa. We went to Cape Town, one of the most beautiful cities in the world. We also visited

Cross Roads, a shantytown on the outskirts of Cape Town, one of the worst slums I have ever seen in my extensive travels around the world. That was when I concluded that no reform of the apartheid regime could bridge the racial divide between the Whites and the Blacks. Any amount of investment to lift up the Blacks would not be enough; and anything taken from the Whites to help the Blacks would be too much. So far, both sides have shown significant understanding and tolerance. How far this will last is a different issue."

"It is in their mutual interest to make it last," the Chairman commented. "Apartheid cannot return, and reversing the tables of racism against the Whites is not a viable option."

"At a social function with De Klerk and his Cabinet after the formal meeting, I said to one of his ministers, 'You know, if I had come to your country during the peak days of the apartheid system, you would have labeled me a Black, my wife a White, and our children Colored. You would have torn my family apart.' Looking at me matter-of-factly, he said, 'You are right; good thing you didn't come.' I was impressed by the honesty of his admission."

"You cornered him. What else could he say? But you are right. His response indicated a genuine change of attitude. He might have been a liberal White. A racist would probably have been evasive."

"Probably. My first encounter with White South African racism actually went back to my days at the University of Khartoum. I was the Secretary General of the St. Augustine's Society. We invited a young White South African Catholic to speak to our Society on the apartheid system of South Africa. Her account was quite emotional and deeply moving. At one point, she could hardly speak. In fact, she sobbed. After some silence, she said, 'Apartheid has to be witnessed to be believed.'

"Later on, while studying in England, I had an eye operation and my nurse was a young, beautiful, and very pleasant White woman. One day, she came to bid me goodbye. I asked her where she was going. She said she was going to South Africa. I asked whether she was going on vacation. She said she was returning home. That's when I realized that she was South African. I could not believe that she was from a country whose very name was synonymous with racism in its worst form. On another occasion, I went to make a phone call when I found someone in the telephone booth waiting for a call. The booth was open. The person waiting for the call greeted me. Then he asked me where I was from. When I told him, he asked how things were there. I asked him where he was from. 'South Africa', he said. 'How are things there?' I asked. He then talked about how good things were in South Africa and how much better off the Blacks were in South Africa than anywhere else on the continent. We both made our calls and I asked him to join me and my South Sudanese colleagues for a drink. We continued our conversation. His main argument was that the Black South Africans were backward and not like us. I asked him how he knew that, since there was no contact between him and the Blacks. The main point is that we had a very engaging discussion, in which race was not a barrier."

"The problem with chauvinism or racism in all its forms is that you dehumanize the 'others' so that, however inhumanely you treat them, you feel no guilt for mistreating a human being. That's why, in the Sudan, Northern Sudanese had a well-deserved reputation internationally as being very kind, hospitable, decent, and noble in their interactions with foreigners, but cruel, inhumane, and brutish in their treatment of Southerners. That was clearly also the case in the attitude of White South Africans."

"What is more, racists genuinely believe in their superiority and the inferiority of others. I recall a very telling event. A colleague who was, I believe, two years behind me in the Faculty of Law, confessed to me his own prejudice by what he presumably intended to be praise for me personally. He said I had liberated him from his racial prejudice. How? He said he used to believe that South Sudanese were intellectually inferior to Northerners. He changed only when he learned that the top of our class was a South Sudanese. Another telling incident was when one Northern Sudanese classmate came to me as we were waiting for the results. He said he came from a poor family and had worked hard to win the prize, which he said he expected and badly needed. It never occurred to him that as his classmate I could be a competitor, presumably because I was a Southerner. But his obvious insensitivity might have made him say the same to a Northerner. Over time, a number of South Sudanese at the University of Khartoum, including several members of my own family, became first in their classes. The myth of Northern intellectual superiority was being repeatedly exploded."

"It's too much of a burden for a people to keep proving their natural equality as fellow human beings," the Chairman interjected.

"What people don't seem to realize is that chauvinism, racism, or ethnocentrism are universally shared. During my second year in England, I participated in an essay competition among foreign students on the subject of race relations. As was to be expected, many students throughout the United Kingdom competed. The ten top essays were selected to receive prizes and be published in a book. Mine was among them. My essay was titled 'Racialism at the Meeting Point'. My thesis was that racialism was universal and that it was a manifestation of pride in one's identity, which was not only natural, but laudable. The problem arises at the "meeting point"—the point where identities begin to compete for recognition and superiority. It then becomes conflictual when one asserts one's superiority and dominance over others. I argued that the solution was to recognize that we are all racists and chauvinists and that we all pride ourselves over all others. Recognizing that shared prejudice could be a foundation for mutual respect: 'They look down on me the same way I look down on them; we are therefore all human, equally proud and prejudiced.'"

"That's quite interesting. But each group would just regard the superiority claimed by the others as simply false and misplaced. They will still consider themselves the justifiably superior group. All the others are false prophets, so I doubt that it would work the way you theorized."

"You are probably right. In fact, the title chosen for the edited volume of essays was *Disappointed Guests*, which of course implied that we were all reacting to White racism. My argument that we were all racists and should recognize that as a shared evil we all needed to address within and among all of us was obviously ignored. I asked for the title to be changed or threatened to withdraw my essay. I was eventually persuaded to accept the title partly because it reflected the theme of the other essays and in any case the thesis of my own essay would speak for itself.

"Going back to White South African racism, I felt that there was a need for dialogue with the White racists in South Africa and Northern Rhodesia (which became Zimbabwe). As Ambassador in Scandinavia, I said to an international conference organized by the Nordic countries that only by talking to the White racists would we understand their fears and explore ways of addressing them. I enraged my African colleagues, especially the freedom fighters in the conference. Later, as Minister of State for Foreign Affairs, I made the same point in the

African–American Conference that we hosted. One representative from the anti-apartheid movement responded rhetorically and, of course, angrily, "Is the Minister suggesting that we talk with the racists of the apartheid regime?' I reaffirmed my position. It was reported in the South African media that our Embassy in Tanzania sent to us as 'a very serious matter'."

"Being right and making one's position public are two different matters. It is appropriate to reveal and argue what may be right, but it may also be appropriate not to make it public until the right time. At that time, Africans did not want to look weak in their fight against racism. You can see that when the time was right, a man who had been the greatest enemy of apartheid was the one who led negotiation with the racists. Even then, it was not an easy initiative."

"I see the point. As Chairman of the OAU, our President, perhaps with my prodding, courageously decided to intercede to try to mediate between the President of Zambia, who was engaging Ian Smith, of racist Northern Rhodesia, and his own more radical colleagues in the region. In Lusaka, in a meeting with the Zambian President, I was shocked to witness the extent to which racism had penetrated the psychology of Black Africans. The President, who had begun to dialogue with Ian Smith, told us that he thought Ian Smith was changing his position in a more positive direction. He said that Smith had come to meet with him and that was waiting in his office while he, the President, was out of his office. When he returned to find his visitor waiting, he said, Ian Smith got up to greet him. 'He actually got up to greet me', he said. I was not sure I had heard him correctly, so I later asked one of my colleagues who had attended the meeting and he confirmed that the President had indeed said that. It was a shocking realization of how domination had lowered the bar of expectation for the Blacks." But I have drifted away from our main topic.

"Actually, all these issues are interconnected. After all, in the Sudan, we also had our own form of apartheid, although less rigid, that required dialogue to resolve," the Chairman commented.

"After my first visit to South Africa, I became closely connected to the country, largely through the activities of the Durban-based Africa Center for the Constructive Resolution of Disputes, or 'ACCORD', and the Cape Town–based Center for Conflict Resolution. The racial problems of the country, while distinct in many respects, became increasingly reflective of problems of racial discrimination and prejudice that are widely shared throughout the world.

"Sometimes, it is not easy to distinguish between racial and class prejudice. I had a rather telling experience on a flight from Durban to Johannesburg. Archbishop Desmond Tutu spotted me as he entered the plane and remarked, 'What are you doing in my country without my knowing?'—which, of course, drew attention to me. Sitting next to me was a White South African who soon engaged me in a conversation that recalled my London discussion with another White South African. The gist of what she said was that, since the end of apartheid, when the Blacks assumed control of the government, the situation in the country had noticeably deteriorated. She specifically stressed the infrastructure. It was as though she was not talking to a Black man."

"That is the class aspect of racism," the Chairman noted. "It does not mean that racism is not at work. It simply means that it is clouded by class emphasis."

"Interestingly enough, the reaction of the Black South Africans to the lingering post-apartheid racial disparities appears to be quite diverse, as I observed on my frequent visits to South Africa. Wherever I go, I usually like to have conversations with taxi drivers to get a sense of what is going on from the perspective of the ordinary person. One taxi driver, commenting on the situation, asked rhetorically, "Is this what we struggled for? That a few Black faces would hold political power while we, the Blacks, remain in the apartheid-like inequalities?' Another said, 'We know the Whites still control the economy and the wealth of the country. But we do not want to shake the system. We know all that will gradually come to us. Let them continue to enjoy it for now.' That seems like a very shrewd and pragmatic attitude."

"It's difficult to tell which of these contrasting positions will prevail in the end," the Chairman commented.

"Of course, inherent in the situation is the usual phenomenon of the dominant group dividing the dominated so that internal conflict will weaken their opposition to the system. I recall a serious clash between the African National Congress and the Inkatha factions. We were having a conference in a hotel in Jo-Burg when we heard a commotion and stepped out to see what was happening. We saw a crowd of young Zulus carrying spears and clubs headed to the ANC Headquarters. At the entrance to the hotel, a man lay bleeding. I asked a policeman who was standing by what was going on. In a calm manner that sharply contrasted with the obvious crisis in the air, he responded, 'Nothing much.'

"Another real paradox of South Africa was an event at which Nelson Mandela, the President of South Africa, was the guest of honor. The event was the launch of a book series by ACCORD on Preventive Diplomacy and my book on the Sudan was the first to be published. The event was held in Cape Town and was well attended by the Diplomatic Corps. As the author of the book being launched, I shared the High Table with Mandela and his Mozambican future wife. We all made speeches as appropriate and Mandela and I exchanged signed copies of the book. Mandela wrote a very flattering inscription about me in my copy of the book, which, needless to say, I was advised to treasure and pass on to posterity. One of my deep regrets is that the book has mysteriously disappeared, either too carefully hidden, or mistakenly given, or, as the Dean of the Faculty of Law in Khartoum once said, in an attempt to conceal accusation of theft, 'unofficially borrowed'."

"Either the person keeping the book has not seen the inscription or has seen it and dishonestly considers the book of material value."

"You are right, it has to be one of the two. The main point about the evening was Mandela's gracious interaction with people at the end. A famous Egyptian Diplomat-Scholar approached him and said, 'Mr. President, my grandchildren will not forgive me if I miss this opportunity to take a photograph with you.' Mandela's response was 'My grandchildren too will not forgive me if I do not take a photograph with you.' He was then informed that the cook and all those who had served wanted to shake hands with him. As they lined up, virtually shaking hands, as I recall almost all White, their leader, the first to speak, said, 'Mr. President, it has been a great honor to serve you.' Mandela responded, 'And it has been a great honor to have been served by you.'

"I was later to have another occasion to witness one of the great virtues of Mandela. A small number, which included his future wife, the widow of the late Prime Minister of Sweden, and several African scholars and intellectuals were gathered. The discussion focused on African leaders about whom much was said of a critical nature. Mandela argued that he had come to know many good African leaders and that the world was unfair in lumping African leaders together as bad. People dismissed what he said as part of his soft-heartedness.

Mandela became visibly irritated, impatiently looking at his watch. Then as he was about to get up to leave, he said, 'Let me tell you, every person, however bad, as a human being, there is some goodness in him. Look for that goodness and build on it to ensure his cooperation with you.' Throughout the discussion, I was in agreement with Mandela, but it was only after he left that I voiced my support for him.

"I have retold this incident on a number of occasions. I told it once in a meeting attended by the Ambassador of the United States who had dealt with the Serbian leaders over Bosnia during the crisis in the former Yugoslavia. After expressing admiration for the idea as noble, the ambassador said, 'There are some people who are just bad, bad, bad, in whom there is nothing good to build upon.' He was of course speaking from personal experience, which cannot be taken as the norm. I personally still believe in this as an aspect of Mandela's wisdom."

"As always," the Chairman said, "the truth must lie somewhere in between. It is like the debate about the death penalty, which is based on total hopelessness in the criminal as a human being, versus other forms of punishment that leave open the possibility of some humane redemption and potential for reform. Neither is entirely wrong or right. And that's why the debate continues. I assume that's why you and your Peace Partner tried to find a solution to our zero-sum conflict with successive governments in Khartoum. As I recall, your mediation initiative began with the government of the sectarian Prime Minister."

"Yes. And that was shortly after the long meeting he had with you in Addis Ababa. I remember what he said about the impression you made on him. He spoke of you as 'head and shoulders' above your colleagues in the movement. He did welcome our initiative and encouraged us to keep moving between the parties. As you will recall, we even planned a secret meeting between the two of you. We were very meticulous in our planning with my cousin, who was your office manager in Addis Ababa. The meeting was to be hosted by the Former President of Switzerland. They even made a plane available to take you to the venue for the meeting in Switzerland.

"We were then in a meeting of all the political parties sponsored by the Inter-Action Council in Harare. As I was quite anxious that everything should proceed as planned, I remained in close contact with my cousin. The Prime Minister announced that he was taking a break

215

for a rest in an unspecified location in Europe. The uncertainty was over you.

"The day before you were to be picked up from a location yet to be specified, we received a wireless message from you saying that you were deep inside the South Sudan's jungles and that even if you were willing to go to the meeting, it was logistically impossible to make it at the fixed time. You went on to say that although you had accepted the principle of the meeting, you had not agreed on the date or the venue.

"Frankly we were outraged, especially as my cousin continued to reaffirm to us that he had kept you fully in the picture, that you had confirmed your agreement with the plans, and that he had documents to back his account. That was the closest I ever got to making a public statement against you. In fact, I drafted a strongly worded letter to you in which we expressed our deep disappointment and anger with you.

"My Peace Partner advised that we should sleep over the draft before sending the letter. The next morning, he was a lot more understanding and forgiving than I was. He said that we should appreciate the fact that you were fighting a war and that priorities while fighting a war were more compelling than those of civilians mediating an end to the war. He asked me to soften the letter so as to be more understanding of your difficult circumstances. He easily persuaded me, perhaps because I did not really want to turn from a friend into a foe."

The Chairman was rather apologetic about that event: "Although it may sound contrived to you, I must have been really absorbed by the war because I do not recall the commitments I made and I cannot say that your cousin was not telling you the truth. I am glad you eventually understood and forgave my behavior."

"Interestingly enough, when we went to Khartoum to report to the Prime Minister, he seemed more understanding than we were, but for totally different reasons. For him, you were not a free agent. You could not attend such a meeting without first clearing with your Ethiopian Host Leader. And the Ethiopian Leader could not agree to a meeting aimed at ending the war in the Sudan, which he was using as a trump card against Sudan's support for the Eritrean liberation struggle. He advised us not to worry about the situation."

"Perhaps we should stop here and in our next session continue your account of the role you and your colleagues played in the cause of peace." With those words, the Chairman ended the session and vanished, quite literally into thin air.

I was quite impressed that I had recounted an incident that almost caused a break between me and the Chairman in a way that was not adversarial and did not at all create any tension between us. Credit went in the first place to my Peace Partner, who was responsible for understanding the difficult war situation the Chairman was in. I was however surprised that the Chairman wanted to hear more about our peace efforts in our next session, which confirmed his genuine interest in what we had done. That added to the depth of my appreciation."

Session Twenty-One: 'Redemption'?

The Chairman was running late by our generally well-established time frame. I began to worry that the separation might be repeated. But I told myself that the Chairman had proved his solidarity with me beyond doubt. Then a sensation rising within me told me that he had arrived.

"Good evening, *Raandit,* I hope you did not think that I was testing you again!"

"How did you know?"

"Is that an affirmation that you did?"

I evaded the question: "Did you have a good day?"

"That is among the questions you do not ask a dead man. Let's get to our subject of the session. You remember that we are to continue to talk about your efforts for peace. And your work on behalf of the movement."

I was quite excited about that, as I had really done much that was not known to our people. This was precisely what the Chairman had in mind in inviting me to record our dual record of achievements or efforts. My motivation now seemed independent of the effect of medication.

In fact, surprisingly, although the dosage of the medication was reduced and the pain was still pretty much controlled, my sessions with the Chairman continued unaffected. I began to believe the psychiatrist that this was something I must have wanted to do and the visitations of the Chairman provided the catalyst. Much of the discussion in the next session focused on developments under the Prime Ministership of the Sectarian Leader.

"Less than two years later, the Prime Minister's failure to solve the pressing problems of the country began to agitate the army. We were attending a meeting in Bergen, Norway, discussing the problems of the country when the army warned the government to either arm the military to be effective in fighting the war or expect a military takeover.

That was the meeting for which I wrote my paper, 'What Is Not Said Is What Divides', in which I argued that what was not openly stated and discussed constituted hidden agendas that were at the root of identity conflicts in the Sudan. You made that article famous by often citing it. While we were still meeting in Bergen, the army issued an ultimatum to the Prime Minister to either equip the army to fight more effectively or expect military intervention against his government. Shortly after, the army seized power in the name of national salvation."

"I remember, you and your friend came to meet with us a few months after the coup. You then chose to go back through Khartoum, against our advice."

"Yes. It was exactly three months after the coup. My principle was to engage with all the parties. You and many others thought it was dangerous to do so, but I insisted as a matter of principle. I learned later that my lawyer colleagues and friends, who were law partners, asked one another whether I had consulted either of them. The answer was No. One of them said 'Let him come, he has never experienced prison.' Both had experienced detention in the famous Kober prison.

"When I got to Khartoum, I went to my senior Dinka colleague, who had led the South under the Addis Ababa Agreement, and he put me in touch with a Dinka officer, one of the three South Sudanese members of the Revolution's Command Council. Through him, I met all the members of the Council. Some of them misunderstood my engagement with them as endorsement. At one point, the leader of the revolution said to me that I would be their ambassador to the United States."

"Was he seriously suggesting that they would appoint you as their Ambassador to the United States? Or did he mean it in a more general sense, such that you would simply speak well of the Government while abroad, rather like an ambassador-at-large?"

"I think it was his way of telling me that they trusted that I would speak well of them and thereby promote their interests. It was probably also an exaggeration of the influence they thought I had in Washington. A friend of mine, who later became close to them at a time when their relations with Washington were at their worst, told me that they thought I was behind all their problems with the United States, another gross exaggeration of my influence. Although I did not in fact tell my friend, it crossed my mind that I should have told him to tell his new friends in Khartoum that we did it together, since I involved him closely in whatever I was doing in Washington. It would, of course, have been a joke.

"I also thought of the Dinka tale of the crocodile and the ball fish. The crocodile used to run away from the ball fish when he inflated himself. One day, the ball fish approached the crocodile in his deflated shape and asked him, 'Why do you run from me, don't you see I have no teeth?' and he opened his toothless mouth to the crocodile. Since then, the crocodile attacks and eats the ball fish. The moral of the story was a careful consideration of whether I should expose the truth to the Sudan government that I did not have the influence to do what they were accusing me of doing or leave them guessing.

"I think he knew that I knew the nature of the role he was playing. In fairness to him, he was very transparent with me. I think he told me this after he fell out with the movement, or he must have known that he was serving two antagonistic sides. As I said previously, it occurred to me later that I should have said to him that he should have told his friends in Khartoum that he and I had done that together. But, of course, he could not have done so in any case, since that would have defeated his purpose. Actually, at the time of my visit to Khartoum, he was still opposed to the new regime."

"You should have told him, to let him know that you were aware of his playing a double role that was inherently ambivalent. I am sure that enhanced his influence on both sides but is also an inherently adventuresome role. As I have said to you on occasion, while I cannot comment on his individual case, such a role can be both useful and suspect by both sides."

"In Khartoum, I asked to visit members of the former government who were in detention in the infamous Kober Prison. The President was taken aback. 'To visit them in prison?', he asked in obvious surprise. I said that since I always met with them when in Khartoum, for them to learn that I was in the country and not visit them, if only on humanitarian grounds, would reflect badly on me. The President approved and asked the council member in charge of security to accompany me. As we drove to Kober, he said to me, 'Doctor, take this as an investment for you to visit us when our turn comes'. The former Prime Minister misread my visit as the government trying to reach out to them for negotiations and began to state their terms!

"The leader of the Muslim Brotherhood was believed to have been also in detention and reported to have been in solitary confinement.

Ironically, it was the Dinka member of the Revolution's Command Council who persuaded the President to have him released. 'Although we differ with him, he is a national leader and should not be humiliated that way,' he said to the President in my presence. He was released from confinement and we met as I was leaving. He was neatly dressed in his white jallabiya and turban, not at all the appearance of a prisoner. All the talk about his detention and confinement was a put-on. As I greeted him, I asked, 'Are you aware that you are seen as the mastermind behind this coup?' His answer was that the Muslim Brotherhood had nothing to do with it, but that he sympathized with the young officers who seized power. 'The country cannot continue in this vicious circle. That's why I support them', he explained."

"In a way, he was right," the Chairman interjected. "The sectarian parties that have alternated control of power since independence never had any alternative to their repeatedly failed policies. The only problem is that the Brotherhood and their proxy so-called revolution were also not offering anything new, only an extreme version of what had repeatedly failed."

"But you joined with them in the National Democratic Alliance? In fact, I never understood how they fit into your vision of the New Sudan, the core of which was separation of religion and state and a refined national identity in which there would be no discrimination on the basis of race, ethnicity, religion, or culture. You know that Islam and Arabism are among the factors that define these sectarian parties. Help me understand."

"I understand why you could not understand. Let me try to explain. The starting point is that New Sudan is an inclusive concept. It embraces all diversities that accept that new framework. The traditional parties accepted the principle of the New Sudan unity framework. How much they would actually live up to the details of the principles embodied in the framework would remain a work in progress. You see, conflict in some form, usually the form of armed struggle, may end, but it continues in other, more subtle forms. The full resolution becomes an ongoing process. I am trying to explain a very complex strategy. I hope I am successful."

"I think I understand. But you are right; it is very complex, and I believe only a few South Sudanese, if any, would fully share your strategic thinking. I was, for instance, surprised that even after you had formed the National Democratic Alliance, you and the sectarian leader, the former Prime Minister, had a falling out and exchanged very acrimonious open letters. In your letter, in which you graciously cited my paper, 'What Is Not Said Is What Divides', you gave a detailed account of the atrocities committed in the South during his two terms as Prime Minister and his unwavering commitment to the policies of Arabization and Islamization. How could you expect to be partners in pursuing your New Sudan Vision?"

"One has to be pragmatic and flexible. Life is an endless search for opportunities to build upon, to borrow your own principle. It is also a pragmatic process of choosing a lesser evil. Our ideal is to make the New Sudan inclusive. Some, like the Muslim Brotherhood, rejected it and we bypassed them. The traditional parties opportunistically welcomed it as a basis for regaining power and preserving national unity and we embraced them. The sectarian former Prime Minister was one of those who obviously vacillated and we also vacillated in our relationship with him and his party. When we had that exchange of letters, he was veering towards an alliance with the Muslim Brotherhood. So, we confronted him."

"It is all fascinating. I suppose that also explains why and how you reached out to the Arab world, specifically Egypt and Libya!?"

"Egypt, of course, has a long historical connection to the Sudan, North and South. And their national interest over the Nile waters takes priority over the commitment to Arabism and Islam, although you can say that Egypt was the champion of modern Arab nationalism. That historical connection, and interest in the Nile, of necessity includes South Sudan. Since the unity of the Sudan, indeed of the Nile Valley, is a high priority for them, our New Sudan Vision naturally appealed to them.

"Libya was a different case. They loved our commitment to unity, but they would have preferred us to embrace Arabism. In fact, when I visited Libya, Gadhafi tried to persuade me to declare myself an Arab as a condition for his full support for our movement. I was too dumbfounded to respond. But President Museveni, who happened to be there with me, came to my rescue by asking Gadhafi how he would respond to being asked to change his color of skin? Gadhafi got the point and ended the matter there. He gave us the support we needed, but I knew that he was erratic and that his support would not last. So, we saved much of what he gave us for the rainy day we knew would come sooner than later."

"Frankly, I am not surprised. This is in fact what I always knew and admired about you: keeping your eyes on the prize and flexibly making use of every opportunity to learn, educate, and gain support. No permanent enemies, hoping for permanent friends, but be prepared to lose some, and welcome them back, should they return, which they often did because their departure was without principle."

"I remember you used to say that Liberation should be pursued through various means: armed struggle; negotiated settlement; *intifada* or popular uprising; development; and diplomacy. It all sounds paradoxical, but I understood and supported your strategy."

"I can see you are a permanent friend."

"I hope so. I have no reason to leave and return. Anyway, let me go back to my visit to Khartoum. One of the members of the Revolution's Command Council with whom I met was said to be the intellectual of the revolution. I was told that he had only fifteen minutes for the meeting. We ended up discussing for nearly two hours. Essentially, I was arguing that the young men and women from the South in the rebel movement represented a new generation, with aspirations for a united Sudan and not just for the South. I said that I had collected their morale-boosting war songs that demonstrated remarkable self-confidence in their struggle for a New Sudan without discrimination on the grounds of race, ethnicity, religion, culture, or gender. He listened to me very attentively. In the end, he said how much he had enjoyed talking to me and listening to all I had to say. 'But just remember that there is another point of view', he said. That other point of view was, of course, their Arab-Islamic vision for the country."

"It boggles the mind that these people insist on a divisive religious identity when unity can amicably accommodate diversity. I always told them to accept that religion is for God and the country is for all, which is in fact the slogan that used to guide politicians in the Sudan. On numerous occasions, I used to say that the state has no religion, that I never saw a state go to the mosque on Friday or to the church on Sunday. On Judgment Day, we will face The Lord as individuals, not as States. But they are obviously victims of blinding Faith and cannot see any other Truth."

"But, to be fair to them, they want to liberate themselves from the yoke of inherited Western systems of government by building their national identity on the basis of their Islamic Faith, which is integrally connected to Arabism as both a racial and a cultural concept. When I visited Khartoum three months after the religiously inspired Revolution for National Salvation, I was asked to address the conference on what they called the National Peace Issues. At first, I was reluctant. I said I was there to learn, not to speak. But the Southern member of the Council, among others, argued that my refusal to speak might be misconstrued. So I decided to speak and frankly stated my views on the national identity crisis behind the conflict.

"After stressing my preference for unity as part of my family background, I presented a choice between what might be called the New Sudan Vision and the partition of the country on the basis of unbridgeable religious differences. If the unity of the nation was the priority, then they had to accept the separation of state and religion. If their version of Islam was their priority, then they had to accept that the unity of the country could not be sustained. In the question-and-answer exchange, a senior Muslim leader, who had been Minister of Religious Affairs when I was in the government, commented that if the choice was as I stated it, then, of course, they would choose their religion over national unity."

"That is a superficial view of a more complex and challenging situation. Sudan is not the only country where different religions co-exist and the people have not been torn apart by their religious differences."

"Perhaps I should have presented the choice differently. It is not a case of preferring unity over religion as such, but a divisive interpretation of religion. After all, in the Sudan, there are different versions of Islam."

"That's right. In fact, the more tolerant Sufi Islam has been the dominant version in the Sudan until the Orthodox versions more recently infiltrated the country and took over."

"I recently heard quite an interesting story that underscores the point you are making. It is said that a leading figure in the Islamist revolution went to one of the prominent Paramount Chiefs of the Hamar Arabs and asked them to support the revolution. The Chief assured him that they were not opposed to the revolution. The Islamist leader said he meant more than not opposing them: 'We want you to join us in the war against the infidel Dinka'. The Chief said to him, 'Sa'atak, Sir, these people whom you describe as infidels are our brothers. We co-exist peacefully, we intermarry, and we trade with them. We have no reason to fight them.' This actually shows that even among the Muslims, there is religious diversity in unity.

"My presentation proved to be quite provocative, praised by some, especially Southerners, who intimated to me later that it had freed them to speak their mind openly, and condemned by others, especially the hardline Northerners. However, I later understood that Northerners were divided between those who argued that my frank talk was precisely what was needed, and those who objected that I was at all given the platform. 'This is the Chairman of the rebel movement himself', they were reported to have said. The hardliners, of course, prevailed. My diplomatic passport was withdrawn, to be returned only later after some prominent personalities intervened on my behalf."

"Typical Northern courtesy or hypocrisy."

"The President himself complimented me by saying that I was reported to have made a very good speech and how he himself would have liked to attend. He said that the downside of the responsibility of the Presidency was that time constraints prevented him from doing many things he would have liked to do, he explained.

"Ironically, despite the initial withdrawal of my passport, shortly after my return to Washington I got a message through the Embassy that the President wanted to invite me back to the Sudan for consultations. But first I was to have secret meetings in London with two members of the Revolution's Command Council, the Southern Sudanese member who had taken care of my program, and the member in charge of security who had escorted me to Kober prison.

"In the meeting, they requested that I renew my mediation efforts for peace. I expressed willingness as a matter of principle, but that there had to be some ground to build upon. What was new in the situation that would provide motivation for undertaking a mediation initiative? That question provided food for thought, but no ready answer. I then suggested to them that we should involve a friend of mine who was residing in Oxford. So we went to Oxford, where we had a very animated discussion.

"The meeting with my friend was socially cordial, and politically very candid. The delegation wanted us to engage in a mediation process between them and the rebel movement. I repeated the point I had already made to them earlier: We needed to find a positive basis for taking a mediation initiative. My friend stressed the oppressive policies the government was pursuing, which could not justify any peace initiative by us. We agreed to observe the developments and, should a positive basis emerge, we would then respond accordingly.

"On my flight back to Washington, I bumped into the US Assistant Secretary of State for African Affairs, with whom I already had close working relations. Although our meeting with the delegation from Khartoum was supposed to be secret, news had leaked to the media and the Assistant Secretary had read about it. He suggested to me that we should meet in the State Department to discuss how we might take advantage of the request of the government for a peace initiative.

"I met him and his staff at the State Department. At the end of the meeting, he made a proposal that was both stunning and intriguing. If the government was seriously committed to federalism, and if the movement about wanting the Sudan to remain united was genuine, then the war should be ended immediately by asking the government forces to withdraw from the South. The movement must then not be allowed to take advantage of the situation toward separatism. He said I should present the idea to the parties as my own, but also tell them that I was quite sure it would be supported by the United States."

"What a revolutionary idea. How did you take it?"

"I could not believe that he was serious. I thought he was joking. For a moment, I reflected without commenting. Then it suddenly hit me that it was indeed potentially the fastest way to peace. Sure, the details of federalism and the precise framework of unity could be worked out. But the war could stop immediately."

"So, how did you respond to him?"

"I said as much. The question was how to pursue the idea that I should present the proposal as my own but tell the parties that I was confident of American support. I left the State Department truly excited by the idea. However, I decided that I should persuade my Peace Partner, the former President of Nigeria, to join me in taking the proposal to the parties. He wanted to know the message. I said it would be better to explain to him in face-to-face discussion. He wanted me to give him at least some idea about it. I decided that we should not talk of the government 'withdrawing' from the South, but rather of 'disengagement' of forces.

"He agreed. We fixed the time for our mission. And he said he would try to get his President's plane to take us."

"You must have felt overawed by the mission."

"Absolutely! But we were also convinced of its potential importance.

"In Khartoum, we were very warmly received, and we held intensive discussions with a wide range of interlocutors. One of our earliest discussions was with a senior colleague who had earlier introduced me to the leaders of the revolution to assess how the government might receive the message. He thought that it would be well received. In the meeting with the President, he asked for a more precise explanation of 'disengagement'. An Islamist physician with a close connection to the regime said, 'If that will end the war, why not?'

"As you will recall, our meeting with you was quite dramatic. With you were three commanders: the two who later attempted a coup against you, and my cousin. After we presented the proposal, frankly explaining that it was an American initiative, you asked the senior member of the three for his reaction. To our surprise, he said that the declared policy of the movement was to preserve the unity of the country. They should therefore not endorse a proposal that might be seen as separatist. You then turned to the second member to respond. He said that his position was the same with that of his colleague. When you asked my cousin to respond, he said, 'No comment'.

"We were quite surprised by their responses. But then you came with a response which we thought was a wise exercise of leadership. You said you were fighting to free your land from the Arabs. If that goal could be achieved peacefully, why should you reject it and risk more bloodshed? What you objected to was having the message delivered by one of your countrymen and a friend. If the Americans were serious about the proposal, they should be the ones to make it directly to the parties. That was the message we took back to Washington."

"The Americans never came to us with the proposal of asking Khartoum to withdraw its troops from the South," the Chairman commented.

"No. Actually they changed their position. I remember the American *chargé d'affaires* in Khartoum coming to my office at the Brookings Institution to discuss the proposal with me. He clearly feared the repercussions on his own situation in Khartoum. He said, 'If that is to be our policy, I should expect to be immediately kicked out of Khartoum. But if that is our position, then we should pursue it openly.'

"Apparently, the idea was opposed by the military advisors. It was eventually watered down to the separation of forces and pulling out of Juba by a specified distance of miles. The proposal appeared both inconsequential to the course of the war and unacceptable to the parties. It became increasingly misinterpreted as my idea, aimed at partitioning the country and promoting the independence of the South. An idea we thought could immediately end the war became a mere smoke screen."

"You ceased to be the Ambassador that the so-called government of national salvation thought you might be for them!"

"Far from it. Over time, as I noted earlier, the regime began to see me as a separatist and the one responsible for all their problems with the United States. At least that was what my friend told me when he was *chargé* in Khartoum during the interim period."

"As I recall, was the regime not hostile to your second novel?

"I don't know whether the regime had a position, but individuals within the regime probably did, as became evident later on."

"Under what circumstances did you write that novel and how was it received by Khartoum?"

I gave the Chairman a detailed account of the process of writing that novel and the gist of the story.

"I wrote it almost immediately after I finished the first novel. It was as though I was under a spell to write. As I said earlier, the narrative flowed as though dictated and all I did was put it down in writing. It was unbelievable. In the second novel, I treated the issue of identity in a much more fictional fashion than was the case in the first novel, which the sectarian former Prime Minister criticized as political. As I noted earlier, the story in the second novel involved two individuals who represented the contrasting models of identity in the country, the Arab-Islamic and the African-Secular visions of the North and the South. They discover at the end of the story that they are in fact half-brothers. The girl the hero was seeking to marry was initially revealed to be a blood relative, in fact a half-sister, but the reality was that she was adopted and not a blood relative. Whether they should marry became a case of conflict between the law and social prejudice. The novel got mixed reactions in Khartoum, both condemned and praised, depending on how people felt about the crisis of identity in the country."

"Although many of your books authoritatively document your ideas about the crisis of identity in the Sudan, your novels proved to be the most effective way of awakening the people's consciousness. I think it was a smart move to have them translated into Arabic."

"Actually, I believe I am more known in the North for those novels than for any other of my numerous books. I remember sitting alone in the waiting area at El Obeid airport on a UN flight to the Blue Nile State. A man approached me and said, "You look familiar. Were you not a minister in the government?' I decided to answer by giving my name. 'By God Almighty! Are you the author of that famous book about *The Bird of Doom*?" He mentioned the Arabic title of the book and I answered affirmatively. Then he heaped much praise on me and the novel.

"But that novel also provoked hostile reactions in some quarters in Khartoum, which is why I said there was probably no unified position within the regime, and that individuals reflected conflicting positions. It was reviewed by a journalist who probably had not read it but described it as another *Satanic Verses* and me as the Sudanese Salman Rushdie. Concerned by the implications, the US Embassy in Khartoum sent a message to the State Department in Washington, which informed me. I jokingly asked the Assistant Secretary of State for African Affairs what a Salman Rushdie without the means to protect himself does. His humorous response was, 'He calls 911'.

"Ironically, shortly after that, I got a telephone call from the Sudanese Embassy in Washington, informing me that the Muslim Brotherhood Leader, the spiritual leader of the ruling Islamic regime, would be visiting Washington, and the Ministry of Foreign Affairs in Khartoum wondered whether I could organize a speaking event for him. I organized a working lunch and among those invited was a diplomat who had served in the Sudan and with whom I had worked closely when I was Ambassador in Washington. He had heard of the reaction to my book in Khartoum. When he received the invitation, he called to tell me that he could not help laughing as he thought to himself, 'Only in the Sudan would Salman Rushdie invite Khomeini to lunch!'

"In the luncheon meeting, I posed a question, prefacing with an apology that we do not shy away from asking our guests tough questions. I reminded the Leader of the Brotherhood what he had said when I met him at the Kober prison, that they had nothing to do with the coup. Now, he was known to be the spiritual leader of the revolution. What had changed? His answer was that the regime was achieving by military means the Islamic agenda that they had not been able to achieve by political means. So they had agreed to enter into alliance with them.

"When I went to Khartoum after that, a journalist asked me how I felt about my book being described as a second *Satanic Verses* and myself as the Salman Rushdie of the Sudan. I seized the opportunity to speak about the book. That's when I learned that the journalist had not even read the book. The Minister of Information and Culture, who was a lawyer and familiar with my works, told me that *he had* read the book and dismissed the journalist's review as based on ignorance. He actually ordered a number of copies to distribute among his colleagues. It is interesting that the ruling National Islamic Front also ordered about ten copies, presumably to inform themselves on how to counter the policy objectives of the book."

"They are certainly very clever and astute. Remember, they have the fundamental principle that whatever you do for the cause of Islam is acceptable even if it violates the moral code of Islam. So, paradoxically, they were promoting your book in order to fight it. Anyway, let's talk in our next session about your efforts in Washington for the cause of peace in our country." And with that, the Chairman vanished.

I have long been aware that the manner in which I related to Northerners, including the Islamists who had just assumed power, was confusing to both sides. Southerners still thought that I was a unionist with a political agenda close to that of the North, while Northerners thought that I was a Southern nationalist and a separatist who was cleverly trying to delude the North into thinking that I was closer to them. That I was from Abyei added a confusing anomaly to the situation. Only a few from both sides fully understood my position and appreciated it. The Chairman was one of those.

Session Twenty-Two: Advocacy

More and more, I was looking quite normal during the day, especially with the medication much reduced. My wife was still aware that my behavior in the evening was not entirely normal, but she accepted it. After all, since the meeting with the psychiatrist, she now knew more or less what was going on and did not try to probe further. I now *wanted* to tell my story and the Chairman provided me with the means for doing that. I was clearly having fun with the exercise.

Interrupting my musings, the Chairman arrived and immediately got to the point: "As I said in our last session, I want us to focus today on the excellent work you did for us in Washington."

"You are right, promoting you in Washington was climbing a mountain, not a hill. But that made our success very gratifying. The starting point is that you were seen in Washington as stooges of the communist regime in Ethiopia. This created a paradoxical situation in which there was much sympathy for the cause of the South and hostility to the movement that was fighting for that cause. The challenge I put to myself was to try to bridge that gap.

"The first step in doing that was to reemphasize what everyone knew: that, while the cause of the South was widely supported around the world, partitioning the Sudan was opposed by the international community. Ethiopia, which was fighting for its own unity, was the only country that was supporting the liberation struggle of the South in a very substantial way. To ensure support not only from Ethiopia but also from Africa and the international community generally, it was pragmatic for the South to fight for justice in a restructured New Sudan, rather than for separation. The socialist agenda of the movement was not an ideological conviction, but a tactic for gaining and maintaining the aid of Ethiopia, the only reliable source of support.

"That argument slowly gained ground. I recall a meeting I had early on with the then Assistant Secretary of State for African Affairs. We were attending a conference about philanthropy at the Rockefeller

Conference Center outside New York. I talked about the myths of identity behind the dominant system that the New Sudan concept of the movement was trying to correct. The Assistant Secretary seemed intrigued and suggested that he convene a meeting at the State Department to continue our discussion of the matter with members of his staff.

"That was the beginning of discussions with successive Assistant Secretaries of State and other centers of power around Washington. I made effective use of my position as Senior Fellow at the Brookings Institution, a leading Washington think tank where I had established the Africa Project and directed it for twelve years.

"The Project covered a number of African policy priorities—including conflict prevention, management, and resolution as well as good governance, human rights, and development issues—on which we organized a series of conferences and discussion groups and produced numerous publications. I placed a special emphasis on the Sudan and created a core group of dedicated friends of South Sudan that eventually became known as 'The Council'."

The Chairman recalled: "I got to know them well. They were truly friends of South Sudan, and very committed to our struggle."

"It started with a surprise visit to me by a man in his forties when I was still at the Woodrow Wilson Center. He wore long hair bound by a rubber band in the back, which made it look like a ponytail. He introduced himself as the Executive Director of the US Committee for Refugees. He said he believed in the just cause of South Sudan and wanted to be of help. I thought he was a wealthy hippy who wanted to offer financial support. But he said that he could not offer material support; he could only assist by gathering and disseminating information."

"You probably got disappointed that he was not offering money!"

"In a way, yes, but I also recognized the importance of educating the Americans by sharing information about the movement. I put him in contact with my cousin who was the director of your office in Addis. He soon proved to be a very useful ally through the dissemination of information and overall advocacy."

"Indeed, a vitally important contribution."

"I recruited the second member of the council when I joined Brookings. He was then a policy analyst with the Congressional Research Services and was well connected to leading members of

Congress. I initially wanted him to join me in the African Studies Program I was establishing at Brookings, but we soon realized that he was playing an important role where he was."

"Being connected to Congress meant access to power."

"Absolutely, especially as he was advisor to the Chairman of the House Sub-committee on African Affairs. The fact that he was originally an Ethiopian who had fled Mengistu's regime and had become connected to the inner circles of the Intelligence community made him a very valuable member of our evolving council. He later explained that his support for the cause of the South went back to his family in Ethiopia, as he observed the sympathy and material support his father gave South Sudanese refugees in Ethiopia. Because his first name was Theodore, which had a Greek ring to it, and came from imperial Ethiopia, prompted me to give him the nickname of 'The Emperor', which he soon took to heart. We enhanced his imperial image by making him our Chairman."

"And he rose to that honor!"

"Very quickly. We were joined in the council by your colleague and friend from Iowa and later by an activist who was with an NGO called Interaction. And then came an academic at a well-known liberal college who initially contributed works of art and became the most prolific writer for the cause. A number of others became members through ad-hoc participation in our luncheon meetings at the Otello Restaurant at Dupont Circle. The council increasingly grew an active profile that informally but effectively helped shape a positive image for the movement in Washington. Years later, an article about the council projected what amounted to a miracle in positively influencing US policy toward the movement and the cause of South Sudan."

"We closely followed that development and the rising profile of The Emperor, your Chairman."

"He rose to the title, often demanding from his 'subjects' that they get up when talking to him on the phone. That extended to you. And after you, your successor inherited the support of the Chairman. He became officially engaged by our government as advisor to the President. He even relished the ritual deference he still enjoyed as Emperor, at one time telling me that his subjects had gone beyond standing up to kneeling down when talking to him on the phone."

"I see that some of your council members have disappeared from the scene while others have now become very critical of the situation in our country, obviously disappointed by our failure to live up to the noble objectives of our struggle."

"The disappointment is compounded by the fact that it really was a hard sell to shift the position of Washington from hostility to genuine support not only for the cause, but also for the movement and your leadership.

"Another institution that played a critical role in supporting our cause was the US Institute of Peace (or USIP). When it was first instituted in the mid-1980s, I was one of the first 'Jennings Randolph Distinguished Fellows' to be appointed. My fellowship resulted in a major book, *War of Visions: Conflict of Identity in the Sudan.* They continued to support my activities on the Sudan and funded a number of related initiatives over the years. A Former Assistant Secretary of State for African Affairs, who was then Chairman of the USIP Board, and I co-chaired a forum on the Sudan which met periodically for quite a while as the peace process was advancing."

"Of course, I knew what you people were doing for us in Washington. I also knew that you were doing all that for our people, not for recognition or any personal benefits. As you well know by now, this was why I wanted us to have these conversations."

"And as you also know, I very much appreciate it. I really think we succeeded remarkably in changing policy perspectives on the Sudan. It was in one of the discussion groups on the Sudan in which many Northern Sudanese intellectuals in Washington participated that my Peace Partner/Former President, with whom I had already been actively engaged in the peace process, asked the group whether I stood a chance of ever becoming the head of government in the Sudan. The unequivocal response from all of them was a resounding 'No'. 'Why?' my Peace Partner asked. 'Because he is not an Arab and not a Muslim' came the response. He then posed a rhetorical question: 'How can you then expect a person who is eminently qualified for leadership but denied that opportunity because of his religion and race to want to be a citizen of that country?' I thought they could have been clever enough to give other reasons that would disqualify me instead of exposing their racial and religious intolerance the way they did. My Peace Partner would often retell that incident in my presence, always apologizing that he did not want to embarrass me."

"I suppose by then our image in Washington had significantly improved?"

"Very much so. But I repeat that it had really been a monumental challenge. I recall a meeting I had with the Assistant Secretary of State for African Affairs and his team in the State Department, when you were still unpopular in Washington. I challenged them to explain what they objected to about the movement. They were vague in their response. I suggested that we list ten specific problem areas in which the US would like the movement to take corrective action. We would then fix a timeframe for action, say six months. After that period, we could then meet with the movement to check the process of implementation, ticking off where action had been taken, and marking areas of failure where action was still needed. The point was well received, although no specific areas were identified.

"Once you were welcomed in Washington, you began to charm the policy makers with your persuasive style, intellect, and humor. As I attended most of your meetings at the State Department, Congress, and other decision-making centers, I observed firsthand how you began to turn the tide. You then visited Washington rather frequently, and eventually established an office and appointed a representative in Washington, supported by the US. We organized meetings and discussion groups at several think tanks and universities around Washington, some of which we held at my institution and which I moderated myself. You and I often appeared together in meetings, including those organized by others. I remember one that was very well attended. At one point you were responding to something Khartoum had said. Angrily, you referred to it as 'bullshit' and I jokingly remarked, 'Mr. Chairman, remember that where we come from, we think very highly of bullshit.' People roared with laughter.

"I remember an all-party conference on the Sudan, convened by the Carter Center and moderated by Archbishop Desmond Tutu. I suggested that they extend an invitation to an Islamic scholar who had in fact written a book about the leader of the Muslim Brotherhood and was a press attaché for the new regime in London. I was asked to prepare and present a concept paper for the conference. An American diplomat who sat next to me in a bus as we rode to the venue of the meeting asked me about developments in the Sudan. After I explained the situation, he asked whether I was a Northerner or a Southerner. I asked him back whether, based on what I had said, he *thought* I was a Northerner or a Southerner. He said he thought I was a Muslim from the South. I then explained that I was neither a Muslim nor strictly speaking a Southerner, since I was from Abyei, between the North and the South."

"You must have really confused him. He must have wondered how you could have the dual identity."

"When I presented my paper, I told the story of my conversation with the American diplomat. In the discussion that followed, one of the Northern political leaders opposed to the ruling Islamist regime responded by saying that I spoke not as a Muslim from the South, but as a Muslim from Iran. I thought that was a testimony to my objectivity, which Bishop Tutu noted and continued to do so with lavish support over the years. But one South Sudanese with whom I later shared the story thought that it was a sad indication of the ambivalence of my position between North and South. That is how zero-sum black-and-white the division of the country had become."

"That is the division that our movement was effectively erasing. I believe we succeeded in changing the mindset from seeing the problem as 'Southern' to making it 'National'. But, of course, the regime worked hard to divide us in the South."

"Interestingly enough, an area in which the gulf between the United States and your movement began to narrow incrementally was, paradoxically, the discord within your movement, which was largely encouraged by the NGO community operating in South Sudan. Most of them still saw you as agents of socialism and began to persuade your critics in the movement that if they came out openly against the New Sudan Vision, declared their commitment to the goal of South Sudanese independence, and advocated respect for human rights and humanitarian principles, they would almost certainly gain the support of the West and take over the leadership of the movement from you. The infamous, vivacious young English humanitarian who eventually married one of your opposition leaders played a key role in the process."

"I read some of the reports and comments of those NGOs and met some of them, including the English humanitarian herself. Their hostility was quite contagious. It eventually erupted in the abortive coup of 1991 that nearly destroyed our movement. The rest is a well-known history.

"We were almost defeated as a result. For a while, we lost the support of Ethiopia—the new leaders stood with Khartoum against us. But support for our cause in the region had become well established.

And some of our friends were allies of the US. So we indirectly benefited from that connection too. That was how we eventually reversed our downward slide. Even Ethiopia came back as a dependable ally to our cause."

"During the coup attempt against you, our group that became known as the Concerned South Sudanese was meeting at Adare, Ireland. The objective was to clarify the position of South Sudan on the Vision of New Sudan and the alternative pursuit of self-determination toward the prospects of Southern independence. Although we supported you against the rebels and sent you a message of our support, I believe there was also sympathy among some of us for their call for self-determination and independence for the South.

"The concept note, background papers on issues, and the declaration I had drafted for the meeting proved to be more controversial than I had anticipated. The controversy was around the objectives of the struggle. Of the whole group, I believe only I remained committed to the Vision of the New Sudan. In fact, a friend of mine later told me that I was the only South Sudanese he knew who shared your Vision for the New Sudan. I could not believe that he was right, but perhaps he was embellishing a kernel of truth.

"As you know, the Concerned Group later focused their efforts on organizing a conference, in which your movement would participate, to discuss and agree on the objectives of the struggle. The idea was, of course, to promote consensus on self-determination. I shuttled between the group and you in an attempt to bridge the differences. When you made your position against the conference unequivocally clear to me, that is when I resigned from the group."

"Then they tried to go around you to organize an alternative conference with the support of your Peace Partner and you foiled that too," the Chairman recalled.

"That's right. These two episodes created a major rift between me and my friend that would take years to mend. But another area of conflict between us was the operation of slave redemption that he was engaged in with a Swiss religious organization. I was strongly opposed to this operation, not only because I thought it was revoltingly doing business with slave traders—in effect rewarding them for their crime instead of prosecuting and punishing them—but, worse, I came to know that the operation had become a morally depraved source of corruption. Children who had never been enslaved were paraded as redeemed slaves. And a brown Dinka was dressed up as an Arab, with jallabiya and turban, to play the role of the slave trader. The operation, which took my friend to the area on a chartered plane every month, became a money-making exercise."

"We were aware of all this and our people were initially torn between appreciating the humanitarian work of the organization and bringing an end to what they saw as a disgraceful business operation."

"I once hosted my friend and his slave-redemption partners, including the President of the Swiss Agency and his field operator, for dinner. When asked for an opinion on the operation, I tried to be polite but frank about my reservations. I put it in terms of feeling ambivalent about the operation. On the one hand, I of course welcomed the redemption of enslaved children. On the other hand, I found it unacceptable that slave traders be rewarded instead of punished. Besides, I said I was hearing that our people were being corrupted by this operation. The Swiss Agency President responded to my comments by saying that if people like me had such reservations, then they should reconsider the wisdom of the operation. My family later told me that they thought I had been too hard on our guests.

"The next morning, my friend told me that he could not sleep all night. He said he would understand foreigners having reservations, but for a South Sudanese to be critical of an operation that was rescuing our children from slavery was something he could not understand. I told him that it was precisely because of my concern for my people that I opposed an operation that was rewarding criminals and encouraging moral depravation among them. We could not find a common ground.

"I remember that my friend and I discussed the case with you in Uganda. We were to go to you together, but I arrived before him. I presented my point of view to you. Then my friend came and made his case. Your response was, 'I see I am called upon to walk a tight rope; but we are used to walking tight ropes.' Later on, the leadership of your movement condemned the operation and you decided to end it. This of course enraged my friend and was the determining factor in his turning against you. He turned from a friend to a bitter enemy.

"Even after that, you tried hard to reconcile us, without much success."

"As you will recall, even the famous marathon meeting you had in London, which I had initiated, but could not attend, did not go far. You remember that I organized a dinner in my house in Washington to follow up on the London meeting with only the three of us. My friend candidly denied that there had been a reconciliation in the London meeting. We ended on a positive note, but even that in the end was a futile exercise."

"As I told you on several occasions, the problem was really his, for I did not think you had done anything to warrant his hostility. So, I was never bothered by his hostility. What about the Swiss peace initiative in which I asked you and him to represent us?"

"Yes, that was when he and I were still working closely together. As you will recall, you said that you wanted those of us who supported the movement without being card-carrying members to represent you. If we succeeded in producing positive results, you would claim us; if we did not, you would deny us. The process involved what became known as The Quartet, with two members from the government side and the two of us. We met several times, with the composition of the Khartoum team changing each time and ours remaining constant. Some of their members later played key roles in the peace process. As you well know, one of them became First Vice-President and he and you became the decisive players in the peace process that resulted in the Comprehensive Peace Agreement.

"But even on that issue, while we worked well together in our dialogue with the government delegation, we had our differences on matters of significant details. My friend's position was that you were not negotiating in good faith. I asked him what he meant by negotiating in good faith and what he thought negotiating in good faith would achieve. I was really surprised by his response. He said that if we negotiated in good faith, he was sure we could get an agreement that was better than the Addis Ababa Agreement. That told me that his expectations of the liberation struggle for South Sudan were far more modest than the call for self-determination that he was vigorously promoting. A strong autonomy would probably have been good enough for him."

"As I have also told you on numerous occasions, those who shouted loudly for self-determination without the tools to bring it about would almost certainly end up compromising on an agreement that would basically have maintained the status quo, with the North still dominating the system. You and your friend also played a role in the Inter-Governmental Authority for Development (or IGAD) peace process."

"Yes. That process was initiated in the early 1990s by an Ethiopian director of an organization committed to addressing African causes. The Resource Persons group initially comprised the two of us and a number of prominent African personalities. Periodically, we invited others to specific meetings. Among those were a former US Assistant Secretary of State for African Affairs and my Peace Partner/Former President of Nigeria.

"I was later told by the director that a concept paper I had prepared for a meeting at the Peace Institute provided the basis for the IGAD Declaration of Principles on which the Comprehensive Peace Agreement eventually hinged."

"Actually, what made the difference eventually was the pressure exerted on us by the Troika of Norway, UK, and particularly the United States," injected the Chairman. "IGAD had become too divided and weakened to effectively pursue the peace process."

"And yet their initiative was crucial not only in starting the peace process, but also in giving it regional legitimacy and laying out the substantive framework for resolution," I resumed. "I remember my first meeting with the Eritrean President in Washington. They had just taken their initiative. The meeting, which was at his request, was scheduled for I believe twenty minutes. It lasted for well over an hour. The President recalled that we first met when I was Minister of State for Foreign Affairs and he was, in his own words, a fugitive. That was when we were negotiating with Ethiopia on the Eritrean problem.

"He then told me that he did not understand why you wanted unity with the North. He said that they had closely observed the racial inequalities against the South in the Sudan. He said the Arabs of Central Sudan were clearly the first-class citizens; Western Sudanese, who, though not Arabs, were Muslims and somewhat Arabized, were second-class citizens; and they, refugees from Ethiopia and Eritrea, followed as third-class while Southerners came last as fourth-class citizens. How could they accept unity in such a country? He could have added the Muslims from Nigeria and other West African countries as falling into the fourth class, leaving South Sudanese as fifth-class citizens.

"I explained in great depth that your position was more complex than that. I told him that you wanted to liberate not only South Sudanese and other non-Arabs in Northern Sudan, but also the so-called Arabs who were in fact culturally Arabized Africans from their distorted self-perception, which they were imposing on the whole multi-racial and multicultural country. I explained further that, even if the South were to be independent, the only way to guarantee that independence was to transform the system in the North. He was fully persuaded to your policy orientation.

"I also met the Prime Minister of Ethiopia and gave him the same orientation. From that time on, I maintained close relations with them. Every time they came to Washington, they requested to see me. And, of course, our Resource Group followed the negotiations very closely and cooperated with the IGAD Ministers in developing strategies and responses to the positions of the government. It was a remarkable partnership.

"Years later, after the war with Ethiopia and the isolation of Eritrea internationally, the Eritrean President attended the independence celebrations in Juba. As UN Undersecretary General and Advisor on the Prevention of Genocide, I accompanied the Secretary General to attend the celebrations. I was in his meeting with the UN Secretary-General in which the Eritrean president, referring to me, thanked him for bringing 'My friend, whom I haven't seen for a long time'. I appreciated his remark, although some colleagues called it a blessing with a curse because of the isolation of Eritrea in the international community."

"You really were at a battle front in Washington, fighting with words. Let us end here and go back to the Washington front in our next session."

"Very well. Good night." I said, forgetting I was talking to a ghost, for which "good night" probably did not apply.

Session Twenty-Three: Negotiations

The visitations by the Chairman were now a routine feature of my evenings, especially since the advice of the psychiatrist. They even seemed to be stimulated by me, with me setting the precise time and the choice of issues to discuss. And I did not mind that. In fact, I felt rather proud that I was able to do that.

I decided to call the psychiatrist to give him an update on the situation. He was very happy to hear my progress report and even seemed to take it as a professional achievement of his. "When you feel the time is right, I would like to sit with you to document your experience. It could indeed be a useful case for others. After all, we are here to help people and what you and your Chairman are doing is to make the record of your experience serve the interests of your people. So, we have a common cause. Good luck, and let's keep in touch."

At the beginning of the session, we reminded ourselves that we were to talk about the developments in Washington.

"Tell us about the efforts to reunite us in the movement. Of course, our friends in Congress initiated the process, but I knew that you were intimately involved behind the scenes."

"We coordinated with our Ethiopian American member of the Council whom we had chosen as our chairman, and for whom I coined the title of Emperor because his first name sounded like that of a Greek Emperor and also because he came from Imperial Ethiopia. As you will recall, the title of Emperor, which started as a joke, became his trademark, even with you in the movement. And it continued after your death to this day. The Emperor was a very influential staff member, assisting successive chairmen of the African Sub-Committee of the Foreign Relations Committee. They had become very good friends to your movement, and to you personally.

"I remember when they invited you and your leading opponent to Washington. Former US President Carter was trying hard to have you both go to his center. Your opponent accepted. You were evasive, actually against going. The President asked me to persuade you. I did not even try, because I knew your position. Your opponent went, for what it was worth, which was not much.

"Before the meeting in Congress, a friend and I went to see your opponent in his hotel, to persuade him to accept reconciliation. I told him that I knew very well the gruesome manner in which my brothers were killed in his 1991 attempted coup. But I was there for the sake of the living. He looked down and did not comment on that part of my remarks. We otherwise had a relatively constructive talk.

"At the talks in Congress, you sat at the podium with key members of Congress, with the Chairman between you and your opponent. The discussion focused on your vision of New Sudan and your opponent's call for self-determination for South Sudan. The representative of the National Democratic Alliance, in supporting your position, said that the Northern parties in the Alliance were committed to the creation of a secular democratic Sudan. An old university colleague of mine, a Muslim Brother, sitting next to me, remarked, 'When the sectarian political parties in the Opposition Alliance get back to power, they will deny having committed themselves to secularism and will say that it was not they who made that statement'."

"As I said," chimed in the Chairman, "for them, the end always justifies the means. To get the peace agreement they needed, they were willing to accept whatever would bring that about. When back in power, the situation would be different, and their new end would require new means."

"That's exactly right. One of the moments I remember very well about that meeting was when your opponent said, 'I could have killed this man', pointing at you, 'but I chose not to'. Still looking down, probably writing, you responded with, "Thank you', which was the most effective way of humiliating your opponent for his shocking comment."

"You signed a statement of agreement that was drafted by the hosting members of Congress, in which they tried to reconcile your respective positions. Your opponent was reluctant to sign and did so only after much pressure."

"Probably not believing what he was signing."

"Signing or agreeing to what is not seriously meant, which we used to associate with the North, has become a pattern in the South. In Nairobi, during the early talks with the government, a friend and I shuttled between your faction and the opposing wing of your opponent and his supporters. In one meeting with him, I reminded him of the meeting my Peace Partner and I had in Addis Ababa with you and your team, and how he had opposed the American proposal for government withdrawal from the South because of the movement's commitment to unity. How could he now turn against you, supposedly in pursuit of separatism? He remained silent, looking down. I asked his rebel colleague who had supported his stance in Addis the same question, separately. His answer was that he was toeing the party line. In a separate meeting with yet another commander who had rebelled against you, I said to him that rights and wrongs were never one-sided. I asked him how he could justify fighting on the side of the Arabs against his people. His answer was, 'It is the Chairman himself who forces people to join the Jallaba.' I told him that there was absolutely nothing, and I repeated 'nothing', the Chairman could do that would justify his joining the Arabs to fight his own people."

"They listed the objective of the struggle and made fighting me their overriding goal."

"That's what I began to observe. I also met in Nairobi with a group of commanders who had been detained by the movement and, I understood, had apparently just escaped from detention. They were clearly very bitter against you personally. One of them went as far as saying 'If you do not remove this Chairman from the leadership of the movement, I will destroy Dinkaland.' I gave him the same response I had given his other colleague earlier, that nothing you had done or could do would justify his destroying his people. But that was what he eventually did. He devastated the land of his own tribe and their neighbors. He kept shifting alliances with the North until he was eventually killed. The remnants of his militia activities are still rampant in our area of Abyei."

"Many of them are disguised in both Sudan and South Sudan, to blend in for personal gain without a national sense of purpose."

"This blurs the national purpose and emboldens the adversaries in the North, who began to believe that there was no core to the cause of the South, only personal interests that could be cheaply satisfied by the North. During the Nairobi negotiations, a friend and I had meetings with the Sudanese delegation, who displayed amazing confidence that they would eventually triumph. In one meeting with a leading Islamist, who spoke very arrogantly about their position, my friend said to him, quite bluntly, that he had heard many bad things about him, but that what he had just heard him *say* was far worse than what he had heard *about* him. I tried to intervene, to moderate the tempers, but the two seemed to relish their mutual animosity."

"Why did you want to moderate positions?"

"Because we were negotiating and looking for a common ground. My discussions with the leader of their delegation were more cordial. They focused on Abyei and he tried to persuade me to revive the proposal I had made, following the Addis Ababa Agreement, to have Abyei play a bridging role between the North and the South. My response was that it was too late, as the divisions had gone too deep and Abyei was too alienated by the North to play that role."

"That's where you should have tried to create a common ground, because that was where our leverage was weakest, because we did not have military presence in the area, for tactical reasons of avoiding destruction."

"Our people would have condemned that as undermining the main goals of the struggle. Of course, we were trying to explore common ground in the wider peace process. Our Resource Group maintained close partnership with the IGAD ministers and heads of state. That was particularly the case at the formative stage in the process. Although the peace process was initiated by the Sudan government, the mediators clearly sympathized with the cause of the South, and Sudan became increasingly hostile to the process."

"We understood that and that is why we strongly supported the peace process."

"It was surprising that the Declaration of Principles emphatically stated that the people of South Sudan had not been part of Sudan's self-determination, that they were entitled to the right of self-determination, including independence, that priority should be given to the unity of the country, but that the government needed to create appropriate conditions for unity. Such conditions should include separation between religion and the state. Failing the creation of such conditions, the choice of the people of the South for secession should be respected."

"That was quite unexpected from African leaders who normally supported the status quo. That made it obvious that the new leaders of the region were freedom fighters for justice. Although we were initially seen as identified with Mengistu by the new leaders in Ethiopia and

Eritrea, we soon stood with them on the same ground. They indeed became our friends."

"Khartoum, of course, rejected the Declaration of Principles. They even arrogantly declared that their mission of Islamization was not limited to South Sudan, but indeed to the whole of the African Continent. That sealed the deal in favor of the South."

The Chairman injected a comment on the IGAD peace process: "Unfortunately, that strong commitment to the peace process and its principles began to wane and eventually came to a standstill, as the IGAD countries became increasingly divided by competing and conflicting national interests. We remained committed to pursuing our cause through various means, including armed struggle. It was the involvement of the Troika—Norway, the UK, and the US—that turned the tide toward peace."

"Even then, as I recall, you did not seem eager to embrace the peace process. And yet, you told me that the regime in Khartoum was probably the right one with which to reach an agreement because, as you put it, they were weak. I remember that, in my meetings in Khartoum with the President and his First Vice-President, separately, I told them that, for reasons I did not need to elaborate, you thought they were the right people with whom to conclude peace. The First Vice-President welcomed my report with, 'That's good to hear'. The President appeared to have realized what you must have meant when he responded with 'People think we are weak, but they are wrong'. He went on to say how they had stayed their course against the opposition of the world, including their fellow Arab countries, and how those who had opposed them were now coming back to them."

"He must have read reports of what I said in Cairo or even in my statements in the field. I certainly made comments about their weakness, and I meant it."

"At the end of my meeting with the First Vice-President, as I was leaving, he said, 'By the way, I am going to meet your friend'. I sincerely did not know who the friend was and asked him. 'The Chairman,' he said. I, of course, understood, but was surprised because you had told me that you were resisting pressure to meet with him. As I recall, you said you did not see what he would tell you that their negotiators could not say. In the end, your negotiating with him is what ended the war."

"Frankly, initially I agreed to meet with him in deference to the many people, including our close friends, who urged me to meet him. I did not expect him to come up with anything new. So, I did not think our meeting would amount to much. I was glad to find out that I was wrong and that my interlocutor was a man of integrity, who genuinely wanted peace for the country."

"Interestingly enough, I was in Durban, in South Africa, when I was informed by ACCORD that a White South African, who had been an ANC advisor, had been appointed advisor to the IGAD peace process. They arranged for me to meet with him. I was joined by a South Sudanese scholar in South Africa who was the movement's representative in the country and later became, successively, an ambassador and then a minister after independence. The South African lawyer shocked both of us by stating at the outset that self-determination was not an option in international law, that the secession of South Sudan was not possible, and that the most South Sudanese could expect was autonomy. Although I controlled myself, I was outraged."

"It was just a case of ignorance about the situation, not bad intention."

"That's what I would eventually find out. I told the South African lawyer that I was a lawyer by training, that self-determination was not only a principle in international law, but that it was the application of that principle that led to the independence of African countries from colonial domination. All he could say was that the exercise of self-determination against an independent country was controversial. I also advised him that the people of South Sudan were allergic to the word 'autonomy'. They had experimented with that system and it had failed them. He must therefore avoid using the word. My Southern colleague also spoke in the same vein. I had the sense that the South African became educated on the situation in the Sudan by that meeting."

"That is often the problem with the international community. They assign people responsibilities in areas they have no knowledge about and expect them to succeed in ignorance."

"I met this man again, after the Machakos Protocol, which recognized the right of the South to self-determination and laid the foundation for the success of the peace process. He was a totally different person, not only much more knowledgeable, but very supportive of the cause of the South. He told me that he advised the

South Sudanese after the Machakos agreement not to go out of the meeting smiling, but instead to look unhappy, so as not to reveal their joy over the agreement. From that time onwards, and throughout the negotiations that ended in the Comprehensive Peace Agreement, he remained a true friend of South Sudan."

"I know the person you are talking about. He did indeed become our friend. But, in the end, I believe the chemistry between the First Vice-President and me was a pivotal factor in reaching the agreement. The more we talked, the more we got to know, respect, and trust one another. These are elements that had never really existed between us and the North."

"I remember what you told me about the strategy *you* used in negotiating. And, ironically, it confirmed something the American Ambassador in the Sudan had said about you and with which I strongly disagreed in your defense. We were at a dinner. The Ambassador praised you as an excellent negotiator and said that you had pushed the envelope to a level that forced your counterpart to make concessions that he would not be able to sell to the Sudanese public.

"I took it as criticism rather than as praise. And I responded defensively and almost aggressively. I argued that you were the aggrieved party and that any successful negotiation must address the genuine grievances of the South, which should involve significant concessions from the North. That was not something to be criticized—it was what was needed for peace to be possible.

"You had explained to me that your negotiating technique was to incrementally raise the bar one step at a time, persuading your negotiating counterpart to take that step, then raise it another step, and continue the process until your opponent reached a point from which he could no longer retreat. That was exactly what they were praising *and* criticizing you for."

Again, the Chairman explained the subtleties of the negotiation: "The process was too subtle and discreet for my opponent to suspect. And as I said, we had become very comfortable with one another, joking and having a good time. In fact, we became friends."

I then turned to what had been the crucial stage in the conclusion of the deal, the signing ceremony. "The signing in the stadium in Nairobi, which I attended, was quite spectacular. The event was attended by several heads of state and many prominent personalities from around the world. Southern Sudanese from South Sudan and

251

refugees and residents in Kenya attended in large numbers. While the VIPs were seated in shaded areas, most people sat or stood in the heat of the blazing sun. Your soldiers marched to the tune of their martial music that brought to my mind the words of their morale-boosting war songs. I remember an earlier meeting with the Sudanese President, when he complained that the movement was corrupting our cultural values. And he gave as an illustration a martial song that had the lines:

Our battalion knows no mercy
Even my father, I would give him a bullet.

"As I listened to the music, reading into it the lyrics, and watched the Sudanese President, I could not help but think of the wide divide between the parties that had just reached agreement. An overzealous South Sudanese Muslim every now and then shouted in the crowd, '*Allahu Akbar!*'—to which an equally excited South Sudanese crowd responded, '*Halleluiah!*'

"I saw the Northerners sitting close to me looking very downcast. The speeches were equally illustrative. Surprisingly, the Sudanese President's speech was quite conciliatory. Yours elaborated in great detail, and with remarkable candor, the reasons behind the war. Frankly, I felt you could have been more magnanimous against your former adversaries, especially in view of the President's tone. But I also realized that your speech had already been prepared and could not be adapted to the unfolding situation. The speech of the President of Uganda was similar to yours. He began by stating that people do not go to war for nothing, and then focused on the distorted self-perception of the Northern Sudanese as Arabs and their attempt to impose that discriminatory vision on the whole of Sudan. It was his familiar attack on the North."

The Chairman responded: "You could say that the agreement ended the armed confrontation, but it had not ended the conflict. The vision of the New Sudan was still alive for me, and the President of Uganda shared that vision. And I had no doubt the President of the Sudan was aware of that."

"In the reception you held later to thank those who had stood with you, especially from the region and the international community, people spoke in favor of the agreement and congratulated you for the achievement. But I was surprised and, frankly, taken aback when one European Minister, who had played an important role in the peace process as a member of the Troika, stressed that the agreement was very good for the South. I was sure that Sudanese representatives or their secret agents were at the reception. If, as the Minister said, the agreement was so good for the South, then it might be misunderstood as not so good for the North. Whatever the truth of the situation, I thought it was unwise of the Minister to say that publicly."

"The Minister took the Agreement as almost a personal accomplishment and she obviously got carried away. She meant well."

"I also recall the dinner you gave the leadership of South Sudan in Nairobi after the reception in which people celebrated with great euphoria. Interestingly enough, the band that played was from Abyei. We all got up to show them our appreciation. That seemed to draw particular attention from the photographers, presumably because of the Abyei connection.

"Again, people spoke with great passion of joy. One of your senior colleagues spoke humorously about the agreement, which he likened to having reached the Promised Land. You spoke of having delivered the right of the people of the South to decide whether to be free in their own independent country or remain second-class citizens in the old Sudan. I found that statement somewhat confusing, as it implied endorsing separation, as opposed to the New Sudan Vision. But, as I had already come to understand, the two were not mutually exclusive in your strategy, as the sustainability of an independent South Sudan significantly depended on the transformation of the North into the New Sudan that would have much in common with South Sudan ideologically."

The Chairman agreed with my analysis. "Absolutely. And that is what most Southerners did not seem to understand. It is the failure to understand that fact which accounts in significant measure for the tragic developments in South Sudan since independence."

"That is what I have tried to document in my recent book, *Bound by Conflict: The Dilemmas of the Two Sudans.* For some reason that I did not understand, your former rebel leaders who were back in the movement urged me to persuade you to go to Khartoum immediately as a gesture of goodwill. I did not see why they wanted *me* to advise you, when, as members of the movement's leadership, they should have felt better placed than me to offer you that advice. For reasons that I also did not know, but thought wise, you resisted that until it was time to be sworn in as First Vice-President of the Republic and President of the Autonomous Government of South during the six-year Interim Period leading to the Referendum in the South. The Advance Team had gone ahead. I joined the movement's leadership in Nairobi, as they were to go to Khartoum ahead of you. It is quite ironic that the very individuals who were urging you to go to Khartoum after the signing of the 2005 Comprehensive Peace Agreement (or CPA) did not come to Juba when the Revitalized Peace Agreement was signed in Addis Ababa, except to join the celebration in Juba later and then return to Khartoum to await the formation of the government in accordance with the Revitalized Agreement.

"In Khartoum, when I arrived at the Hilton Hotel, where most of the leadership was accommodated, the first thing that drew my attention—and I felt it was a major mistake—was to see your photograph and that of Ali Abdel Latif, the 1924 South Sudanese leader of the revolt against British colonial rule, put up together high on the front face of the hotel. It was obvious that the picture would be read to mean that your revolution was a continuation of Latif's Black Revolution against foreign domination—which even I thought was offensive and posed an imminent threat to the ruling Arab minority."

"Why did you want us to deny our revolutionary brother? What was wrong with making it clear that ours was a continuation of what they had started that far back?"

"I thought it would do what you were trying to avoid: polarize the country along racial grounds. Yours was a liberation struggle for *all* the Sudanese, not only for the Blacks."

"But so was the rebellion of Ali Abdel Latif. The only factor you seem to have been concerned about is our color, not our objective or message."

"I guess you are right. In fact, I recently read something about this point in a very good book about you by one of your comrades who knew you well and is a staunch supporter of your vision for the nation. He wrote that digging deep into the chronicles of time, one sees no difference between what individuals in the long line of Black African Sudanese leaders from the South *and* the North—beginning with Ali Abdel Latif and up to yourself—wanted to achieve. He said that they all agreed, for instance, that it was divisive to apply Sharia laws in a religiously diverse country. Those leaders stressed that power should devolve to the regions through a democratic and equitable distribution of powers and resources. They also emphasized the importance of allowing people to freely practice their cultures. But this author said that you had a different style and direction, arising from a broad-based political movement. According to him, all that the others saw, as a framework for unity, was only being a Sudanese or an Arab, whereas you emphasized the concept of 'Sudanism' as the uniting framework. The difference is subtle, but important. One adopts the exclusive identity of one group to cover all, while your approach is inherently all-embracing."

"He—or should I say both of you?—got it right."

"After my missing it a bit! The experience of your return to Khartoum since 1983 was truly extraordinary. The whole country waited for you in anticipation, in a manner that had not been seen in the Sudan in my memory. The reception at the airport was impressive. But everything that followed was beyond any expectation. It seems that the Advance Team had made superb arrangements. You were to address *the nation*. As far as the eye could see, it was as though the whole of Khartoum, joined by masses from elsewhere in the country, gathered to hear you. Those of us who were not out there were glued to the television. Then something that seemed very fishy happened: The sound system failed and could not be made to work. So, you could not address the gathered crowd. Suspicions were obvious and credible. It is unbelievable that massive riots did not take place."

The Chairman gave an explanation I had already suspected: "That was why I deliberately played down the suspicion of sabotage. I still don't know what actually happened. But if it were sabotage, it was a very ill-conceived plan, since it risked generating a calamitous reaction."

I resumed my observations. "I really think they felt desperate because you had clearly won the political struggle. It was like what a drowning person does, trying to grab anything he sees that might help him to survive. I heard that the President's reaction to the way you were received was to say, 'I think I will be the last Arab President of the country.'

"The swearing-in was in many ways reminiscent of the Nairobi signing of the Agreement. The speeches were quite representative of what had transpired in Nairobi. The President was conciliatory while you again gave a full account of what the war had been about. You made two points that I thought were particularly confrontational. You said to the Sudanese people that they were now free. 'Put on your wings and fly to greater freedom', you said. Then you said that your movement would establish offices in all the states of the Sudan.

"As you will recall, back at the hotel, later that day, you called for me to see you in your room. We talked about the events of the day. I recalled in particular what you had said at the swearing-in. I asked you, 'When you said the Sudanese people were now free and you called upon them to fly to greater freedom, from whom were they free but from the same people with whom you have now agreed? How will they take that? Again, you said you would open offices in all parts of the country. Would you not be competing with them?' Your answer was again a repeat of what you had said about your speech in Nairobi, that although armed confrontation had ended, the conflict continued. You also told me that you had qualified what you said by adding that it was a way of promoting the unity of the country. In any case, you were clearly calling the shots."

The Chairman commented: "This was a struggle that had lasted for half a century and in which millions of our people had sacrificed their lives. We should not mince our words about the cause. We must be clear-headed and candid in making our case. We might not have won decisively on the battlefield, but we had the cause of justice on our side."

I agreed and added: "And there is no doubt that at that moment you were clearly on a moral high ground. It is quite telling that, in a recent meeting of the leadership council of the movement, now party, the President very movingly said that, at independence, we held our heads high as a proud nation, but that we are no longer a proud nation because of the way we have mismanaged the affairs of our independent country. He asked the rhetorical question, 'Why have we done this to our people?' It was a voice of moral courage and a call for going back to the moral high ground of the liberation struggle.

"What I observed about your activities and the response to your leadership among Northerners indicated a new page in the political evolution of the Sudan. My colleagues, the lawyers with whom you spoke, were euphoric. They complained to you that the system was so chaotic and confused that there was virtually no legal system in the country, and you encouraged them to submit to you their proposals for the reform of the legal system. That is what I mean when I say that I thought you already had the Sudan on a course of no return. I now see that I was wrong."

"I understand what you are saying,' he replied, "but the destiny of a people and the struggle for their dignity cannot be tied to the life of an individual. If it is, it should be viewed as only temporary. In the end, it is the people themselves and their determination that will achieve the objectives of their struggle."

"You are right," I admitted. "But the loss of a leader can also lead to the loss or dimming of the vision and direction. I may be biased, but this seems to be the case, especially with regard to Abyei. A side event that was challenging to your new joint leadership for the country related to the issue of Abyei. The Abyei Boundary Commission (or ABC) had completed its work and presented it to your joint Presidency. It seemed quite favorable to the Ngok Dinka. A group of Ngok representatives came to the hotel to share their happiness with me. They said they had been 'given' areas that were on their borders with the Missiriya. They told me that they planned to stage a public rally to welcome the report and were also planning to slaughter bulls and arrange festive celebrations of the report.

"I advised them against any public display of their happiness, as that would almost certainly provoke a hostile reaction from the Missiriya. I told them that even their speaking of having been 'given' areas suggested an unexpected outcome from the ABC. They were adamant. Among some fifteen of them, only three agreed with me. Some of them even spoke to me quite angrily for opposing the people's expression of joy. I suggested that we should consult the leaders of the movement that had liberated the area for advice. Fortunately, two of the leaders were nearby. They both advised against any public display of happiness with the report. One of the members of the Commission gave the same advice: 'Celebrate quietly in your homes', he suggested. When I raised the issue with you in your room that day, your advice was the same."

"In a conflict, one should not demonstrate pleasure at a solution, as it implies that you are the winner and your adversary the loser. That's grounds for the resumption of conflict, if only through other means."

"I recall what you told me about the way the President reacted to the ABC Report. 'We will have another rebellion in our hands," he said. You told him that the two of you would face that challenge together. As we discussed the situation, we agreed that you should meet with the leaders of the Missiriya. But you advised that the request for the meeting should come from them. I was able to steer them into requesting the meeting. But then I left and read reports later that misrepresented the situation, even about my meeting with them. Apparently, Sudan's security agents aborted the meeting.

"Reports about your impact on Khartoum indicated that your leadership was proving transformative. Then suddenly, tragedy struck."

"I know what you are about to say. But I suggest that we stop here and leave that subject for our next session."

The tragedy of course was the Chairman's own accidental death. I had come to see the future of our people of the South and indeed of the whole Sudan to be in the hands of the Chairman. In a way, it was like seeing the security and the destiny of our Ngok Dinka people without the protective role of our father as their Paramount Chief. The Chairman was the emerging Paramount Chief of the Sudan. I did not know how we would talk about this tragedy. But it was a central topic in the saga of the Visitations.

Session Twenty-Four: Death

I was not sure how I felt about discussing the subject of our next conversation. How do you discuss with a dead man his own death? Should I inform him about his death or would he himself talk about his own death? What about the impact of his death on the people and the country? The meeting hour approached, and the Chairman was running late by my timetable, but I was okay with that, as it postponed discussing this painful subject. Suddenly, the Chairman announced his arrival. We exchanged salutations.

I decided to be transparent. "Frankly, for the first time since we began our conversations, I have not looked forward to the next session."

"Why?" the Chairman asked in a way I thought was part of his teasing mannerism.

"You know why."

"No, I don't."

Was he still teasing, or oblivious to his own situation? I decided to get to the point. "You remember that in this session we are to focus on the impact of your death on our people and on the country as a whole."

"So that is why you did not feel comfortable about today's session? What about the old saw that there is no point crying over spilt milk? I am dead. You should all move on."

"I don't know how to talk about your own death," I confessed. "Should I be *informing* you, on the assumption that you do not know the details of your death—and how people have responded to it? Or did you watch it all?" I then added, "After all, you came to me because you have been watching what has been going on in our world of the living!"

"Remember, *I* did not come to you; *you* came to me," the Chairman surprised me.

"I don't understand. Of course, you came to me!" I asserted.

"How do you know? Do you even realize that I am now not with you? Can you actually see me or touch me? I am a figment of your imagination."

I really felt confused and frightened. Once again, I doubted my sanity. "Don't tell me that all these conversations have only been illusions in my mind!"

"I am not telling you that. After all, what is reality and what is illusion? Reality is perception and perception is reality. Does God exist or do we believe that God exists? Did God create us or did we create God? I suggest you continue with your story about my death and you will tell from our conversation whether I witnessed it or not."

"You put me in a very awkward position. But I will tell you what I witnessed." I took a breath. "Word of your death first circulated like a rumor that the plane that was flying you from Uganda to your post at the New Site was missing. I believe it was our 'Emperor' who first informed me. The prospect was so shocking that the instinct was to dismiss it in denial. But the 'rumors' kept coming from all over, so we began to worry. Then came the shock that the plane crash was confirmed. It was still difficult to believe the confirmed news.

"Once the news was confirmed beyond doubt, I decided with some friends from the 'Council' to immediately leave for the New Site where your body lay. I was able to connect for the New Site in Nairobi, so as to accompany the body as it was taken around to several towns in the New Sudan. The response to your death was unbelievable. And it differed remarkably from area to area, according to the cultural values involved.

"As you know, culturally, the Dinka do not cry, far less wail, over a leader or a warrior killed in action. In Rumbek and Bor, the silence of masses of people who turned up to pay their last respects to you was overwhelming. Now and then, a woman who broke the silence with wailing was promptly whizzed away and silenced. In the non-Dinka areas of Kauda in Nuba land, Yei, and Juba, the contrasting cries and wailing were deafening. Some people, mostly women, threw themselves on the ground. In Khartoum, the news provoked spontaneous attacks against the Northerners by the Southerners, who suspected foul play. The police responded with greater brutality against the Southerners. Many people died. I must say that it crossed my mind to wish you were there to witness how beloved you were. But seeing how you are alive in death, perhaps you witnessed it all."

"Remember, I am the one who died, not a spectator. Coming back as ghost or a spirit is a different matter. It also took time."

"Even among the Northerners, people genuinely felt that your death was a calamity, a grave loss for the nation as a whole. A Northern classmate who had been a Muslim Brother told me that his wife wept when she got the news. A leading Islamist who had been an active member of the government's negotiating team told me how his mother cried, saying, 'We hated him when we did not know him, and loved him when we got to know him, and suddenly he is taken away from us.' Many world leaders said to me that your death was a severe loss not only to South Sudan, but to the IGAD sub-region, the African continent, and the world at large. I don't want to embarrass you."

"You cannot. Remember, I am dead. I cannot shed tears. I cannot even blush—that is, if I ever could," the Chairman mused.

"The question is why God saved you for decades amidst obvious dangers, and then ended your life in this senseless manner. That was why people generally could not believe that it was an accident. But who could be responsible for such a horrific assassination is, of course, a mystery."

"Don't ask me why God does what He does. I am dead, but I am not privy to His thoughts. And don't ask me where I am. I myself do not know. I am only here as a ghost ... if I am really here."

"What I find incredible was that your wife is said to have tried to persuade you not to fly back at night, but you insisted that you had been assured that the plane was safe."

"Remember, I was the Commander-in-Chief of our army. I had confronted death on innumerable occasions. How could I be expected to fear something I could not even see coming? Besides, remember, hindsight is perfect."

"You remind me of a lyric we used to chant as children. It depicted the goat calling out to the sheep: *'Sheep, sheep, beware, there is a crocodile in the river!'* The sheep responded, *'Goat, you with your lies! Does a gentleman run away from a danger he does not see?'*

"There is a difference between what is not seen and what is seeable. I think the danger of flying at night into a somewhat uncharted sky is foreseeable, as indeed your wife presumably did. What was also foreseeable—but not foreseen—was the possible action of those for whom you posed an existential threat."

"Nothing will bring me back. So, what's the point of knowing who did it and risk triggering another conflict that will lead to more deaths? Let the sleeping dogs lie."

"If it were truly an accident, then God operates in a mysterious way, as they say, and must have His own wisdom unknown to us. I have on occasions said that, dreadful as your death was for our people and the world, perhaps, for you personally, the timing was opportune, as you left at the pinnacle of your success, for which you will be remembered. You would probably have done more, but your position would probably have been contested and might in any case have been controversial. And our people were divided, a fact that, in itself, would have continued to challenge your leadership. Who knows?"

"In the wisdom of God, my time was over. Who knows what my continuing to live would have meant, whether it would have been for the good of our people and country, or a source of some tragedy? We do not know and will never know, thank God."

"The question often asked is whether you might have been more successful negotiating with the Sudan the credible implementation of the Protocols on Abyei and the two border Northern areas of Nuba Mountains and Blue Nile. There is now a total impasse on Abyei. The popular consultations that were to be held in the two Northern areas, to determine the system of government they want, have not been held. Quite the contrary, they went to war with Khartoum shortly after the independence of the South. And despite the good intentions of South Sudan, they have not been able to help them in any significant way. They are now virtually defeated. And they are sharply divided organizationally and ideologically. The New Sudan Vision has become purely a slogan that requires clarification, both in terms of the concept and of the means for pursuing it."

"Throughout the negotiations, my position was that if we deferred the solution of the problems of these areas, they would not be resolved in the near future. These are people who were our comrades-in-arms. They suffered and died with us. It is morally and even politically untenable to abandon them."

"In Abyei, the referendum that was to be held simultaneously with that of the South never took place. And since the independence of the South, the case of Abyei has been increasingly marginalized. The Report of the ABC, which the President saw as a source of potential rebellion among the Missiriya but which you strongly defended, was unceremoniously shelved because the government claimed that the Commission had exceeded its mandate. The case went to the Hague for the consideration of the International Court of Arbitration. The Court revised the borders determined by the ABC and reduced Ngok Dinka territory by about a third. Even then, Khartoum insisted—and still insists—that the Missiriya must participate in the referendum and must share power equally with the Ngok Dinka during the interim period. This would mean that the Missiriya administer themselves and then go to share the administration of Abyei with the Dinka. Where is justice in that?"

"There is none," murmured the Chairman. "And the North knows that. Theirs must be a position of negotiation. And that requires knowing what their real interests are. We assume that those interests are rooted in the oil of the area. If that is the case, it should be openly stated and negotiated. After all, that's what we did with the oil of the South. As you said in your now famous article, what is not said is what divides."

"Although the government of South Sudan supports a semblance of administrative structure and its core personnel, Abyei is now in a state of virtual statelessness without the protection, services, and development activities normally provided by the state. Twice, Abyei was attacked by the armed forces of Khartoum, risking potential return to war between the now two independent countries. The United Nations intervened and established the United Nations Interim Security Force in Abyei, or UNISFA, which now provides much appreciated protection, but only in a small portion of Ngok Dinka territory. Much of the traditional land of the Ngok Dinka now remains deserted."

"After a while, it will be a subject of historical claims that this was once the land of the Ngok Dinka."

"That's what I tell our people. Our plains are now covered with shards of broken decorated pots which belonged to the Lueel or Girma, the people we displaced. Besides, the identity of the Ngok Dinka as South Sudanese seems to be under assault. Most of the leaders of the Ngok Dinka in the government and the army have either been dismissed or marginalized and prominent voices have spoken of Abyei as part of the Sudan and Abyei citizens as Sudanese and 'not yet' part of South Sudan. This is despite the fact that the Abyei Protocol provides for dual citizenship for the inhabitants of Abyei and the

Interim Constitution of South Sudan makes them full citizens of South Sudan. The situation is very much a case of the history of the disregard of the Addis Ababa Agreement on Abyei repeating itself. You used to say that if the South were to postpone the issue of Abyei to be addressed after solving the problem of the South, the South would lose Abyei. This has sadly become a reality."

"That's very unfortunate."

"That is why I have come up with an initiative similar to the one I proposed when the government refused to implement the provisions of the Addis Ababa Agreement on Abyei. I proposed a program for the Interim Stabilization of Abyei, which would build on several pillars:

- provide full security over the entire territory of the Ngok Dinka as demarcated by The Hague;
- establish an autonomous administration of the Ngok Dinka with all the three conventional organs of government;
- generate a robust program of social services and economic development activities; and
- promote peaceful coexistence and cooperation with the neighbors of the Ngok Dinka, especially the Missiriya.

"The Ngok Dinka feel that your death turned them into orphans. They are confident that, if you were alive, you would not only have ensured the implementation of the Abyei Protocol, but would have turned Abyei into a model of cross-border development and nation-building between the North and the South, in line with your New Sudan Vision. The government of South Sudan is doing its best for Abyei but is overwhelmed by the many crises, both internal and with the Sudan, that it is trying to resolve. Perhaps you too would have been equally overwhelmed."

The Chairman was obviously moved, although I could not observe his nonverbal cues. "What can I say except that people should distinguish between personalities and the policies they postulate for the nation? Although the vision of the movement tended to be associated with me as a person, it should substantively stand on its own and be judged as such. As for the causes of the two Northern areas (Southern Kordofan and Blue Nile) and Abyei, it has always been my view that it was not only our moral obligation to support them, but that our interests are intimately interconnected. Peace and security, and even the independence of South Sudan, will never be assured and sustained without achieving and sustaining the legitimate rights of these kith and kin at our Northern borders."

"That indeed is the point I have been making to those who seem to continue to fight your legacy. But that is a big issue, which I suggest we discuss in our next conversation."

The Chairman agreed and we ended the session.

The Northern areas of Southern Kordofan and Blue Nile and the contested border area of Abyei are among those areas most affected by the Chairman's death. And, in a way, their cases are symptoms of the failure of the Chairman's Vision of the New Sudan because they represented the link between the North and the South. While the Principles of the New Sudan would apply to any country characterized by diversity—which is virtually every country in the world—the principle of national unity which it entailed was particularly applicable to the Sudan. The separation of the South therefore demonstrated the failure of the New Sudan agenda. But as we will see in the next session, there was more to the death of the Chairman than the partition of the Old Sudan.

Session Twenty-Five: Aftermath

I was now reconciled with discussing the death of the Chairman and its aftermath with the Chairman himself. But he apparently remembered my reticence to discuss the matter in our last session. So that was what he began our next session with.

"*Raandit*, I am here for our next session and I hope you are now willing to discuss my death without shedding tears all over again—that is, of course, if you ever did cry."

"You are welcome. But remember that the Dinka say that adult men cry inside, not with tears. And that is worse than shedding tears. Anyway, I am ready to discuss your death.

"Our last conversation covered the impact of your death on the two Northern border areas and Abyei. In a way, we overshot the sequence of events. In this conversation let's go back to the crisis at its root, the immediate response of the movement to the issue of secession."

"That sounds interesting. I am interested in hearing what you have to report."

"I am sure you know it all. But there is no harm in hearing it again. The movement demonstrated an impressive sense of unity and discipline in managing the implications of your death. The leadership immediately decided unanimously to elect your deputy to succeed you. Your funeral was attended by several heads of state and prominent personalities from around the world. The speakers—national and world leaders, and family representatives—all gave you your due as a great leader and a loss to your family, country, Africa, and the world. I was forewarned that I would be called upon to speak, and I indeed prepared myself for that, but the list of speakers was too long and the available time ran out."

"At least I believe I know what you might have said. And although you did not say it, let me thank you for your intended, though unsaid remarks."

"You are most welcome. Two or three days after your burial, I had a very open discussion with your successor about the implications of your death for his leadership. Of course, I remembered the 2004 conflict between the two of you, which ended with magnanimity on both sides. I urged him to be a force for unity in the country. He assured me that he would reach out even to those who were viewed as particularly close to you.

"What was particularly problematic is that the Agreement which you had so carefully and successfully negotiated proved very difficult to implement. The interim government of National Unity proved dysfunctional. Members of your movement in the national government were marginalized and rendered mere figureheads, while their Northern deputies or undersecretaries ran the ministries. Once, they withdrew from the national government in protest. The management of the oil revenues was so skewed against the South that the interim government of South Sudan decided to shut down oil production, which paradoxically deprived them of their only source of revenue and exposed them to severe international reprimand."

"If the amounts of oil revenues that had been pouring into the country had been used to boost agricultural production, along with the construction of main and feeder roads, the hardship might have been ameliorated."

"The agreed-upon referendum itself became a subject of intense controversy at both the regional and international levels. Khartoum continued its campaign against it and, in particular, the risks of potential Southern independence. They argued that, once the uniting opposition to the North was removed, South Sudan would be torn apart by tribal conflicts. It would become a failed state and a source of instability in the region. I remember intense discussions with the leadership of the African Union and IGAD, who also argued that the independence of South Sudan would set a bad example for the African continent. Even the Secretary General of the United Nations was opposed to the referendum and the potential of South Sudanese independence. After a long discussion, he asked me to write him a note on the issue, outlining my arguments in favor of the referendum and respecting the will of the people of South Sudan. I wrote a piece which I later included in my short book, *Sudan at the Brink,* on the challenges of unity and self-determination in the Sudan."

"Did your note change his position?"

"I don't know for sure. But I was told by his speechwriter that the book was very helpful to him in writing the speeches of the Secretary General. My main arguments for holding the referendum on time and respecting the outcome was to invoke the theme of the famous sub-title of the book of the respected South Sudanese statesman, Abel Alier, *South Sudan: Too Many Agreements Dishonored,* and made the point that if that latest Agreement was dishonored, no other agreement would be possible between the North and the South in the Sudan. Besides, I asked, what reasons would lead to the collapse or failure of an independent South? Would they be internal or external, and could they be prevented?"

"The answer, of course, is: both… with the external factors perhaps being pivotal. Isn't that what actually happened with the militias that constituted the bulk of the rebel forces?"

"That was clearly the case, although I doubt the international community fully understood that. As the date of the referendum was approaching, the United Nations organized a symposium in Khartoum about the prospects of giving national unity a chance and asked me to give an opening statement. I argued that it was too late to give unity a chance. But I was urged to address the meeting, if only to make that point. I did address the symposium and made my arguments for why it was too late to make unity attractive, but stipulated what could be done, even at that late hour, to improve the grim prospects of unity. This meant expanding the principle of 'One Country, Two Systems' into 'One Country, *Multiple* Systems' to meet the demands of all the regions of the Sudan. When I made that point to the Secretary General of the UN, his response was that providing for *two* systems within one country was challenging enough, which should rule out *multiple* systems within one country."

"He obviously did not grasp the issue."

"No. He took accommodating diversity as a step toward separatism. That probably has to do with his background in such a homogeneous society as Korea. Ironically, while I was in Khartoum for the symposium, I had an intense discussion with a friend of mine who supported the Northern Sudanese argument for the postponement of the referendum for the North, namely, that it was to give unity a chance. For my friend, it was probably to enable the South to prepare itself better for independence. Although he had been one of the leading proponents of the referendum and the prospects of Southern independence, he now opposed both, fearing that the South would be torn apart by its own internal conflicts and its continuing conflict with the North. His reason was that he could not recommend Southern independence if it would mean continuing the conflict with the North or risk tearing the South apart through tribal warfare. I asked him whether he was implying that the South should remain under Northern domination to avoid the risks associated with independence. His answer was that he did not mean that. But he did not explain what he therefore did mean."

"I am not surprised. It calls to mind what your colleagues of the Concerned South Sudanese Citizens said when they called for the referendum without clarifying how they would bring it about. And far less, they did not explain how they would bring about the independence they wanted. The same applied to wanting to postpone the referendum or opposing independence without explaining how to otherwise achieve the objectives of the struggle."

"I subsequently published the book, *Sudan at the Brink,* in which I included my 1989 address to the peace conference in Khartoum and the keynote address to the UN pre-referendum symposium in Khartoum. In that book, I saw independence to be unavoidable and began to advocate post-separation cooperation between the two independent neighboring countries. Until the end, the option of independence was still controversial and indeed undesired by the international community.

"What our people do not seem to fully realize is that it was the United States, and specifically President Barack Obama, that eventually turned the international tide. In a side event in the United Nations General Assembly in October 2010, which he jointly hosted with the UN Secretary General and which was attended by world leaders, including the heads of state of our sub-region, it was decided that the referendum should be held on time and the will of the people of South Sudan should be fully respected."

"It is indeed ironic that the friends who made independence possible are now being seen as the enemies. And that is because they are most disappointed and therefore the most critical of what we have done with independence."

"That's exactly what I say. After the near unanimous vote for independence and the enthusiastic international acceptance of the will of the people of South Sudan, there was euphoria about South Sudan's independence. The Secretary General and the President of the General Assembly both attended the celebrations of independence in Juba. I was invited to join them. The attendance of both was said to be exceptional in the history of the United Nations. So was the speed with which South Sudan was accepted into the UN.

After independence, I published a book titled *Bound by Conflict: Dilemmas of the Two Sudans*. In that book, I argued that, despite the separation, the two countries were still bound together negatively by their respective internal conflicts that spill over across their international borders. With the conflicts in the Nuba Mountains and Blue Nile as well as the conflict over Abyei all remaining unresolved, South Sudan could not turn its back to them without some form of support for their cause. For its part, Sudan would continue to suspect South Sudan of supporting its rebel groups and retaliate by supporting South Sudan's opposing militias. The two countries needed to cooperate to resolve their internal conflicts and transform being bound-by-conflict into being bonded-by-solutions. The threat of internal conflicts within South Sudan turning the nascent country into a failed state loomed even closer but continued to be denied by the leadership."

"On numerous occasions following the independence of South Sudan, I reminded our leaders of the fears of the international community that South Sudan would be a collapsed or failed state, and that we must not be complacent about our success, but instead must prove the prophets of failure wrong every day.

"Sadly, the prophets of doom have been proven right. Even my friend, whatever his motives at the time, has been proven right in his belated opposition to the referendum and the independence of the South. Not only the country, but also the movement, have become violently divided. The dreams of the liberation struggle have been shattered. The question now, to quote what you used to say about the Islamist National Congress Party, is whether your movement is too deformed to be reformed? And I might also ask whether the country is too divided to be viable? On both questions, and for the sake of the country, I certainly hope not."

The Chairman put a more optimistic spin on the situation. "The movement has always been challenged by its detractors. It is all part of the struggle for leadership. Everyone wants to be the leader. Of course, it is all a question of how the leadership manages the struggle for power. There is nothing wrong with ambition for leadership, provided it is constructively and democratically pursued and managed."

I chimed in with my observation. "That's exactly the issue. It all began when your former opponent started to openly criticize the leadership of your successor. He listed seven specific areas of alleged failures and declared his intention to run against him for the Chairmanship of the party and the Presidency. Others, specifically, the Vice-President and the Secretary-General of the Party, also declared their intention to run. The division within the party glaringly entered the public domain."

"That is something I always tried to avoid. The first layer of response is to contain it internally. But if it breaks out into the open, the next response is to deal with it decisively and end it."

"My cousin began to mediate for a resolution of the differences. But ironically, he was alleged to have been the source of the conflicts. He had supposedly heard the President say to some African heads of state that he did not intend to run again for the Presidency. My cousin indeed confirmed that to me and even said that the heads of state concerned said to the President that he would provide a good example to African leaders and that they would hold him to his word. My cousin told me that the President had shared his decision with his family and told them to prepare for his exit. It was, however, argued that the President's remark was said in a lighthearted, jocular manner and not intended to be taken literally or seriously. The Second Vice-President told me that my cousin had created the problem he was now trying to resolve."

"He could not have created the problem by simply reporting what he heard said in front of others. The source of the problem was saying something that was not seriously meant."

"That's right. Amidst this confusion, the President decided to dismiss his First Vice-President. And shortly afterwards he also dismissed his entire Cabinet. He quickly reappointed the Minister of Foreign Affairs, but otherwise left the ministries to be run by the Undersecretaries.

"On a visit to Juba, I met with all the main parties to the conflict. The President confirmed what I had already suspected and had shared with others in discussing the situation. He said he was reacting to the perception of his adversaries that he was weak. He wanted to show them that he was not weak. And explaining to me a military strategy with apparent relish, he said he had decided on a massive attack that probably left them whining helplessly in their houses. "

"I told him that what he told me was what I had surmised. However, I said I had told people that if I were to advise the President, I would say that, while his reaction to his opponents was understandable, he should not be forced to compromise the virtues for which he was known, and for which I have often described him as a Dinka gentleman. This is not because I am being a Dinka chauvinist, but because of the qualities I know the Dinka associate with being a gentleman and a leader: cool-hearted, calm, uniting, and forgiving. I would advise him not to let his enemies define his character. The President nodded in agreement and told me that he would reach out to them."

"Was it a nod of courtesy or a persuaded response?"

"In retrospect, it was probably both, and over the years that followed, he did demonstrate both toughness and conciliation. In my meeting with the dismissed First Vice-President, he initially impressed me as remarkably calm and understanding. He told me that it was the President's right to dismiss him or any of his appointees. However, he asserted that the President had become a dictator. I told him what I had told you and your successor, that our society is a highly segmentary lineage system, described by anthropologists as an acephalous and egalitarian society in which everyone and every family all feel at least equal to all others. It is a society where, in the language of Professor Evans-Pritchard, no one can 'lord it over others'. This indicates a democratic culture in which dictatorship cannot work. The First Vice-President reacted by asking me to 'please remind the President again!'"

"That's because he was not the one dictating."

"In the meeting with the Secretary General of your party, he reiterated the position of the First Vice-President that it was the President's prerogative to dismiss members of his government, but that he had no doubt in his mind that he wanted to be a dictator and was indeed already becoming one."

"That was another case of pointing fingers away from one's own potential for dictatorship. We all have that propensity. It's all a question of tactical or strategic balance."

"Probably both. As people who have long been in the trenches, sometimes you feel the danger coming without knowing where from and precisely when."

"The anticipated violence erupted on December 15, 2013, generated by the climax of the political differences that were mounting among the leaders. The reported trigger was whether election to the party positions should be by secret ballot, which dissidents wanted, or by open show of hands, which was preferred by those holding power. Shooting began around the Presidency, but soon spread like wildfire throughout Juba. The First Vice-President fled the Capital and declared armed rebellion. Violence soon spread deep into the country, increasingly taking an ethnic dimension between the Dinka and the Nuer.

"The government alleged an attempted coup, while the Nuer alleged genocidal atrocities against their people. The so-called White Army of Nuer youth marched toward Juba, seeking vengeance against the Dinka. The blood bath in Juba was horrendous, described by many observers as genocidal against the Nuer. The expected revenge would certainly have resulted in genocide against the Dinka. That was prevented not only by a strong resistance by the Dinka-dominated army, but also by the intervention of Uganda.

"Many of those with whom I had had discussions in my cousin's house, including my cousin, were among those arrested and charged with the attempted coup, a treasonable offense. I was then back at my post in New York. While the official version remained that what had occurred was an attempted coup, the international community was skeptical and resisted endorsing the government's claim."

"Which version did you yourself believe?"

"I kept an open mind. Of course, I would not contradict my government's position, but I was also influenced by the international response, since I was far from the scene. But I could not believe that my cousin's group could have been involved in a coup attempt. A briefing meeting of ambassadors was convened in Juba to reaffirm the official version, for South Sudan diplomats to promote internationally. The ambassadors were instructed to make the case to the outside world. Anyone who disagreed with the government's version and was not prepared to promote it was encouraged to resign. None did. Eleven of those alleged to be responsible for the coup were detained. Anyone wanting to visit them had to submit a written request to the Minister of Justice, stating the reasons for the requested visit. The ambassadors were reminded that the detainees were accused of a treasonable crime that the Minister of Justice emphasized was punishable by death.

"That was presumably a way of discouraging contact with them that might reveal facts the government did not want revealed, such as their possible non-involvement with the allegedly attempted coup. At my request, I was granted audience with the President. Toward the end of our meeting, I said to him that there was no way of knowing whether the detainees agreed with the First Vice-President on armed rebellion, since they were not being heard from. The President said to me that he did not think they were in agreement with him. I told him that although we had been told that visiting them was discouraged, I would like to meet them and hear their views on the situation. I would then, of course, report to him. The President immediately granted me permission. He instructed his security advisor to facilitate the meeting."

"It is good that you succeeded and that the President allowed you to see the detainees. But that is also how the decisions of the leadership get undermined and lose credibility. It's a dilemma."

"Perhaps the President gave me permission because, by the time I was to meet him, the government had agreed to release into the care of the government of Kenya seven of the detainees, including my cousin. The President decided to meet with two of them, including my cousin, both Dinka. As I was entering the President's office, they were leaving to go to the airport for their flight to Nairobi. So I went from the Presidency to the airport to bid them farewell and then went to meet with four of their colleagues who were still in detention in Juba.

"In my meeting with the four, I heard what I had expected. They did not believe that there was an attempted coup. Certainly, they did not agree with the use of force. However, they maintained their position that major reforms of the system of government were urgently needed. I found their detention facilities quite comfortable and, although a security officer sat at a distance, watching over us, the conversation was very open and frank.

"On my way back to the United States, I stopped in Nairobi to meet with the other detainees. Their story was essentially the same as that of their colleagues in Juba. I was persuaded that they were definitely against resorting to violence but shared the call for reform. Once back in New York, I wrote and sent my report to the President about my meetings with the detainees."

"Did you recommend any action by the President?"

"I don't quite recall what recommendation I made, if any, but I did emphasize that the detainees had told me that they did not participate in the alleged attempted coup, and that they did not believe there was a coup attempt, but that they strongly disagreed with Riek's use of force. For me personally, I thought the debate over a coup attempt was futile. The fact that Riek immediately resorted to violence made the distinction between a coup attempt and armed rebellion almost insignificant.

"As you know, the civil war triggered by those events of 2013 lasted for two years, during which IGAD, the African Union, and the UN endeavored to end the violence. Understandably, the international community was deeply disappointed by the tragic developments in South Sudan. The independence of the South had been very controversial and was eventually possible only because of the support of IGAD and key actors from the international community, specifically the Troika countries. Once independence had been accepted, high hopes and great expectations were placed in the new state. Our friends were therefore among the most disappointed and pained by our descent into ethnic violence, which was a realization of Khartoum's self-fulfilling prophecy."

"It is said that the most obvious model for the oppressed is the oppressor. That is why an abused child is most likely to be an abuser. Averting that requires being both introspective and objective, to remember the pain you have suffered, and the risk of inflicting it on others."

"As a case of history repeating itself, the IGAD peace initiative was a virtual repeat of the one that had resulted in the CPA. By 2015, they reached the Agreement to Resolve the Conflict in the Republic of South Sudan. But, unlike the CPA, this was a very controversial agreement, which the parties, specifically the President, signed very reluctantly, only because of international pressure, and only with serious, documented reservations. The core of the reservations had to do with the recognition of two armies, two commanders-in-chief, and virtually two governments in one."

"Was it not you who once told me that co-heads is no-head?"

"Yes. I was quoting a famous American diplomat who was the strongest supporter in the Security Council for my work as Representative of the Secretary General on Internally Displaced Persons. He was reacting to the choice between designating one agency to be in charge of the internally displaced and sharing the responsibility through an inter-agency collaborative approach. He wanted the UN High Commissioner for Refugees to assume sole responsibility.

"Barely a year later, the fears that the agreement would not be implementable were realized. Minor incidents culminated in another violent eruption of uncertain origin, again alleged by the government to be another coup attempt, triggering yet another escalation of mass atrocities. The President himself later explained to me how the street lining the Presidency was covered with bodies and streaming with blood. He said he ordered the bodies to be immediately removed by trucks and buried in mass graves, and the streets washed at night so that the blood would not be seen by the population in the morning.

"The First Vice-President again escaped to wage yet another armed rebellion. Initially fleeing into the Democratic Republic of the Congo, he tried to get asylum in a number of countries but was rejected. As has often been recited, the general reaction seemed to echo Elvis Presley's 'Return to Sender'—no such number ... address unknown ... we had a quarrel ... etc. Eventually, South Africa became the sender to whom he was returned. By agreement among the regional leaders, he was placed under discreet 'detention', euphemistically described as 'protection'.

"A number of initiatives have since been taken, both nationally and internationally. With the leadership of IGAD, the international community embarked on an initiative for the revitalization of the 2015 Agreement to Resolve the Conflict in the Republic of South Sudan. The President of Uganda also took the initiative to reunify the SPLM/A. South Sudan's President initiated a national dialogue aimed at ending the war and addressing all the challenges facing the country at all levels, national, regional, and local, through a top-down/bottom-up process. The goal was to promote comprehensive peace, unity, stability, and prosperity in the country."

"You have a role in the leadership of the steering committee, don't you?"

"Yes, I am one of the two Deputy Rapporteurs and designated the spokesman and the one responsible for the quality control of all publications. What I find very sad is that the Revitalization Forum talks became about power sharing, largely concerned with the division of positions in the executive and legislative branches at both the national and state levels. Related to that is the number of states in which people monitor what their area or even tribe will get. I hear no talk about the country or nation we want to build. Is that what the South Sudanese struggle of over half a century was all about? It is really sad."

"You are right, it is sad. I thought I had done a better job at inculcating in my comrades a more strategic political understanding of what liberation was about and what peace would mean to us and our people."

"Actually, you really did your part. Recently, as I was pondering over the crisis, I was deeply moved by something I read in the good book about you that I referred to earlier. It just happens to be here near me. When I turned on the light next to my bed, I still could not see the Chairman, but I went ahead to read, believing that the Chairman would in any case not want to be visible, remaining obscure in the dimness of the room. Let me read it. It quotes you as saying:

So what does Peace mean to us in the SPLM? What does it mean to me personally, not as a leader, but as a brother, an uncle, a father and a child of God? There are many—here and elsewhere—who think that peace is about job allocation, is about appointments to positions of authority, is about lining pockets through misuse or abuse of public assets, or about lording it over others. Those who thus think must be reading from a different script than mine. We have more supreme goals and loftier ideals and alternatives. My script is that Peace is about what people believe Peace should hold for them. Peace to my mind and in the depth of my soul is a promise of a better living to the young, middle aged, to the individual, to the unemployed and the destitute, to the sick and unlettered, all over the Sudan. It is also a promise to the men and women of Southern Sudan, the Nuba Mountains, Southern Blue Nile, Abyei, Eastern Sudan, and other marginalized areas of Sudan who suffered in a dignified silence the loss of their dear ones in the war of liberation or who felt and still feel a sense of helplessness, a promise that we shall never betray the cause for which those martyrs have made the ultimate sacrifice. And theirs is a cause of better and more honorable living. It is also a promise to martyrs and to those who lost their dear ones on the other side, a promise that a just and honorable Peace shall heal all the wounds that we have inflicted on ourselves on both sides.

"I see these words as a most moving summary of the noble principles and indeed ideals for which you led the movement."

"Thanks! I hope my colleagues who assumed the mantle of leadership have not lost sight of that."

"Anyway, going back to the peace process—or, more accurately, processes—the various initiatives now underway remain uncoordinated, far less integrated. Indeed, they are characterized by mutual suspicions and acrimony. The opposition groups outside the country and in the international community see the national dialogue as a ploy by the regime to distract from the implementation of the 2015 Agreement through the Revitalization Forum. The proponents of the national dialogue see the Revitalization Initiative as a regional and international strategy to *undercut* the national dialogue for their own ulterior motives. The opponents of your ruling party see the prospects of reunification as a means of resuscitating a movement or party that they see as a threat and wish would disappear."

"I believe that, whatever its failures, the movement has become too much a part of the political consciousness of the people in the country for it to disappear. What the opponents want will remain wishful thinking. And the role of the international community can only be as good as the will of the people."

"Unfortunately, our people have become so paranoid towards the international community that they invent a hostile sinister plan that does not exist. Some go as far as believing and saying that the international community is against us, that it does not want the war to end, that it is somehow serving its own interests through the suffering of our people, that it is supporting the rebels, and that it wants regime change.

"I tried to remind them—based on my own insights into the perspective of the international community—of a few items: many of those in the international community supported our liberation struggle and independence when there were very strong forces opposed to the division of the Sudan; they had a very ambitious agenda in support of the reconstruction and development of our nascent country; the UN mission in the country was indeed envisaged as a tool for pursuing that agenda. The international community is deeply disappointed by our failure to live up to the noble aspirations of our struggle. It is profoundly concerned with the suffering of our people and does not believe we care about our own people, whom it feels morally bound to protect.

"My message to the international community is that we appreciate its concerns about our people and our country, but that we too obviously care about the suffering of our people and the devastation of our country, perhaps even more than it does. We should see each other as standing on the same ground and pursuing the same goal; rather than weaken ourselves through mutual acrimony, we should join hands and enhance our collective capacity to be more effective in achieving our shared objective.

"On the national dialogue, my message to well-intentioned skeptics is that no one can object to the principle of a national dialogue, that no leader who can claim any moral or political legitimacy would *not* want to see an end to the suffering of his people or the destruction of his country, that the real challenge is how to observe the principles of inclusivity, credibility, transparency, and integrity of the process to ensure its success, that this should be a shared objective and responsibility, and that joining our efforts in promoting the national dialogue would reinforce it and strengthen it, so that it may have a life of its own that can impose itself even on those who might have planned it as a ploy for pursuing other ulterior motives."

"The skeptics on both sides have a point, though. It is easy to say that there is a common ground and a shared objective. But these are lofty ideals. The reality is that different people have different and often competing vested interests. These should be identified and realistically addressed. That's what we did in negotiating the CPA. And that's why we decided to share the oil revenues equally."

"You are right. Obvious as the logic of cooperation toward a common goal is, it is proving to be a hard sell, presumably because of vested interests. For the international community, there is apparently deep mistrust about the political will of the leadership. For our people, there is equally deep suspicion that the world is against us. It reminds me of a discussion I had with you when I wondered why Southerners were afraid that Northerners joining the movement in large numbers might take it over instead of seeing it as success. Your response then was, 'That is the psychology of people who have been oppressed for far too long'."

"It all goes back to a deficit in self-confidence, which sometimes translates into an exaggerated, compensational display of confidence. Anyway, you have given me a great deal of insight into the situation. So, where do things now stand and what is the way forward?"

"The tragedy is that the country is disintegrating. The suffering of the people has really become totally unbearable. Almost throughout the country, there is rampant violence and insecurity. Warfare, not only between but within tribes, is the norm. When I think of how we used to go to school on foot or on horse for days on end, sleeping in the wilderness, fearing no dangers from humans but only from wild animals, and assured of peace, security, and harmony everywhere, and then compare it with what is now going on, you wonder what has become of humanity. This must stop.

"I might have already told you this anecdote and, if so, I apologize for repeating myself. When I left the UN and the Secretary General gave a farewell lunch for me, I asked him whether he was optimistic or pessimistic about the state of the world? I quickly added that we, of course, had to be optimistic—the question was: on what basis? He paused, looking up, and then responded, 'There has been too much suffering'. It was as though he was thinking of South Sudan."

"Sadly," said the Chairman, "witnessing grave human suffering does not seem to give warring factions a motive for peace. To make peace you must cater to what they perceive as their vital interests."

"You are right. And in our case, these vital interests seemed to be merely 'pie in the sky'. Meanwhile, they appear to be blind to the massive suffering on the ground.

"When our people used to speak of the time the world was spoiled, a total destruction of the world as they knew it, I thought they were referring to a catastrophe or calamity that was a thing of the mythical past that would never occur again. Our people now use the same terminology to describe what is happening in their world today. Is humanity descending into the past, or moving forward into a better future?"

"Let me try to respond to what I think is a rhetorical question. Of course, humanity must progress into a better future. But a better future will not come by itself. It has to be achieved by the will, the way, and the endeavor of the people. And that needs leadership. And that in turn needs global partnership. No country can achieve any progress in isolation. The saying that no man is an island unto himself is not just a cliché; it is a truism."

"You are quite right; the world *is* progressing forward. That is why the world is demonstrating deep concern about what is happening to our people. But the different strands of initiatives remain parallel and not sufficiently coordinated, far less integrated. If they are to be effective, then they must be made complementary. My view is that, in the short run, the Revitalization agenda and the national dialogue must intersect and overlap in favor of an immediate end to violence through sustainable ceasefire and power-sharing arrangements. The national dialogue can then continue to comprehensively address the problems confronting the country at all levels, from the grassroots to the national.

"The critical question is: where will the process lead? What is the end game? I believe we have three main options about the system of governance we should aim to establish and consolidate. We can choose to continue with the current system, which is based on the Western model followed by most African countries—of course, with appropriate reforms; adopt a novel system that is based on our cultural values and institutions; or develop an integrated model based on both. In my earlier study, you might recall, I proposed a strategy of transitional integration that aims at applying precisely such a model.

"In a way, the Swiss-sponsored proposal, aimed at establishing a House of Nationalities, reflected an element of building on our traditional institutions. As you will recall, I was inclined toward supporting it, but you were somewhat reluctant to endorse it."

The Chairman explained the grounds for his objection to the proposal. "It was a politically motivated tool to support the agenda of the opposing individuals who portrayed themselves as representatives of an ethnic minority. The Swiss funded the project as a way of encouraging pluralism and multi-party 'democracy'."

"Yes, I recall your telling me that we would develop our own way of utilizing our cultural values and institutions. But we never did."

"We had no time."

"I still believe that we are dealing with a paradoxical development in our contemporary world. As you know, the people of South Sudan have been thoroughly studied by anthropologists and are known to be exceedingly proud, egalitarian, independent-minded, and intensely resistant to domination. Until recently, when they have been exposed to new standards of scientific advances and material advantages in other societies, they considered their race and culture the ideal models of God's creation. They regarded their cattle as the most noble model of wealth, a source of envy by others, and their land the best in the world. Their myths of creation provided justification for their sense of racial and cultural superiority.

"I have always argued that the notions of wealth and poverty, from a cultural perspective, should be viewed as having objective and subjective components. While our people objectively lack many of the resources associated with wealth in the modern world, subjectively they never considered themselves poor and would be insulted to see themselves described as such. Their popular songs are—without exception—always in praise of their ancestral wealth, social standing, pride, and dignity. It is because of their ethnocentrism and cultural chauvinism that they initially resisted modern medicine, education, and the market practice of selling and buying, which they viewed as repugnant to their spiritual and moral values."

"That, at least in part, explains why they have been left behind by the train of progress."

"Absolutely. It was only when they came to realize that their traditional sense of pride and dignity could indeed be enhanced by these modern resources and practices that they radically embraced change and modernity. That is when migration into towns in search of employment, previously despised as depraved, began to be popular. But that is also when they began to see the comparative disadvantages of their traditional life. Negative self-perceptions began to grow. People began to accept, though reluctantly, that they were indeed 'poor' by modern criteria. But even then, if we take the current standard of one US dollar a day as the poverty cut-off point, then it is still difficult to see how a person with a hundred heads of cattle, with a polygamous family, living in relatively well-constructed homes, with cattle byres for their herds, and with ample land to farm can be said to live on one dollar a day.

"But feelings of deprivation increasingly grew, especially in light of European Christian and Arab Islamic domination. Myths of superiority began to be reinterpreted to explain emerging deprivation. One myth, which had proudly presented the Dinka as choosing the cow against the mysterious thing called 'What', began to be recast as denying the Black man that potentially enriching 'What'. God then gave 'What' to the White man and Arabs and it became the source of scientific inventiveness and prosperity that have given them advantages over our people. Another myth, which had favorably portrayed the Black child as more loved by their mother than their White and Brown siblings, whom she did not adequately nurse, now has the father asking God to take care of His deprived children, thereby giving them more benefits than the Black child."

"That is paradoxical because it makes God a party to injustice, when humanity looks up for divine justice."

"But that paradox is built into religion. Does the Bible not say that to those that have, more shall be given, and to those who do not have, even the little they have shall be taken? Where is justice in that? I am reminded of the song by Ray Charles that says it is 'them that got are them that get; how you get the first is still a mystery to me.'"

"I told you not to question me on the ways of God. All I can do is repeat the popular saying that God helps those who help themselves."

"In that respect, you did indeed help our people with enriching ideas. You found them sliding into a self-perception as poor and downtrodden. Someone interpreted the Bible as meaning that God helps those who help themselves.

"This was the situation that your liberation movement effectively began to reverse, by making the marginalized non-Arab peoples of the Sudan revive their sense of confidence and demand full equality. In their war songs, they began to tell the Arabs, 'O people, the land is our land'. They told the Arab rulers, 'Back to your original home, the land is being claimed by its legitimate owners'. As a result of this moral reorientation, our people's sense of confidence, pride, and dignity began to be revived and revitalized. It was a most gratifying development to watch. Now, all this is once again being reversed. Our people are being both objectively and subjectively impoverished and humiliated through mistreatment by their enemies and their own leaders."

"Remember, as we just said, God helps those who help themselves. And leaders also help those able to help themselves. I did not give our people any material gains. All I did was to try to inspire them to enhance their self-image and to realize that self-image through their own efforts of self-enhancement. You are right—we did that with ideas."

"That's my point. What is missing is that leadership of ideas, the inspiration for lifting themselves up and sustaining their upward march to prosperity and dignity. You led a war of liberation that was uplifting. Now, the humanitarian tragedy imposed by the conditions of a prolonged chain of wars has made them destitute. Unable to cultivate or keep their herds within utilitarian reach, since they must be kept far away from potential raiders, people are now largely living on international food aid, mostly from the United States. This is surplus food from subsidized overproduction which would otherwise be rotting in storage. Food aid is, of course, saving lives, which is much appreciated, but it is also impoverishing them, making them dependent and killing their incentive to produce."

"This is an area that has been of grave concern for me," he said. "No one can become rich on charity and everyone wants to get wealthy if they can, not be a beggar."

"You have just rephrased what I have always said, that no one can be rich by begging in the church yard. You are in fact reported to have said that relief was harmful to development because it plants laziness and dependence on foreign hands. You also said that after liberation from domination, people should no longer expect to receive assistance from the government. The situation would indeed be paradoxical, as the government would not have money to give, since people would have no money to support the government in the first place. You said that poor people have weak states while rich people have powerful states."

I concluded my account of this jigsaw process of racial, ethnic, and cultural progression and retrogression by telling the Chairman: "This is what your leadership in life and the implications of your death have brought to our people: first a redemption from enslavement and self-denigration, then a return to objective and subjective impoverishment that was alien to them even in their unadulterated traditional life. It is a deeply painful development to watch.

"That book about you which I referred to earlier has a very pertinent statement about how you reversed the negative self-image of our people. Let me read what the author said:

The Chairman refused to be seen or treated in a self-defeating context of being an inferior South Sudanese, second- or third-class citizen. Though some politicians from South Sudan preferred to see him as a 'sell-out to Arabs', he stood out [as an] articulate, sincere and a dignified fighter. The Chairman did not address the problem as the 'Southern Problem' from an angle of intellectual bankruptcy and poor logic adopted by the Northern Arab-Islamic elite. Those people set their parameters around personal gains and apprehensions, and some Southern elites allowed themselves to be subjugated because of what to eat.

"In another area of the book, he wrote:

The Chairman succeeded in liberating Southern Sudanese minds from the bondage of 'inferiority complex', which subjugated people behind borders demarcated between South and North by colonialists; keeping our people behind the savannah curtain blocked Southern Sudanese 'political mind' in the bondage of backing for rights. The Chairman went on logically to emphasize the problem, saying, 'Who would really be the problem, the one carrying a person on his back, or the one being carried?' In those words, the Chairman succeeded to articulate the 'Sudanese problem' with excellence like nobody did before. He applied the analysis in similar situations in the Nuba Mountains, Blue Nile and Darfur where the same conditions of domination existed. He applied the same analysis to Eastern Sudan and to Khartoum itself, which made him more Sudanese than those claiming to be citizens of Khartoum.

"Sadly, all this now looks like history. South Sudan appears to be plunging back to the time our people used to describe as when the world was spoiled. The pride our people used to have—even when they suffered the humiliation of foreign domination, from which you had begun to liberate them physically and mentally—is rapidly eroding. The President recently lamented this, by pointing out that, at independence, we were a proud nation and we stood tall and held our heads high, but that we no longer are because of what we are doing. He ended with the rhetorical question, 'Why are we doing this to our people?'"

Dead silence followed. The Chairman did not say a word in response. "Are you still with me?" I asked.

"Yes, I am with you. What do you want me to say? Part of me does not want to believe you because it is too painful to listen to you. But I have never heard you tell a lie. Besides, what you are saying is glaringly visible. You describe it in a vivid and traumatizing manner that is too distressful to react to. All I can say is I hear you."

"When I used to hear you talk about the village in which you were born as the Biblical Garden of Eden, and refer to specific verses of the Holy Bible to justify your claim, I used to marvel at your audacity in making such outrageously mythical claims. I also thought it utopian for you to say that, in the New Sudan, you would plant all the varieties of the trees in the world to line the miles of the streets in your village. I learned only recently that the Garden of Eden is said to have indeed had all the varieties of plants and trees in the world. I now see these ideas, which I used to consider absurd and utopian, in a different light. They are elements of extraordinary perceptions of a visionary leader who was set to positively transform our country, and perhaps the lands beyond.

"Another South Sudanese who is a committed member of your Movement and a devoted believer in your leadership wrote a powerful book on your ideas, with a focus on the New Sudan Vision. He traces the identity of our people to ancient Kush, using Biblical and other archeological sources to substantiate the connection. His scholarly documentation of these historical claims to Kush represents a reconstruction of identity through myth creation that is not different from the manner in which the Northern Sudanese claims to Arab-Islamic roots evolved. He envisioned the New Sudan Project as a way of utilizing what he described as the illustrious history of the Kingdom of Kush to achieve the ideals of freedom, liberty, and dignity.

"If I remember his words correctly, he wrote that you 'brought down the walls of injustice and marginalization by securing our mental liberation from the self-imprisonment we suffered in the jails of ignorance, hatred and jealousy. This mental liberation came through the truth about our rich historical heritage that the thousand-year empire of the Kushites bequeathed to us.'

"After citing Genesis and archeological research that confirm that Kush/Cush was the first recorded kingdom to be established in sub-Saharan Africa, the author observes that, because of 'our lazy thinking', we have not been able to dig deeper into our history, but that you did that. He then proceeded to quote sources establishing Kush as a Black Kingdom that wielded considerable tools of power—military and governance—without having a system of writing, an extensive bureaucracy, or numerous urban centers. Alleging that historians have mislabeled Kush as a vassal of the state of Egypt, the author went on to say that the challenge is for our historians to join hands with world-renowned archeologists in their quest to dig deep into the Kushite system of governance, because 'the ugly face of racism and prejudice concealed this reality'."

"I can see that you still hold doubts on the legitimacy of our historical claims to Kush as a Black Kingdom and Civilization to which we belonged!?" The Chairman posed a challenging question.

I was quite candid in my response: "To tell you the truth, this reconstruction of identity, which was, of course, a pervasive aspect of your promotion of the New Sudan Vision, was one which I initially viewed with skepticism as too contrived. But I grew to understand, recognize, and appreciate it as a creative mythology of identity formation. I do not use the word 'myth' to connote lack of reality, but as a concept that is well established in the social sciences to mean frequently occurring or recurring ideas and practices. And as I have noted, this mythical shaping of identity mirrored in many respects is reminiscent of the way the Arab-Islamic identity was shaped.

"My own works, based on extensive interviews with Dinka Chiefs and elders in the early 1970s and published in two books, *Dinka Cosmology* and *Africans of Two Worlds: The Dinka in Afro-Arab Sudan,* indicated the connection to the Biblical and Koranic scriptures and religious practices, a connection that has also been documented by anthropologists. Centuries of intervening hostilities have, however, overshadowed this connection. Perhaps for the same reason, I don't think this revivalist reconstruction of bridging identity resonates with most South Sudanese. This is, however, not a reason to stop the scientific search for knowledge on the issue. So whatever reservations I initially held, I became converted to your strategic reconstruction of national identity."

I ended with an equally challenging question: "How could you leave such a powerful vision to remain just an illusion?"

"I know you want me to respond," said the Chairman, "but I can't. All I can say is that a vision is a human creation and therefore can be realized by humans. No one can say definitively when that realization will happen. But faith is a vital motivation in human endeavor and attainment. So, hope and hope and keep on hoping!"

"We will—hopefully, with your inspiration. I recently heard some fascinating reflections about the Agreement you negotiated with the North. It is said that you skillfully and very successfully negotiated an agreement that is in many ways the best that could have been done under the circumstances. Even the interim arrangements gave the South virtually all it wanted, with virtual independence combined with a share of power and wealth at the Center. However, it is said that you negotiated an agreement whose implementation in the way it was intended only you could have ensured. You certainly would have consolidated Southern independence while also pursuing the transformation of the Center to both guarantee the independence of the South and create a compatible twin system in the North. That is too good an arrangement for anyone other than the one who created it to implement. Why did you leave it half-cooked?"

"You are exhausting my capacity to absorb and respond. I find everything you say painfully fascinating. Much of it I know or recognize. Some of it I believe to be your creative expansion of what I did or intended to do. But I cannot comment on what all this means now. There is nothing I can do except hope and have faith that ideas do not die. As I said earlier, they merely become dormant and wait for the right leadership at the right time to make them rise and bloom into fruition."

"The question is often raised as to what you would have done in the country, had you lived. I will spare you the need to go back that far. What would you advise your colleagues in the leadership of South Sudan to do now to address the crisis they are in and move the country forward?

"Before you answer, I should say that what moved me quite profoundly by the end of the book I have just referred to is how the synergy between your ideas and those of your expert advisors became so developed and close to implementation by the time you assumed the position of First Vice-President of the Sudan and President of South Sudan. The detailed account of what you and your advisors did during this brief period can be summarized in two clusters: conceptual and operational. Five conceptual issues relating to governance and management capacity can be identified:

"Decision-making capacity, which refers to the ability to make decisions;

"Policy reform capacity, which, in the context of a post-conflict environment, refers to the ability of war-to-peace transition leadership to put in place a set of rules, policies, and strategies for good governance;

"Implementation capacity, which is the ability to translate policies into action and implement formulated policies, strategies, and associated programs/projects within given resource constraints, including time and human and financial resources;

"Service delivery capacity, which is the ability of newly established administration to provide basic public services—for example, security and administration of justice, including human rights protection, education, health, water, and physical infrastructure; and

"Accountability capacity, which is the ability to ensure equity in the allocation as well as efficiency in the utilization of public resources, including development assistance and effective coordination of donors' support in the immediate aftermath of the peace agreement.

"Foreign policy featured significantly in your plans, which stipulated a foreign policy that would take account of the unique and strategic location of the country as an important link or bridge between Africa and the Arab world. A Sudan at peace with itself and its neighbors had the potential of becoming a regional powerhouse in the light of its size as the largest country in Africa, its natural resource endowment, and its historical military might since the time of the Kingdom of Kush. The framers of a new foreign policy for Sudan were to take these parameters into account in formulating the strategic role of Sudanese diplomacy in the geopolitics of the twenty-first century.

"Now, let me go back to my question: What would you advise your successors?"

"Again, you are asking a question which I have already answered. My time has passed, and the responsibility has also passed on. I cannot be a competing dead man. You have already answered your question on what should be done. If the parties agree to end the war, as they must either by their willful choice or in response to international pressure, then they will need to immediately alleviate the suffering of the people. The army must then be turned into a force for ensuring peace, security, and stability throughout the country. Conditions should be created for the voluntary return of the people to their areas of origin. They should be given urgent services and assisted with the tools to resume their normal self-reliant way of life. Oil revenues must be invested in development and not in fighting futile wars. Socio-economic development programs in areas of health, education, agriculture and infrastructure should be expeditiously prepared and implemented. The objective should be to take the amenities of the towns to the villages to reduce the impoverishing influx of the rural population into urban centers, where they get subjected to the humiliating tales of cities divided between the dignified rich and the denigrated poor.

I elaborated: "We must return our people to their previous subjective view of themselves as wealthy. If a person thinks he is rich, why make him think that he is poor? And if he believes he is rich, why not challenge him to use his wealth to invest in production to become even richer? And why not alert him to his becoming poorer if he does not use his wealth to get richer?"

"It is fascinating you say that. After the Addis Ababa Agreement, I interviewed a number of Dinka Chiefs for a book I was writing on the

Dinka worldview. It was later published under the title of *Africans of Two Worlds*. The book begins with myths of creation and original leadership and earliest migration, moves on to contact and interaction with the outside world, leading to wars with invaders, slave raiders, and various forms of foreign domination that seemed to have ended with the Addis Ababa Agreement. Throughout that whole historical account, despite the challenges of foreign aggression and oppression, what came through was a high degree of self-esteem and confidence. The lamentations of war were shifting to the positive aspirations of post-conflict development. And they described their society as wealthy and able to support their own development.

"They asserted that their very identity connoted wealth, that their wealth was cattle, that because of their cattle wealth they were admired and envied by others, and that with that wealth they were now prepared to support their development and construct schools, hospitals, and roads. They said that they did not need money from anyone, as they were ready to sell their cattle to acquire the money needed for development. All they needed was technology and equipment, such as tractors, for which they were ready to pay.

"I knew that all this indigenous pride reflected a grossly inflated ego, but I also took it as a potentially useful resource. Why not build on that positive self-perception until they recognize their limitation, in which case they themselves would then accept with appreciation any complementary input into their development? And, after all, development should not be viewed as something falling from the sky or a gift from outside benefactors. It should be seen as an incremental improvement of what you do anyway and can do better. People have always built their own dwellings; they can build better housing. People have always grown their own food; they can increase the production and quality of what they grow. People have always reared their livestock and benefitted from animal products; the quantity and quality of those products can also be improved. People have always needed pathways; they can upgrade those into roads needed for better means of transport. In other words, development should be viewed as a process of self-enhancement from within, self-generated and self-supported, with external complementarity as needed."

"This external complementarity as needed can be a potential trap, as it can incrementally lead to dependency. It begins with innocuous terms like *interdependence*, *cooperation*, and *equal partnership*, but the richer and more powerful soon become 'more equal' than others. And partnership becomes grossly uneven in their favor. Even assistance means proudly giving with the right hand and discreetly taking much of it back with the left hand. Traditional self-perception of pride and dignity turns into a demeaning and self-deprecating acceptance of poverty, begging, and indignity."

"You are absolutely right. It brings to mind the way our traditional method of resolving conflicts—which was part of our culture, practiced by our chiefs, leaders, and elders as part of their functional role in society—was turned into a project for which foreign funding was being solicited. This is the famous case of the Wunlit Peace Conference, in which Dinka and Nuer chiefs and elders negotiated a peace agreement between their communities. The intellectuals who were associated with the process soon turned it into a model project, which they used to raise funds in Europe and particularly in the United States.

"I attended some of their presentations in Washington and New York and listened with mixed feelings. On the one hand, I was glad that the practice was recognized, documented, and made known internationally. On the other hand, I was disturbed that what was a normal cultural pattern, practiced as part of the responsibilities of leadership in our traditional society, was being turned into a professional skill that needed foreign funding. Reinforcing the practice with foreign funding was paradoxically undermining the practice as an indigenous voluntary function. I made my views known without restraint."

"I fully agree. The question now is what to do about it. I do not mean this specific issue of traditional methods of conflict resolution. I mean the whole issue of dependency."

"I think the starting point should be making better use of our cultural values and institutions as resources in our development strategies. I have been interested in observing the experiences of other countries, especially in Asia, specifically Japan, South Korea, and China. And one of the areas of conversation I consistently raised was how they approached *their* development from a cultural point of view. All of them related their development patterns to their cultural values. The details of what that meant may not be easy to articulate, but its contextual manifestation was quite evident."

"I would be very interested to hear what was said."

"I am happy to share that with you, but I hope it does not sound too academic or intellectual."

"Are you suggesting that I am not up to that? You think my mental capacity has been compromised by death?"

"*Benydit,* you are the last person I could dare to say that about! Remember, when I was accused by some reviewer of my book, *War of Visions*, that it was obvious I was the theorist for your movement, I protested that he was putting me in trouble with my friend—*you*—as you did not need a theorist, being yourself the thinker for your movement. As for the impact of death on your thinking, I hope nothing in our long series has suggested that I entertain such a thought."

"You are taking me too seriously! I was joking"

"Actually, I thought so. On the other hand, as we have agreed, this material is for a wider audience than yourself. So, it should not be too theoretical or intellectual."

"Well, I should also warn you not to insult the intelligence of your potential readers. But this has been a long session. Let us leave it for our next session."

"Point well taken. I will tell the story and make no intellectual assumptions."

"Or assume that the reader is fully with you."

"That too," I said as we ended the session. It had been quite a substantive discussion of approaches to development and, although related to what the Chairman would have done, the ideas that were generated were pertinent to what is doable generally. And the experiences of other countries were quite relevant to that discussion. That was to be the subject of our next discussion.

Session Twenty-Six: Development

A s we were to discuss issues related to development, the sensitive issue of the Chairman's death did not feature directly. So, when he announced his arrival, we exchanged greetings and went directly to the topic of the session.

The Chairman began by reminding me to tell the story of my visits to Asia and my observations about their development strategies. He also reminded me to talk straight and not 'talk down' to my audience.

"You remind me of an anecdote," I opened. "A Swedish friend who was something of a renegade in his society and was writing books that were very critical of the Swedish welfare system, which he wanted me to contribute to, was telling ladies in a well-known aristocratic family about his latest book. One of them said, 'I hope you will make your next book simple enough for us ordinary people to understand.' My friend's reaction was, 'I will try!'

"I didn't want to say I will, but I get your caution. I went to China in 1986, at a time when the Chinese saw themselves as a developing country and did not even want to be acknowledged as a leader in the developing world. They said they needed Western technology for their development but wanted to develop in the Chinese way. When I asked what 'the Chinese way' was, they could not specify, and reacted only by saying jokingly that I asked difficult questions. When I told them that I thought their cultural revolution was a strategic withdrawal from the international community to come to know themselves and then rejoin on their indigenous cultural terms, they reacted against that. The cultural revolution experience was a very painful one in which they saw nothing positive. But I still meant what I said. I wrote a report about that visit which I titled, 'China: A Giant at the Cross-Roads', in which I documented my comparative observations about China and Africa."

"Did you clarify what roads they were crossing?"

"No, I did not, but I thought it was implicitly the Western way and what they vaguely called the Chinese way."

"Fair enough. So, continue with the other cases."

"Japan and South Korea, of course, benefitted from the West, particularly the United States, in supporting their development after the Second World War, but their distinctive cultural orientation has also been a major factor in their development pattern. One distinctive difference with Africa is the respect the world accords to Asian cultures, contrasted with the condescending view of African cultures.

"Two countries in Africa stand out as relatively successful models of building development on indigenous cultures. The first is Botswana. Although I have never visited the country, from my reading in the early 1960s about their customary law, which has been well documented by anthropologists, and a book about Seretse Khama, who led the country to independence, and from my more recent readings about their system of government, Botswana has been quite successful in developing on an indigenous cultural foundation. Although a small country with rich mineral resources, especially diamonds, I believe their success has much to do with making effective use of their cultural values, which, like those of South Sudanese Nilotic societies, are dominated by cattle."

"Actually," mused the Chairman, "they were among the countries most sympathetic to our cause. They believed that South Sudan was the northern front line of Black Africa from historical times and that we were the buffer against the spread of Arabism and Islam into the African heartland."

"What I found remarkable," I continued, "is that Seretse Khama, the leader of the independence movement and President from 1966 until his death in 1980, was married to an English woman. Interestingly enough, she was his partner in the development of the country on the basis of indigenous African cultural values."

"It shows that the issue is not race, but ideas and principles, as you know from your own example."

"That's right. Many of my relatives praise my wife as more Dinka than most Dinka wives in the family, maybe an overstatement, but I believe a justified compliment."

"Very much so!"

"Going back to my account of African examples, Rwanda's case is another interesting model. I visited the country in the 70s, 80s, and 90s. I went there only several months after the 1994 genocide on my UN mandate on internal displacement. And I visited again more recently. The transformation is remarkable. Rwanda now looks like a modern

European country in the heart of Africa. When I asked how they did that, the gist of what I was told was that they invoked their cultural values to stimulate their model of development. And the cultural values they mentioned to me were almost identical to those of our people."

"I am not surprised. They *are* actually our people. If you noticed, although the Tutsis are considered generally light skinned, many of them are as black as we are, with features identical to ours."

"Interestingly enough, one of my brothers was supposed to go to Rwanda on a UN human rights mission, but it was decided that he would be mistaken for a Tutsi. So, he was advised against going. During my visits, I was often mistaken for a Tutsi and people spoke to me in their language. I recall one evening at dinner with a number of Tutsi leaders. I made a comment that made one of them, the Minister of Foreign Affairs, a very black Tutsi with a sense of humor, remark, 'Listen to this Tutsi'—meaning me.

"I was told that in their development strategy, they invoked, for instance, their notion of dignity, which was the same as what our people call *dheeng,* a concept that has esthetic, physical, moral, social, and spiritual connotations. The argument they presented to their people was that you could not have that dignity if you are not physically clean, if your house is not well built and neat, or if the areas surrounding your house are not clean and tidy. Not only are the houses in Kigali well built and well kept, but the city as a whole is meticulously clean, with flowers and well-trimmed hedges prominently featured.

"Another cultural value I was told they built upon was a concept of unity, harmony, and solidarity, which corresponds to what our people call *cieng baai.* This concept was used to mobilize people to help each other in building their houses and public utilities, cultivating their fields to increase production, and constructing roads, all with modest state contribution as a stimulus. In a way, this collective work was applied by the British in the Sudan using the age-set system in our traditional society but was abandoned after independence as colonial exploitation of forced labor. What I found striking about the Rwandan model is that their culture, which is cattle-oriented, is quite similar to ours in almost all aspects."

"As I said, they *are* our people. What you left out of your analysis is the role of leadership. I knew the Rwandan President well. He and many of his colleagues were personal friends. They had a deep commitment to their cause and the ideals of their struggle. They are trying to live up to those ideals."

"Actually, I was told that one of their guiding principles is zero tolerance of corruption. I was told that many generals were languishing in prisons. One of the factors in their favor is what you might call blood money paid by the international community over the guilt of withdrawing the peacekeepers while genocide was underway and abandoning nearly a million Tutsis and liberal Hutus to be slaughtered. Even three months after the slaughter, bodies lay as shrunken skins plastered on skeletons. In one location, on a rainy day, my helicopter landed some one hundred meters from the site, a church. To enter the churchyard, I had to go through an archway where bodies were piled up. People trying to flee from the adjacent rooms to the left of the archway had fallen dead, in a line, as they tried to escape.

"Entering into the churchyard meant literally stepping over the bodies. Fortunately, someone had given me rubbers to wear over my shoes and which I, of course, discarded as soon as I left the scene. Going through the churchyard littered with bodies and then into the church where bodies also lay scattered, with unforgiving stink, was an experience I can never forget and, hopefully, will never see again. I could not believe that human bodies could be treated worse than dogs. And I wondered why the Rwandan government allowed the bodies to be so defiled by leaving them to rot unburied for months. However, I learned that it was a deliberate way of keeping the evidence, later moved into the now famous museum in Kigali. For days, I could hardly eat, as the sight and the smell continued to haunt me. I am sorry, I got carried away. It was a painful experience."

"No, please, do not apologize. These are vitally important experiences from which to learn. Such atrocities are not unique or totally isolated. They are potential horrors that loom upon humanity at large. Please continue."

"You have actually indicated the direction for continuing with my narrative. The Rwandan genocide was an aggravated replay of the most horrific crime humanity keeps repeating. I was in former Yugoslavia two years earlier at the peak of the Bosnian war in 1992, also in connection with my UN mandate on internal displacement. It was a case of experiencing the Nazi concentration camps that I had watched in documentaries. Skeletons plastered with skins appeared literally like walking dead or bodies lying motionless on hay in sometimes roofless barns, soaked with the cold rains of the winter season.

"The world keeps saying 'Never again', only to see genocide or similar atrocities repeated again and again. The only optimistic aspect to it all is that every time we *say* 'Never again' and it *happens* again, the guilt level rises and with it the determination to do better. And yet, people shy away from even mentioning the word genocide. Denial immediately sets in, not only by those alleged to have committed the genocide, but also by those who would be called upon to prevent it or to punish the perpetrators.

"That is why, in discharging my UN mandate on the prevention of genocide, I decided to demystify the crime, describing it as an extreme form of identity-related conflicts. What causes conflict is not the mere differences, but how we manage the differences. In most countries afflicted by identity conflicts, the country is divided between the in-groups, whose members enjoy the rights of citizenship, and the out-groups, who are discriminated against, marginalized, denigrated, excluded, and denied the full rights of citizenship and human dignity. If they react against this gross indignity, the dominant group retaliates with a vengeance that can become genocidal."

"So, what do we do about it?"

"You know very well what we do. I believe in your approach to our problems in the Sudan: you created the framework for a preventive strategy, one that I sincerely share. From the analytical perspective I have just presented, it follows that the best strategy for preventing genocide or mass atrocities is constructive management of diversity to promote inclusivity, non-discrimination, full equality, and enjoyment of the rights of citizenship and human dignity. Does this sound familiar?"

"Are you asking me or your potential reader? Yes, of course; that's our New Sudan. But from what you say about what is happening, you are as far from it now as we were in the Old Sudan."

"Unfortunately, yes. Although the crisis of identity in the Old Sudan sharply dichotomized the country into clear-cut lines of race, ethnicity, culture, and religion, South Sudan, which had been assumed to have no such divisions, is now torn apart by tribal differences that are proving just as deadly—and, some believe, worse. This shows that identity conflicts are relative. After all, Somalia, one of the most homogeneous societies, is now torn apart by clan conflicts. Differences can go even lower down, to the family level and between individuals.

But the prescription is the same—recognition, acceptance, mutual respect, and equality. In South Sudan today, the Dinka are being seen in much the same way as Southerners saw the Arabs in the Sudan. Since partition is not an option, New Sudan, now New South Sudan, is the only option."

"And the core of that is to make every group feel in control of its own affairs and destiny, while also enjoying equal participation in the sharing of national power and wealth. The world is moving in opposite directions at the same time. People are broadening their horizons into larger identity frameworks, and countries are becoming members of larger communities. At the same time, people find solace and greater security in being part of smaller, more close-knit circles, in which loyalties and solidarities are more intimate and tangible."

"I suppose this takes us back to our earlier discussion about building development on indigenous values and institutions. For me, this has meant studying the Dinka in depth and through a variety of disciplines, including customary law, oral history, anthropology, and folklore. The paradox is that, while this particularistic approach is essential to our understanding of our composite national identity configuration, it runs the risk of being seen as chauvinistic and tribalistic. What is interesting is how much our understanding of the particular reveals how much we have in common. A South Sudanese scholar from Equatoria told me that my ethnographic study of the Dinka was very reflective of his own society. And a Somalian told me that my ethnography on the Dinka applied very much to his Somali society. Even as far away as the United States, people told me how struck they were by the differences as much as by the similarities between Dinka culture and universal values and principles. That only goes to show that humanity is as diverse as it is unifying."

"I have, of course, read your works and how you applied Dinka culture to culturally oriented development. Why don't you give us a brief summary of your thesis?"

"As you know, my approach to this subject is documented in my doctoral thesis, which became my first book, *Tradition and Modernization: A Challenge for Law Among the Dinka of the Sudan*, published in 1971. In that book, I propounded what I called a 'Strategy of Transitional Integration', very much along the lines of what I said about Rwanda. But I covered the values, institutions, and patterns of behavior comprehensively. Even the overriding traditional concept of immortalization through procreation, *kooc e nhom,* which the Chairman of my doctoral committee called the myth of permanent identity and influence, could be invoked to foster developmental achievements for which one can be remembered after death. It is interesting that when I published my doctoral dissertation, which was my first, one of my brothers, a medical doctor, wrote to congratulate me and said, 'This is the immortality in which I believe.'

"Very well said. What more is there to be said?"

I detected that the Chairman was hinting that it was time to end the session, which had been quite long. We had pretty much exhausted the areas we needed to discuss in the conversations. But I was totally surprised when the Chairman suggested that it was perhaps time to end our program of his visits. "Ever since your visit to the psychiatrist, I see that our meetings and discussions have caused concern in your family. I see no need for us to cause so much anxiety to your family. In any case, I think we have exhausted many of the issues we wanted to discuss."

Although the Chairman's suggestion came to me as a shock, I could see his point. In fact, the initiative could just as well have come from me. My reflections went back to the very question that continued to haunt me ever since the psychiatrist raised the issue of whether it was the Chairman or me who wanted our experiences recorded. In a way, it no longer mattered now. We had recorded our experiences, mostly mine. We were now both exhausted. I felt quite ambivalent about what the Chairman said, sad about the prospects of ending the program, but appreciative and even relieved that it was a wise course of action.

However, the Chairman, in his gracious mannerism, did not want to abruptly end this unique and remarkably enlightening experience. He suggested that our next session should perhaps gently lead us to the end of the series. We parted on that note.

Session Twenty-Seven: Termination

The suggestion the Chairman made at the end of our last session still haunted me. And although I accepted what he said, I still entertained the hope that he might change his mind and that there was still some room for discussion. This added to my usual anxiety in anticipation of his arrival. The more I thought that our sessions were coming to an end, the more I appreciated what they meant to me and the more I looked forward to our next one.

The time was 8:00 pm, which was the usual time for his arrival. But as we did not go by the strict hour, I waited for 8:30. Then my anxiety increased. By 9:00 pm I began to worry. At 9:30, I began to suspect that something had happened again. What would it be this time? Was the Chairman again testing me? But I had assured him of my interest. And we had ruled out health concerns as irrelevant to the dead. By 10:00 pm, I began to reassess the whole program of visitations. Why should I allow myself to be a victim of the whims of the Chairman? Did I really need him that much? And even if I needed him earlier, had we not talked enough? Was he perhaps already acting upon what we had agreed, that we should end the program? But he had suggested that we should ease ourselves out of the program. Should he just decide by himself without further consultation? More questions flowed for which I had no answers.

I was tempted to call my wife and share the development with her, not only for the sake of company, but also in the chance that she might persuade me to free myself from the bondage of the Chairman's visitations. But no, that would not only be weakness, but failure. Why did I allow myself to tell the Chairman all that about my experiences? What good did that do me? What will he do with it anyway in his world of the dead? And what will it do for me? If I shared the information widely, would I not be risking being considered self-promoting at best and crazy at worst?

The bottom line was that the Chairman had not turned up for a second time. Since he had an explanation last time, perhaps he will also have an explanation this time too. I should give him the benefit of the doubt, as they say. The Arabs say that an absentee has his reason. I tried to convince myself that the Chairman must have his reason.

The flow of questions without answers exhausted me into gradually fading into a restless sleep. I woke up in the morning with the same questions in mind. I told my wife that I had barely slept. She wanted to know why, but I ignored the question and changed the subject. I spent the day repeating the questions in my mind without answers. And as I persuaded myself that the Chairman had disappeared for good, I did not even look forward to the usual time of his arrival. Dinner with the family offered an occasion that I wanted to help reorient me, away from the distorted view of the world my own lifge had become through the visitations of the Chairman.

Session Twenty-Eight: Progress

As I lay in bed planning to go to sleep, the thought crossed my mind that the visit of the Chairman would have been about that time. But although we had missed only one night's session, my thoughts and reflections of denial made the experience quite distant. It all seemed like a long dream from which I had awakened.

I gave myself the consoling thought that at least our last session had been a rich discussion about cross-cultural approaches to development. There was not much else to add. In fact, we had pretty much covered all the issues that were to be addressed. And, as the Chairman had suggested, perhaps the next session was only to lead us to the conclusion of the visitations.

Then, to my utter surprise, the familiar sound of the Chairman announced his presence. *"Raandit,* good evening! I have returned."

I almost behaved like a child disguising his pleasure with a contrived somber look. "What happened?" I asked without returning his greeting.

"Won't you at least greet me first before asking?"

"Well, I don't know whether you have actually returned or I am dreaming. I need to know by asking why you did not come?"

"I told you that I was getting concerned about your family. You can say that I was again testing to see whether this program was something you can begin to be less dependent on. Missing another session would provide you with the opportunity to begin the process of ending the program."

I saw the Chairman's point, although I resented the fact that it was a unilateral decision without consultation. But it did not make sense to quarrel with a dead man. Besides, he was back and we had two concluding sessions to conduct.

"Let us be more constructive and move on with the substantive conversation."

"Very well. What would you want us to talk about?" I asked.

"The choice is yours," the Chairman responded.

I thought of one more area for discussion. I began by telling him that in my chronic propensity for optimism, I wanted this session to focus on recent developments in the peace process.

"That's a very good idea. So why don't you begin with the progress of the High-Level Forum for the Revitalization of the 2015 Peace Agreement?"

"That's precisely what was on my mind. What is striking is that Sudan has assumed the leadership role in the IGAD mediation and the talks have been held in Khartoum now for over a month. Usually, these talks held in Addis last for a week, at most ten days. What is now going to almost a month and a half is clearly a record, which most people see as a reflection of the seriousness of Khartoum to get positive results.

"I will not go into details about the issues being discussed, what has so far been agreed, what is still being negotiated, and what the prospects of full success are. What has so far transpired as positive progress is that Sudan and South Sudan have reached a bilateral agreement on oil production, including securing the oil fields and revising revenue sharing. Most of the parties have signed the security arrangements and initialed the power-sharing agreement, and those still reluctant to join are still negotiating an arrangement to bring them on board. The final agreement is expected to be signed on August 8, 2018, to be witnessed by the regional heads of state. Sudan and Uganda have undertaken to guarantee the agreement with a peacekeeping force.

"While there is some controversy over the motivation of Sudan and Uganda in playing this leadership role and the fear of a potential threat to the sovereignty of the country, many see it as a positive step toward improved bilateral relations between Sudan and South Sudan. Some people go even farther and see it as a move toward reunification, which is welcomed by Sudanese generally but suspect—indeed strongly opposed—by most South Sudanese."

"Of course, no country is going to be a do-gooder without serving its national interest. What is important is to ensure the mutuality of interests in the cooperation."

"For me, I see this as an opportunity for the two countries to help one another by resolving their internal conflicts, which continue to poison their bilateral relations. Should Khartoum succeed in its mediation efforts, it will be a welcome step. But their cooperation in addressing internal conflicts should be widened and deepened. South

Sudan should also help the Sudan in resolving the conflicts in Southern Kordofan and Blue Nile. After all, none of these regions wants to secede. A formula akin to our proposal for a 'One Country, Two Systems' arrangement can be extended to make for multiple systems. Relations between Sudan and South Sudan could also develop into some closer association between two otherwise independent and sovereign states."

"What about the case of Abyei? After all, without resolving the issue of Abyei, bilateral relations between the two countries will never be cordial or normal."

"You are absolutely right. As you know, my effort for de-freezing the impasse has been to work toward the interim stabilization of the area by providing full security coverage over the entire area through UNISFA, facilitating the return of the displaced populations to their areas of origin, providing them with essential services and socio-economic development activities, and fostering peaceful and cooperative relations between the Ngok Dinka and their neighbors to the South and the North, in particular the Missiriya nomads. I have been promoting this agenda with international donors, who are generally favorable but would want to be assured of the consent and preferably the cooperation of the two countries. Of course, South Sudan would be supportive. The question is with respect to the Sudan."

"The evolving good relations between the two countries should create a conducive climate for addressing the issue of Abyei."

"That's right. In fact, I have also been working on that and making progress. I am particularly encouraged by the response I have recently been getting in my discussions with the authorities on the side of the peace talks. I met with the leadership at all levels, and with the leaders of the Missiriya community. The results were most encouraging. We signed a joint statement agreeing on the stabilization proposal and developed a program of action to be adopted and implemented by the two governments, hopefully in partnership with international donors. Of course, we should guard against the dangers of dependency, which we discussed earlier, but international support is also imperative."

"Agreed. But what about the issue of the final status of Abyei?"

"The Stabilization agenda does not in any way touch on the existing agreements and arrangements that the parties are still called upon to implement. It is only an interim arrangement. But my idea is that the stabilization of the area is an urgent necessity. But, if accomplished, it could have a positive impact on bilateral relations and might even help in ensuring a mutually agreeable arrangement over the future status of Abyei. In my discussions with Sudanese interlocutors, we also agreed that stabilization in all its aspects is an imperative, whatever the final status of Abyei—whether it remains affiliated with the Sudan or reverts to South Sudan."

"It makes a lot of sense. Let's hope that good sense continues to prevail. Perhaps we should end the session here."

"Good, and good night." I was glad we added that aspect. The Chairman's untimely death happened shortly after he had just ended a devastating war. And since then, South Sudan has been devastated by a civil war that was undoing all the promises of the peace the Chairman had negotiated. I thought we should end on a promising note for the peace process.

Session Twenty-Nine: Legacy

As I anticipated the end of our conversations, I wondered whether there was some way of lifting up his spirits, if that were possible for a dead man. Discussing his death and its impact on his people seemed too dismal an end to what was in many ways a glorious achievement. It crossed my mind to focus on developments since my last visit to the Sudan. In many ways, this would shed some light on what I believed was to be his legacy.

The Chairman seemed to have sensed my thoughts when he appeared. *"Raandit,* I suspect you are concerned how we should end our conversations. I must say I was rather intrigued by your observations about the situation in the Sudan. Perhaps you could say more about the developments, since you were there."

"It's amazing you say that because I have been thinking precisely about what to talk about. I think what you suggest is perfect. Recent developments in the Sudan that began in December 2018 indicate that your ideas and vision did not die with you; they live on. The final phase of the peace process, which the Government of the Sudan played a pivotal role in mediating, ended with an agreement initialed by all the parties in Khartoum and finally signed in Addis Ababa on September 12, 2018."

"I am particularly interested in your observations about the background to the popular uprising that erupted later," the Chairman injected.

"Thanks." Another insightful remark. "Alongside the formal meetings of the revitalized peace process, I engaged in intensive and extensive discussions in Khartoum and saw surprisingly keen interest in my books, which, as you know, have a lot to say about identity conflicts in the Sudan, an issue on which you and I have similar views. I was invited to give talks and lead discussion groups at the University of Khartoum, think tanks, and other forums. The media—television, radio, and newspapers—were equally interested in interviewing me. Discussions focused on the politics of identity, management of diversity, the role of religion, the circumstances that triggered rebellion in several regions of the country, and the exercise of self-determination that resulted in the independence of South Sudan. People seemed to have read my works on the identity crisis in the country and were keen to engage in eliciting and discussing my views. Even on the chronic crisis situation in the Abyei area, there seemed to be renewed interest and a degree of willingness at all levels of the leadership to engage in finding a mutually agreeable solution."

"What do you think is the reason for that change of attitude?"

"Nothing explicit was publicly stated, but, in private conversations, it was unequivocally said that the Islamic project had failed. I dismissed that as the usual complaints against any dominant group. And I was also impressed that Khartoum appeared to be flourishing. Impressive buildings lined up streets that glowed with flashing lights at night. The bank of the Nile was laced with a highway with an increased number of bridges connecting the Three Towns of Khartoum, Khartoum North, and Omdurman. I once made a favorable comment to the President about the impressive development the city had undergone. His reaction was, 'And yet people are complaining that they have nothing to eat when they own several houses. Why don't they sell their houses to eat?' Of course, it was intended as a joke."

"A bad job. It sounds like the Queen in the French Revolution reacting to the demand for bread by wondering why the people were not having cake instead."

"He obviously did not find any ground for complaint. But I believe even the Islamists began to sense that things were changing and that their nationalist project was being seriously questioned. Among those who invited me to address them was an organization of Islamist Youth, who wanted me to speak on the role of religion and the state. My initial response was to wonder what they wanted to discuss with me, since I knew what they stood for and they obviously knew what I thought of their stance. I was proven wrong, for I found that they had comparatively studied and considered in depth the challenging issues involved. They were also well informed on my works in the area and were very interested in my ideas. We indeed had a stimulating exchange of views."

"Don't forget that the Muslim Brotherhood had actually prepared themselves to seize power and rule by sending their youth to universities, ironically, in the Christian West, to learn and equip themselves, particularly in technological skills. It was in fact by effectively using information technology that they campaigned so successfully to challenge the traditional parties and gain a third position in the elections, despite being numerically in the minority."

"I believe there was also a deeper cause behind their rise. As I had long concluded, for them, the Islamization agenda and its related Arab nationalism were elements of their efforts to rid the country of the lingering remnants of the Western Christian colonial system of governance and constitutionalism. My response was that I understood and appreciated their motivation and that there was a similar call in Black Africa to build governance and constitutionalism on indigenous cultural values, institutions, and operational principles. I then raised as a challenge to be addressed the question of how they proposed to reconcile their Arab-Islamic ideology with the challenges of diversity in the country. I explained how I had favored the vision of New United Sudan, which aimed at a secular system of full equality, without discrimination on any grounds; how I had contributed to the stipulation of the 'One Country, Two Systems' formula as an alternative strategy for managing unity in diversity; and how I had accepted partitioning the country as the inevitable result of failure to create a mutually agreeable basis for unity. I believe they appreciated the dilemma."

"You should remember that their version of Islam does not represent the majority of the Muslim community of the North. As we discussed earlier, traditional Islam in the Sudan is very liberal. Even the leaders of the Muslim sectors who led the politics of the independence movement believed in the separation of religion and the state reflected in the well-known slogan, 'Religion to God and Nation to All'."

"That's right. Besides, despite the independence of the South, internal conflicts of identity in the Two Sudans continue to negatively impact bilateral relations. In my discussions in Khartoum, I frequently referred to the thesis of my book, *Bound by Conflict: The Dilemmas of the Two Sudans*, in which I argued that, despite the independence of the South, the two countries remained negatively bound together by internal conflicts that spill over their borders and fuel conflicts between them, as each suspected the other of supporting their rebels. What the situation called for, I argued, was for the two countries to cooperate in solving each other's internal problems, and thereby turn being bound by conflict into being *Bonded by Solutions* (the potential title of a book still to be written). What Sudan was doing in mediating the civil war in South Sudan was, therefore, in my view, a step in the right direction. If it succeeded, it would then be for South Sudan to resolve the internal conflicts of the Sudan, which would not only bring the two countries closer together, but also foster peace and unity throughout the sub-region."

"But that did not address the contradictions imposed on the country by their Islamic-Arab agenda."

"No, but I thought that, by presenting it as a dilemma that needed to be addressed, they would at least think about the need for alternatives. And that was in fact the core of my discussions with scholars and intellectuals. I had several video-taped discussions with two Khartoum University professors and a series of tape-recorded interviews by Khartoum University Radio that were intended to be transcribed and published in a booklet. The themes were similar: the challenges of managing diversity in unity, the factors that led to the partitioning of the country, and what needed to be done to promote comprehensive peace and unity within and between the two countries as prerequisites to improving bilateral relations and fostering regional peace and security. Although I did not foresee the popular revolution that would break out several months later, it seemed obvious to me that a process of soul-searching and scrutinizing the course the country was following was underway. People seemed to acknowledge openly or overtly the mistakes that had not only led to the secession of the South, but had triggered seemingly endless armed conflicts in regions of the North, prominent among which were the rebellions in Darfur, Southern Kordofan, and Blue Nile."

"You are right, but, characteristically, perhaps overly optimistic in thinking that the Islamists would voluntarily change their policies without being forced out of power."

"I remember that you used to say that their regime was too deformed to be reformed. You also often mentioned *intifada,* or popular uprising, as one of the tools for change. What I observed was, unbeknown to me, a precursor of what was to occur less than three months later, when what started as protests over fuel and food prices mushroomed into massive demonstrations throughout the country. Professionals, women, and youth played a pivotal role in the uprising. The demands of the masses crystallized into a call for the resignation of the leadership and a radical change toward the vision of a New Sudan.

The regime was criticized for the regional wars raging in the country and the loss of South Sudan. Some South Sudanese have interpreted this to mean that any new regime that might emerge from this revolution will try to reverse the situation by undermining the independence of the South to restore the unity of the country. I disagree. The criticism of the past regime is not over its allowing the South to secede, but over creating the conditions that led to the regional rebellions and forced the South to secede. The implication of this is that any subsequent regime would strive to create conditions that would achieve peace and unity within the Sudan and prompt the two states of Sudan and South Sudan to improve bilateral relations and move towards a new form of association."

"Again, while I share your aspiration, I fear that there is a normative ambiguity in what you are saying. There is an element of what *should* be rather than what *will* be in what you are saying."

"I have long accepted that I am an incurable optimist. I believe that is also a strategic motivation for action to work for change. Anyway, after a protracted period of negotiations and maneuvers, the military eventually sided with the people. The President and his government resigned, and a new military council assumed the mantle of power and pledged to hand over full control of the government, after an interim period of partnership between the military and the civilian leaders. The leadership of the revolution insisted on immediate total transfer of power to civilian rule. All this sounded very much like your reaction to the overthrow of the military regime in 1985 by a junta that tried to bridge between military control and civilian rule during the interim period. You refused to negotiate with them and insisted that they immediately hand power over to the civilians. The revolutionaries are responding as you did, perhaps with the benefit of hindsight. At the moment of writing (mid-May, 2019), negotiations continue."

"It is difficult to see how a regime that has vigorously endeavored to shape the character and destiny of the nation can be totally eliminated. Besides, total surrender by the military may be feared as suicidal, since such a radical change might lead to reprisals or vengeance on the part of the many interests that have been severely impacted by their misrule."

"I agree. In fact, I say that if there were a seventy-five percent change, with twenty-five continuity, that would be change enough."

"Here you go again with your strategic optimism. I will let it pass without comment."

"I take that as a degree of approval. And no further comment is called for."

"Not even 'Good!'?"

" 'Good' is most welcome. And I believe there are sufficient grounds for optimism. But let me add another aspect of the situation that you might label as characteristic optimism. I understand that leaders of the former regime are now in the infamous Kober Prison. You will recall that when I went to the Sudan three months after the so-called Revolution of National Salvation, I requested to visit the leaders of the former government who were in Kober Prison. I was given permission. And as the member of the Revolution's Command Council in charge of security escorted me visit the prisoners, he said, 'Doctor, remember that this is an investment for you to visit us when our time comes.' Well, their time has now come, and I feel a moral obligation to fulfill that prophetic request."

The Chairman's only response was, "No comment." But I surmised that, since he had advised me against going to Khartoum then, he might again counsel me against going to Khartoum under these circumstances. Although I would wait and see, I felt that I would once again go against such advice and visit the prisoners as a matter of honor, conditions permitting.

"Although the final outcome of the developments in the Sudan is still uncertain," I continued, "it is obvious that a major search for the soul of the country—which you had championed—is underway. While your liberation movement was not specifically identified as a principal actor in the revolution, members of the Northern sector of the movement have featured prominently in its leadership and the slogans of the demonstrators are reminiscent of the movement's call for a New United Sudan in which there would be no discrimination on the grounds of race, ethnicity, religion, culture, and gender. You used to say that the people of the marginalized regions of the Sudan had struggled and suffered for far too long, that people should not mince words in defining the problem and explaining the objectives of the struggle. You therefore have reason to say, 'That's what we were saying... the chickens are now coming to roost... too late to save the unity of the country... but better late than never.'"

"You are putting words in my mouth, but that's alright, no objection."

"Another approval, thanks. Where all this will lead is still a matter of conjecture, but I agree with a South Sudanese scholar, one of your committed followers who wrote a powerful book on your ideas and vision. If I remember his words correctly, he said something along the lines that he was directing his message to young people and future generations to provide them with what he called 'critical tools of analysis' and to use the body of knowledge acquired through these tools, the body of knowledge based on these critical tools of analysis, to pursue the vision of New Sudan that you had defined and pursued with conviction, courage, and consistency. He would like the young generation to know that the commutative policies of successive regimes in Khartoum have finally broken the back of the Sudanese 'golden camel', splitting the country into two independent states. He argues that if this young generation internalizes your vision, they can avoid further disintegration of Sudan into the smaller states of Darfur, Nuba Mountains, Funj, Beja, and Kush. Addressing the youth of South Sudan specifically, the author goes on to say that this calls for a nation-building project that looks beyond our tribes and geographical locations on the map of South Sudan. They must focus on the unifying factors of the people of South Sudan, not on what divides them. He ends his book by stating that your ideas will continue to inspire successive generations to come and motivate members of your movement to protect your legacy and pursue your vision, as they had pledged to do."

Dead silence followed. I wondered whether I had lost the Chairman or he had been moved beyond words. He spoke rather abruptly, "Good night, *Raandit*. I hope to see you tomorrow."

Session Thirty: Retrospection

As we approached the close of our conversations, I thought a great deal about how we would end what had become an important part of my nights and for which I always waited with great anticipation. And if, as the psychiatrist had said, I was indeed the initiator and the primary beneficiary, then why would I want the conversation to end? I reminded myself of the popular saying among my people that there is nothing that does not end. It is also universally said that all things must end. There is no exception.

I decided to pose one last question for a more in-depth discussion with the Chairman when he emerged for the session. "*Benydit,* as we approach the end of our conversations, I would like to ask what you would have done in the event that your death had been aborted? But first, let me share with you what I have heard people say in speculating over what you might have done. The main question people debate is whether you would have remained committed to the unity of the Sudan or accepted the independence of the South? Connected with this question is whether you had the ambition to lead a United Sudan? What would be your answers to these questions?"

"I am now in a different world. I can no longer think the way I might have thought in the world of the living. All that is now for the living. But I would be interested to hear what people are saying about that."

"The very popular way you were received by masses of people from across the country leads most people to believe that you could easily have won Presidential elections. That is why the President was reported to have said that he would probably be the last Arab President in the country. I have heard one person who knew you well say that he did not think you wanted to be President, even though he believed you were seriously committed to unity. This is presumably because he thought that despite your rising popularity in the North, the dominant Arab-Muslim elite would not allow that.

"One person thought that if you became President, you would have been assassinated within one month of your Presidency. The same person, however, thought that you would probably have extended the interim period before the referendum of the South to give unity a chance or at least prepare the South to develop its capacity to be a more viable independent state.

"What I find quite interesting is that people think of you as both idealistic and pragmatic. They see idealism in your vision of a New Sudan, that would transform the country from a grossly inequitable system dominated by the Arab-Muslim minority, which they believe is too entrenched to concede to a democratic secular system in which the denigrated non-Arab majority would seize power. But they also see you as realistic enough to recognize that you would not be accepted by the Arabized Muslim North to lead the country, being both non-Arab and non-Muslim."

"It is indeed a contradiction. You remember what I said to you when you told me that you had said to some Northerners that I would look for a likeminded Northerner to lead the country, as I was realistic enough to know that I would not be accepted by the North to be President? You were surprised when I asked you why you were denying me the Presidency? You simply laughed it off as a joke. You see, all this is the result of a long history of domination in which people accept the status quo as sacrosanct. Our vision of the New Sudan was to shatter that myth and we were well on the way to achieving that vision. My reception by an estimated six million people from across the country was a clear testimony that the goal was in sight."

"But then what went wrong? You died?"

"Since I died, how do I know? You tell me."

"I will tell you something quite extraordinary and which I believe is an aspect of the impact you had on the political landscape of the Sudan. Amidst the excitement of the 2010 presidential elections in the country following the 2005 Comprehensive Peace Agreement, I received a surprise phone call from a representative of the Northern Sudanese branch of your Movement informing me that I had been chosen to be the nominee of the Movement to run in the elections. The news came as an utter surprise to me. How could that be possible when I was not even a member of the Movement? Was it perhaps a joke?

"Apparently, the initiative came from a group of liberal-minded Northern Sudanese members of your Movement, most of whom belonged to the progressive Islamist Republican Brotherhood, whose pious founding leader had been executed years earlier by the then 'born-again' Islamist President for the contrived crime of apostasy. Other parties to the initiative were leftist-leaning young intellectual activists, scholars, and academics. They wanted my permission to register me and pledged to campaign for me.

"The call was soon followed by a visit to my office by one of their members who was serving in the UN Secretariat. His visit was to confirm the initiative. He even confided to me that he himself had opposed my nomination on the grounds that I was too much of a bridge builder for such a contentious political process. He said he was overruled by those who saw that as an asset and not a liability. He said that the 'Big Man', meaning the Head of the Movement, who was First Vice-President of the Sudan and President of the then autonomous South, had given his approval.

"Of course, my instinct was to tell them that while I was honored and flattered, I could not accept the invitation for a variety of reasons. Then I thought that it was more prudent to reflect on the matter before giving a response. I thanked them for the confidence and the honor they had bestowed upon me but told them that I would have to think it over and get back to them. The more I reflected, the more I was intrigued by the idea and the challenge it posed. Eventually, I decided that, although, in all likelihood, I could not win, I might play the role of a guinea pig to ascertain the extent to which attitudes in the North had changed. But there was the remote possibility that a miracle would occur and I might win. I therefore thought seriously what I could bring to the leadership of a New United Sudan. I took that remote possibility very seriously for a brief but most intense period.

"I was then at the UN in the position of Undersecretary General and Advisor of the Secretary General on the Prevention of Genocide. To avoid having the news get out into the media before informing my superiors, I told the Chef d'Cabinet, a former Ambassador of India to the UN, who responded very positively, taking it as an encouraging indicator of a positive change of attitude in the North. He encouraged me to accept. He in turn informed the Secretary General, who also responded very positively and congratulated me.

"But then I learned that the Deputy Secretary General of the Northern Branch of your Movement, a Northerner and ironically a relative of the President, was running. He also happened to be my brother-in-law, whose marriage (to my half-sister from the same father) I had supported, over the objections of relatives who had protested that he was a Northerner. He and I became very close, both personally and politically. Since he was a senior member of the party and I not a member at all, I thought that there was a disconnect somewhere and, in any case, I could not stand against him. That was the end of that remarkable initiative."

"You have just provided evidence of our success", the Chairman commented. "Your brother-in-law was one of my closest comrades with a vitally important role to play in the North. The Movement could not have chosen a more worthy candidate for the cause of the New Sudan. But the fact that Northerners would nominate you, a Southerner, to run for the Presidency, was a very significant sign of the progress we were making toward the New Sudan Vision. I can't say that you should have accepted to run, but I am glad that the initiative was taken."

"Ironically, nearly a decade later, while I was in Khartoum during the Revitalization talks, I had a minor accident on my foot that took me to a prominent hospital for emergency attention. After being X-rayed, I was led to the surgeon, who surprised me by getting up, calling my name, and hugging me with great warmth and expressions of pleasure for the opportunity of our meeting. He seated me and immediately got into politics without any reference to the reason for which I was in the hospital. With obviously jocular criticism, he said, 'I am angry with you.' I was somewhat taken aback. Why? I thought, without asking. Then he proceeded to give the answer. 'I was one of those who wanted you to run for the Presidency. The country needed you. Why did you let us down?' I was dumbfounded. I could not say anything, other than awkwardly acknowledging the flattering confidence with humble gratitude. We eventually got to the issue of my foot. He listened to my complaint and looked at the X-Rays and examined my foot. He assured me that there was nothing serious and prescribed medication for the pain and the swelling. He also instructed his Secretary that I was not to be charged. While I was still with him, his phone rang and I heard him say, 'Yes, he is here with me.' He explained to me that the call was from the Director of the hospital, enquiring about me. A professor of medicine from Khartoum University to whom I had talked about my accident had talked to them.

"Of course, my nomination for the Presidency of the Sudan is now ancient history. Sudan has since broken up into two countries. The question now is whether there are lessons to be learnt from your leadership that led the country that far toward a New United Sudan and suddenly left the mission unaccomplished.

"My personal view is that two factors must have been at work. The first is what we have already talked about, that the people of the South never really bought into your vision of a New Sudan. They only accepted it as a clever ploy for achieving Southern independence. And you allowed that ambiguity to persist in order not to lose support. The other factor is that, like most charismatic and towering leaders, you never really prepared a successor who genuinely shared your vision and was capable of at least sustaining the ambiguity after you departed. Your movement was too much of a one-man show."

"You once raised this issue with me and I explained to you how I had assigned tasks to my top three comrades: one for the army, another for the party, and the third for the civil service and the economy. Unfortunately, they did not deliver as I had hoped."

"I reported this to your successor shortly after your death, and he told me that he had delivered his plan to you as you had requested."

"I hesitate to react to what he told you. Since I cannot have a face-to-face discussion with him, my reaction would be too one-sided. In any case, all this is a lot of food for thought, not for me, but for you the living."

"Another area people speculate about is what you would have done to develop the South? Some people, including members of your immediate family, say that you had a blueprint for the development of the country. It is said that you wanted South Sudan to be a model in Africa. What the leader of Rwanda has done in his country is often cited as an example. And that is a small country without much in the way of natural resources, while South Sudan is known for its rich natural wealth that still remains to be tapped. Is this not yet another instance of your not having prepared a successor who was fully 'on board' with your plans?"

"You have raised a lot of questions. Remember, I am no longer of your world. You have colleagues in charge. The responsibility and the challenge have passed on to them. I don't want to lead from another world. In any case, I cannot. Why don't we stop here and then conclude our conversations in our next session, which will be our last?"

"Sadly, but as we agreed last time, all things must end. I look forward to one more session before we conclude our program of conversations."

Session Thirty-One: End

When we met for our last session, I reflected on what to say, and decided to focus on what was happening to the movement that he had successfully led to liberate our people. That movement was not only fractured and marginalized, but its vision and programs were almost entirely shelved and forgotten.

The Chairman announced his arrival with the usual greetings, and added, "*Raandit,* as I assume you know, sadness is not a condition that applies to the dead. But I didn't want to speak about that. I will only express the hope that as we end our program of conversations, you have found the experience rewarding and worth the time we have spent on it."

"Mr. Chairman, I have no words to express how I feel about what this experience has meant to me. I always knew how much our friendship meant to both of us. But that you should choose to spend such valuable time with me among the multitudes of people who are much more deserving of this honor than me is something no language can adequately acknowledge and appreciate. So let me just use the simple old words, 'Thank you'.

"Without opening new areas for discussion, I just want to say something very close to my heart. What I find very disturbing about where we are now is the extreme hostility against your movement in influential circles, even though, as you know, I was never a member of the movement. Of course, the movement itself has become acutely divided and weakened, compounded with its marginalization by the dominant wing. I often recall a conversation I had in New York with leading Northern Sudanese members of the movement. They said that even with the independence of South Sudan, your movement and the ruling Islamist party in Khartoum are incompatible and can never co-exist; one will have to destroy the other. I wonder which of the two is winning this existential war.

"It looks as though the wing of your movement that is now in power has come to the conclusion that their survival depends on their cooperation with Khartoum. But I wonder whether the balance of power is not tilted against your movement.

"I once posed a question to a colleague on what it would take to get the country out of the predicament it is in. His answer was that, as long as the movement remains in power, there can be no solution to the crises confronting the country. Conversely, once the movement is eradicated, all the problems would be solved. In his view, shared by many, the movement is beyond reform. I find the hostile sentiment against your movement a total obsession. I have often said that to some people I know, even if a man quarreled with his wife at home, some will say it is caused by the movement.

"This hostility is paradoxical for a movement that liberated the country with a noble vision that should continue to inspire the independent state of South Sudan. Although what divides South Sudanese is not as stark as what divided the Sudanese, there are still differences to be reckoned with. After all, identity is a relative term. I always give the example of Somalia, which is recognized as one of the most homogeneous countries in the world and yet is torn apart by clan conflicts.

"That is why I believe that the Vision of the New Sudan—of equality without discrimination on any grounds—is as valid for South Sudan as it was valid in the old Sudan. And I wonder why your strategy of taking the towns to villages or using oil revenue to fuel the engine of agriculture, and your development goal of prioritizing roads, roads, roads, appear to have been buried with you. So, you see why you are so sorely missed?"

The Chairman reacted again with an attractive balance between confidence and modesty: "I will conclude by repeating what I have just said. Ideas cannot be buried with a person, nor can they die. They may lie dormant, or hibernate as many creatures do during certain seasons, until they are revived, spotlighted, and reactivated by timely intervention, stimulation, and direction. What is required is faith, backed by patience, and creative search, as always, for the suitable leadership."

"Are you saying that your ideals cannot be pursued, far less realized, now, under the current leadership, or in our own lifetime?" I probed a challenging question.

"I did not say that. For one thing, I no longer have a say about your leadership. Besides, to whom does 'our own lifetime' refer?"

"Well, I hope it excludes our own children," I said.

"That is soon enough!" the Chairman responded.

The conversation brought to mind two principles that had always guided me in life. One is that strategic optimism generates motivation for constructive action while pessimism leads to a dead end. The other is that in crises there are often opportunities to be tapped and pursued.

"What is your last word to our people and to the world?" I asked the Chairman, hoping that his answer would lay a basis for my two guiding principles.

"Why the last word? Although we are ending these sessions now, let us keep alive the principle of the conversation into the foreseeable future," concluded the Chairman. "I will again visit periodically and alert you in time."

While I felt that we had exhausted the issues for discussion for now, I was glad to hear the Chairman say that we would periodically resume our conversations. It would now be for me to reflect on all that we had discussed and what I should do about those reflections.

For now, I thought I should share the information widely and hope that the Chairman, even in his death, will continue to inspire people, including contemporary leaders. After all, new leaders emerge, and existing leaders might be renewed.

In change there is also continuity. And in death, there is continued identity and influence through the living. So, I end by saying: "The Chairman is dead; long live the Chairman!"

Session Thirty-Two: Epilogue

The visitations of the Chairman and my conversations with him had ended. But I had a final discussion with my wife on the experience. She had shared it in confidence with my Dinka cousin who lived in Virginia about an hour from Washington D.C. and visited us fairly regularly. Although my wife did not tell her fully what I was going through, after the session with the psychiatrist, she gave her a general appreciation of the situation.

After the last session with the Chairman, my wife clearly felt relieved, especially when I stopped the medication and she saw no sign of withdrawal, which would have been a consequence of addiction. She must have felt the urge to share these positive developments with my cousin. My cousin was in turn quite excited. She told my wife that ever since she learned about my condition, she had been praying to God and our ancestors for me. And my wife, although she did not make such a claim, sensed that my cousin took the positive development as evidence that her prayers had been answered.

My cousin even had formal ideas about applying our cultural and spiritual values and practices to my situation. "Among our Dinka people," she told my wife, "certain rituals are performed to separate a dead person from the living relatives. A ritual is performed three days after the death for a male, and four days for a female, by which an animal is sacrificed and cut into two parts, one kept at home while the other is thrown away. The idea is both to cleanse the family of the evil spirit of death that had taken the life of the relative and to separate the world of the dead from that of the living."

My wife was somewhat confused by this information. She thought Dinka culture ensured the continuation of the dead through the memory of the living. This was done through a concept of immortality known as *koch e nhom*, "standing the head" of the dead person upright through the children and other relatives he or she had left behind and all those the dead person had deeply touched in one way or another. "I understood that the dead even own cattle and that animals are sacrificed for them and other offerings made to them periodically. Why then should they be ritually separated from the living? I don't understand."

"You are right that our people believe in that form of immortality through the memory of the dead by the living. Although it may seem like a contradiction, they also believe in separating the dead from the living. That is why, when a dead relative comes to a person in a dream, a sacrifice must be made to clear that person from the effects of the dream. If the dead relative makes a request through the dream, that request must be granted along with the ritual of separation from the dream. The ritual of separating the dead from the living is a form of closure, a reckoning with the reality of the loss."

My cousin then explained the custom in relation to the Chairman and me. Although the Chairman is not a relative, he and I had a close relationship, so that he was like a relative. Not carrying out the ritual of separation therefore created an unresolved situation.

My wife recalled another Dinka practice, which my maternal uncle had told us about. When his father, to whom he was very close, felt that his death was near, even though it was not apparent to others because he looked well, he asked his son to fetch a lamb for him to sacrifice in a ritual of separation between him and his son. "My son," my grandfather spoke to my uncle, "they say that a dead man sometimes misses his favorite son so much that he returns to fetch him to join him in the world of the dead. I don't want that to happen between you and me. I want to separate us when I am still alive."

My uncle told us that he questioned his father's move. "Father, how can you think of separating us when you are still alive and indeed looking well? I have never heard of a ritual of separation between people who are still alive."

But his father insisted, and a lamb was provided. His father then invoked the lamb in prayer, "I am sacrificing you to join me after I die. I want you to be my witness and to remind me, should I try to fetch my son to join me in death. Remind me that I had sacrificed you to stop me from fetching my son." The lamb was then sacrificed and cut into two parts, one part kept at home and the other part thrown away.

My cousin then proposed that a ritual of separation between the Chairman and me be carried out. She feared that, although we had terminated our program of visitations, there was no telling whether one of us might initiate the program some time in the future. My wife gave no opinion on the proposal, but she suggested that my cousin herself be the one to present the idea to me.

My wife joined me in the meeting with my cousin. My instinct was to dismiss the idea off-hand as superstition. But I quickly reflected on the proposal and gave it a more favorable verdict. After all, having gone through various schools with different religions, I had long decided that all religious beliefs and practices have elements of superstition and that our traditional belief system had more merits than we had been led to believe. I came down with the decision that, as long as that was what our people believed, and considering that applying it would do no harm, I should respect it. My only condition was that after appropriate invocation and prayers over the lamb, we would hand it to a professional butcher to perform the slaughtering and cutting of the animal into halves as prescribed by the tradition. I said we should not worry about what he did with the meat. That was agreed.

The ceremony took place in the backyard of our house. Present at the ceremony were several members of our clan and a few other members of the Dinka community in Washington, including one from a spiritually prominent Ngok Dinka clan. My wife was there. The lamb was brought and tethered in front of the people standing in a horseshoe formation. I was made to sit in a chair located at the center of the horseshoe. Although the initiative came from my female cousin, only men were expected to pray in accordance with the Dinka practice.

One of the cousins, a towering, slender, and gentle middle-aged man, was the first to pray. "God, our clan spirits, and you our ancestors," he began, mentioning the names of our forefathers in the long line of ascendants in our lineage. "It is to you all that I say this, my word. It is not for a bad reason we are gathered here. It is for a good reason. Our brother and our beloved late Chairman were very good friends. And for us, the Dinka, relationships, including friendships, survive death and continue into the world of the dead. But God willed that the living and the dead live separate kinds of life, even when their relationships continue.

"Our brother recently broke the barriers of life and death by developing a close connection with our departed Chairman. We worry that this breach of what God had ordained poses a threat to his well-being. We appreciate that you all continued to protect him and nothing bad happened to him. But we are worried that evil might befall him for violating your will and creating abnormal bonds between the world of the dead and that of the living. And we worry that the same relationship and the threat it poses might return to our brother and the Chairman. That is why we ask you to accept this sacrificial lamb as a symbol of our prayer. We will sacrifice it in the custom of our people to sever the connection between them.

"As for you, the lamb chosen for this sacrifice, you are not dying for a bad cause. You are being sacrificed to save life. From Creation, God ordained that the lives of the animals we keep are interchangeable with the lives of humans. So, accept your destiny in good grace. It is for a good cause. That is all I have to say."

Another cousin, a medium-height, sporty young man in his thirties, took the floor. "I am a child compared to my brothers, but I have something small to add to what they have said. God of our fathers, spirits of our clan, and you our ancestors and forefathers, I do not have much to say. I just want to add my word to that of my brother who has just spoken. All we want is to obey the order of things you have ordained for human beings in this life and the one to come after death. You want these worlds to be separate. Our brother transgressed this separation. We are here to atone for that violation and to pray that it does not occur again. We are not against their friendship continuing. We just want them to do in the manner you have laid down for the living and the dead. That is my word."

I felt uncomfortable with the notion that what had happened was a wrong against God and our ancestral belief system. I raised my voice and asked to speak but was hushed down. "Do you really believe that I have commuted a wrong?"

The oldest cousin responded: "No one is accusing you of having committed a moral wrong. All we are saying is that you have crossed the boundaries separating the dead from the living. We are saying that this is against what God has ordained. Nothing bad has happened, but we are concerned that, if it continues, it can destabilize your life. That is what we are praying to prevent. And you do not have a say in this."

The man from the renowned spiritually powerful family decided to speak: "What I want to add to what has been said is a small word. It is often said that with modern education, we have lost the ways of our people, including our ancestors. They say that those who become Christians no longer believe in our traditional religious beliefs and practices. No one abandons what his father and the forefathers before him have bequeathed to their descendants. We are all created by the one God. But He gave us different ways of relating to Him. Our Ancestors have their own way that has come down to us through the long chain of ancestors from the Byre of Creation.

"What our brothers have said is the truth. So, You God, Father of all people, and you our ancestors, all we are asking of you is to bless our brother so that he avoids crossing the lines you have drawn between the living and the dead. That's all I have to say."

My cousin, a tall, confident, and imposing lady in her mid-forties, announced that she wanted to say something. At first, there was dead silence. Then the oldest cousin responded. "This is a male function, not for women."

My cousin was visibly enraged. The idea had been hers from the beginning, and here she was, being discriminated against on the grounds of gender! "What keeps women away from matters of life and death? Am I alien to the ancestors you are invoking? Which of you is the son of a father without a woman? And why did I not hear the name of a woman in the long line of our clan ascendants? Where is Achai of Noh, whose sacrifice to the spirits of the river by Jok, our original father, made the waters of the river separate so that our people could cross on dry land? Have you forgotten that our people sacrifice to Achai in the river every year? So, please do not insult women by saying that this is a male affair."

My wife raised her hand to speak and was acknowledged," I just want to say that the idea for this event actually came from our sister. Some of you know this, but I thought I should announce it in view of this exchange."

"Thank you, Sister," my cousin rejoined. "All that aside, I want to add my voice to the brothers who have spoken and call on God and all the spirits of our clan, ancestors *and* ancestresses, that we are asking for good health for our brother. Communication with the dead comes only in occasional dreams. Continuous visitations and conversations of the type our brother has been having with our Chairman is not normal. It is a sign of something wrong. Fortunately, nothing disastrous had happened. But it is a bad omen that we pray you to not let it be repeated. That is the word I wanted to add."

The oldest cousin responded in a conciliatory tone. "Sister, I want to assure you that no offense was intended. We were just following tradition. But you are right, there is no reason why praying for good health and wellbeing should only be a function of men. Along with the cultural continuity we are exhibiting here, there must also be change. And gender equality is one of the areas in which there must be change. So, we apologize."

"Apology accepted," my cousin graciously responded.

Suddenly, the lamb bleated and urinated, which the Dinka interpret as the animal having accepted being sacrificed, although I have always taken it as evidence of panic and despair in the face of imminent death. Fortunately, the animal was not slaughtered in our house. The butcher was called to come and take it to be slaughtered and its carcass severed according to the requirements of the rites of separation.

To substitute for severing the carcass of the lamb, a rope was unwound to symbolize the unfolding and severance of entanglement. The representative of the spiritually powerful clan took a bowl of water and said a few words of prayer that the water which he was about to spray on me should bring the 'coolness of good health' and cleanse any impurities in my mind. He then sprayed the water on me and the assembled group. The group was then invited into the house to share a meal of communion to conclude the event.

So, the saga of my reunification and visitations with the Chairman came to an end through a ritual I thought I had left far behind in my journey through cultures and religious belief systems. I still do not know whether what I experienced was real or a figment of my imagination—a fiction. Nor do I actually know what is real and what is fictional. What I know is that the ghost of the Chairman no longer visits me. Which of us has left the other? I do not know. He had advised me that it was time for us to end our meetings and conversations because he realized that it was a source of anxiety in my family. The family now saw to it that the program ended through a ritual whose effect was apparently on me, not on the Chairman. But the experience confirmed to me that the boundary between the dead is both rigid and malleable and that by the will of God we are both separated and continue united. Yes, the Chairman is dead, and through this severe ritual he is separated from me, but he will continue to live in my memory and in the minds and hearts of his people forever and ever.

www.ingramcontent.com/pod-product-compliance
Lightning Source LLC
Chambersburg PA
CBHW021849020426
42334CB00013B/245